The Clinton Presidency

THE CLINTON PRESIDENCY

Campaigning, Governing, and the Psychology of Leadership

EDITED BY

Stanley A. Renshon

The City University of New York

Westview Press

Boulder • San Francisco • Oxford

Copyright © 1995 by Westview Press, Inc.

Published in 1995 in the United States of America by Westview Press, Inc., 5500 Central Avenue, Boulder, Colorado 80301-2877, and in the United Kingdom by Westview Press, 36 Lonsdale Road, Summertown, Oxford OX2 7EW

Library of Congress Cataloging-in-Publication Data
Renshon, Stanley Allen.
  The Clinton presidency : campaigning, governing, and the
psychology of leadership / Stanley A. Renshon.
    p. cm.
  Includes bibliographical references and index.
  ISBN 0-8133-1976-5. — ISBN 0-8133-1977-3 (pbk.)
    1. United States—Politics and government—1993– —Psychological
aspects.   2. Presidents—United States—Election—1992—
Psychological aspects.   3. Clinton, Bill, 1946– .   I. Title.
E885.R46   1995
973.929'01'9—dc20   94-27952
                                                                          CIP

Printed and bound in the United States of America

      The paper used in this publication meets the requirements
(∞) of the American National Standard for Permanence of Paper
      for Printed Library Materials Z39.48-1984.

10   9   8   7   6   5   4   3   2

Contents

PART IV   Public Psychology and President Clinton

**PART V   The Clinton Presidency and the Psychology
of Public Policy: Dilemmas and Opportunities**

Preface

Debate on public issues and candidates' stands on them have traditionally represented the bulk of knowledge sought about presidential candidates. In recent decades, however, an important change has taken place. Rather than ask presidential candidates where they stand, the public now wants to know who they are. As Susan Estrich, Michael Dukakis's 1988 campaign adviser, noted, "Ultimately, most presidential campaigns are about character, broadly defined; they are a choice between two men, and which one the voters decide to trust with their future" (quoted in Elizabeth Drew, "Report from Washington," *The New Yorker,* July 4, 1988, 71).

The 1992 presidential campaign offered three rather different choices in this regard. One purpose of this book is to explore those choices from the standpoint both of public psychology and the individuals themselves. George Bush, Bill Clinton, and Ross Perot offered very different diagnoses of the public's needs. They also differed on their plans for resolving these public dilemmas. And they differed dramatically in the kind of leadership they offered to the American public.

On the basis of all these considerations, a plurality of the American public selected Bill Clinton as president. Did the election campaign reveal important and useful information about the personal psychology and leadership abilities of presidential candidates?

The importance of this question lies in its relationship to the quality of the judgments that such information facilitates in making choices among candidates. It is anchored by the expectation that the basis on which judgments are made has real importance for actual presidential performance. Given this fact, it is somewhat ironic that, although presidential elections increasingly turn on issues of character and leadership, the relationship between campaign and presidential performance remains unclear. Even if campaigns allow the public to see something of the candidates' psychology, judgment, and leadership skills, a major question remains: Are these the same elements that will be important once a person assumes office?

We first focus on the 1992 presidential campaign itself from the standpoint of both public and candidate psychology. We then focus on the relationships among campaigning, governing, and the psychology of political leadership as they emerged from the 1992 presidential election, the postelection/pre-inaugural transition period, and roughly the first year of the Clinton administration.

Our purpose here is twofold. First, we wish to offer some preliminary assessments of the Clinton presidency informed by theories of presidential leadership and political psychology. Second, we wish to draw some theoretical inferences about the relationships between presidential campaigns and in-office performance. These twin objectives are reflected in the title of this book: *The Clinton Presidency: Campaigning, Governing, and the Psychology of Leadership*.

We examine the emerging Clinton presidency from a broadly psychological perspective, and that deserves some comment. The contributors to this book, among whom are political scientists, psychologists, and psychiatrists, hold different theoretical perspectives. Some approach their work from a broadly psychoanalytic perspective, others from a social psychology, cognitive, or personality perspective. Still others in this book approach issues from the perspectives of mass political behavior and presidential politics. Most contributors draw on several of these perspectives.

The issue of what is learned regarding candidates' psychology, judgment, and leadership and its implications for presidential performance cannot be approached from a single theoretical perspective. The same is true for analyses of presidential leadership and behavior once a candidate assumes office. Individual psychology and public psychology play important roles, but so do political leadership and the politics of governing.

At the original presentation of these chapters, differences among the contributors were evident. Sometimes there were differences in the weight or meaning accorded to various data. Sometimes contributors from different theoretical perspectives brought new data to bear on our joint efforts. Yet there was also a surprising amount of agreement given the different theoretical (and perhaps personal) perspectives.

No effort has been made to resolve all these differences for the sake of a premature consensus. One possible contribution of this book lies in the fact that many congruent understandings and explanations emerged from our different theoretical perspectives. But our differences may also lead to a deepening appreciation of the complexities of these processes and a continuing interest in exploring and understanding them.

Thanks are due to my assistants Carol Remond and Grayson Williams for their help at many stages of the production of this book. I wish to thank Nancy Carlston, senior editor at Westview Press, for her interest in and support of our work. She has been a skillful and understanding collaborator, helping to get this book to publication in minimal time. I also wish to thank Libby Barstow, senior production editor, for her able assistance in bringing this book through the production process with skill and responsiveness. Thanks are also due to Jan Kristiansson for her very skillful copyediting of the manuscript.

Lastly, I want to thank my wife, Judith, and my children, David and Jonathan, whose love and support have been my cherished companions throughout.

Stanley A. Renshon
New York City

1

The Psychological Context of the Clinton Presidency: A Framework for Analysis

STANLEY A. RENSHON

The purpose of this book is to explore and develop an initial appraisal of the Clinton presidency. Our effort is framed by an exploration of the 1992 election and by theories of political leadership and psychology. The chapters herein draw on a diverse body of theories, including psychological theories of character and personality, cognitive psychology and communication theory, theories of presidential leadership and performance, and theories of public psychology. Our goal is to examine the many facets of leadership and governing that constitute the modern presidency and to locate Bill Clinton's emerging presidency within that framework. One result, we hope, will be a clearer, more objective framework in which to evaluate the man, his approach to political leadership and executive power, and their consequences than has been available in the past.

There are several reasons that a clearer, more objective framework is needed. First, Clinton himself is and will likely remain a controversial president. Throughout his public life he has generated intense feelings, ranging from idealization to distrust and dislike. Many admire him. He is clearly smart and knowledgeable about many aspects of domestic policy and has focused attention on and put forward plans to resolve long-standing public problems, such as those in health care. He is clearly determined to leave his personal and political imprint and has proposed the most ambitious schedule of policy initiatives in twenty-five years.

Yet many distrust him. During the presidential campaign he evaded and dissembled when asked about his avoidance of the draft during the Vietnam War, his smoking of marijuana, and his extramarital relations. Since he has become president, a number of questions have arisen about his candor, leadership, and even competence. One major columnist (Herbert, 1994) recently characterized Clinton as a "truth sculptor," whereas another (Peters, 1994, 21) noted "a history of difficulty with the truth." It is unusual for a president to come into office with the public holding such strong and contrary views. There needs to be some systematic and more objective analysis of the basis, if any, for each of these feelings and their implications for Clinton's presidency.

Second, these strong and conflicting views have to some degree limited what we have come to understand of Clinton and his approach to political leadership and social policy. For a man who has been in elected public office for almost all of his adult life, there is surprisingly little objective, systematic knowledge of Clinton as a political figure and leader. Clinton, like other presidents before him, has supplied a number of details about his life and career. However, presidents' views of their own record are not necessarily the most reliable guide to understanding them.

Third, reporters and other analysts covering the Clinton presidency tend to focus too much on particular policy victories or setbacks. Did the budget and the North American Free Trade Agreement (NAFTA) pass? Did Clinton backtrack on his commitments to Haiti or to the reforming of policy toward gays and lesbians in the military? The problem with treating each discrete issue in terms of winning or losing is that it obscures patterns not only of outcomes but also of approaches to Clinton's presidential leadership. One purpose of this book is to step back from the day-to-day analyses of each discrete event and attempt to locate them in a broader theoretical context.

Understanding the Development of Clinton's Presidential Style: Sources and Cautions

In some respects we have a great deal, but in other respects not nearly enough, information and analysis to help us develop our understandings of Bill Clinton. We now have data available from five different but accessible periods that are relevant to this book's concerns: (1) Bill Clinton's terms as governor of Arkansas, spanning the twelve-year period 1978–1980, 1982–1992; (2) the 1992 primary campaign, stretching from the meeting of the Democratic Leadership Council in the spring of 1991 through July 1992; (3) the presidential campaign, spanning July 1992–November 1992; (4) the period of transition from November 1992 to January 1993; and (5) the first twelve months of the Clinton administration.

In some respects, of course, data from each of these periods are limited. Nonetheless, although I use the word *initial* to characterize these analyses, this does not mean there is a paucity of data to make these preliminary inquiries. The last four periods cover more than two years of highly visible public events that were widely reported and analyzed. Clinton frequently and publicly responded to and commented on these events, first as a candidate and then as president. The highly public and overtly political nature of the Clinton presidency is one early characteristic of the administration that helps anchor these analyses. Indeed, Clinton shows few signs of developing a "hidden-hand" presidency (Greenstein, 1982).

Clinton as Governor

Surprisingly little emerged during the presidential campaign about Clinton's performance as governor. One major problem for researchers interested in more systematic analyses of the development of Bill Clinton's governing style is that his gubernatorial papers are not easily available to scholars. They remain in the custody of President Clinton at an undisclosed location.[1] Another problem the interested researcher encounters is that there are very few in-depth scholarly analyses of Clinton's performance as governor. One exception is Charles Allen's (1991) analysis of Clinton's educational policy as governor. It is one of the few analyses not undertaken by individuals with close personal connections and feelings about Clinton.

There are two reasons we can identify for this dearth of objective material. First, Arkansas is a small state in which the elites of the various sectors (governmental, legal, educational, financial, and so on) are very well known to one another and often have close personal as well as professional ties.[2] Second, Clinton's approach to leadership reflects a very strong interpersonal emphasis. He has been known to travel many hours and more miles to meet small groups of voters in his home state. It is probably an exaggeration to say that everyone in Arkansas has met Clinton. But Clinton has made a three-decade-long point of meeting people of the state in his quest for political office and has been especially sensitive to meeting elites and opinion makers. That he knows and is known by, and in many cases has developed close personal relationships with, many of these individuals has complicated assessments of his tenure in office. Thus, good theoretically focused analyses of Clinton's approach to leadership, his performance as governor in specific policy areas, and the implications of both for his performance as president remain to be accomplished.

Clinton as President

In examining the Clinton presidency at this stage, we must exercise prudence. The Clinton presidency is in its initial stages. Much of what we learn about a president's approach to governing and political leadership is found in specific undertakings, and these are in the process of unfolding. Also, even though Clinton's public behavior and commentary provide us with important preliminary data, public presidential behavior, however plentiful, cannot be the sole basis of analysis, because such behavior may well reflect as-yet-unknown strategic political calculation. Such behind-the-scenes calculations may modify our understanding of the meaning of an actor's public behavior and thus its place in any framework for analysis.

The inner workings, debates, and understandings of presidential administrations ordinarily come from several different sources: (1) interviews with top administration officials both during (on and off the record) and after their terms of service, (2) memoirs of officials who served in the administration, (3) records of the deliberations of the administration both formal (e.g., transcripts of meetings) and informal (e.g., summary memos with or without participants' notations). When these data emerge, they will doubtlessly enlarge our understanding of the Clinton presidency and may well modify the analyses of Clinton presented herein. Appropriately, therefore, we are still collecting data.

Uncovering emerging patterns does not guarantee that they will continue into and through a presidency. Changes in external circumstances may elicit new elements of a president's psychology or require modifications of the old ones. (These circumstances can, of course, reinforce older psychological patterns.) Although we have substantial data, our initial theoretical impressions about what these data mean and where they fit in specific appraisals of Clinton's presidency will be refined, modified, and perhaps abandoned as the Clinton administration both initiates and responds to events.

A president may also try to consciously discontinue unproductive patterns. Or, alternatively, a president may for political purposes at least appear to be doing so. Sometimes, as in the case of Clinton's widely publicized and analyzed "shift to the center," symbolized by his hiring of David Gergen, it is not yet clear whether we are witnessing the former or the latter.

As a general rule, however, it remains to be seen whether short-term politically motivated corrections can fundamentally alter presidential tendencies that reflect basic psychological patterns. For example, Sidney Blumenthal (1994), in interviewing Clinton about his first year in office, offered a number of areas in which the president learned from his experience. Among other lessons Clinton reported is the understanding that political capital is renewable and not fixed (32), his confidence that his vitality can carry him through his trials (33), and his recognition that at times he tried to do too much and became overscheduled (39). The last of these has been a perennial problem for Clinton since his days in Arkansas, and the implications of the others for how his presidency will evolve are at this point unclear. Given these facts, the analyses that follow can be offered only in the spirit of exploration, not validation.

The Clinton Presidency: Framing Questions, Dilemmas, and the Appraisal of Performance

The Clinton presidency faced a basic set of public questions at the outset regarding its real intentions, strategies, and competence. These questions persisted throughout the first year of his presidency. Clinton was elected president with a plurality of the votes cast while claiming a mandate for change. But almost all of his policy initiatives have been controversial, some extremely so. Why?

One reason is clearly related to emotional and political resistances to change. It is not only that systems in operation tend to build their own constituencies, although that is certainly true. It is also that even relationships that do not work well become preferable because their nature and limits are known. Another reason is that people question whether the change they wanted is the change they are getting. There is a concern that Clinton is not being entirely candid with the public either about the real costs of his policies or their impact, a concern fueled by the elastic estimates of the costs and savings of some administration initiatives.

There is also a related concern about Clinton's attempt to change the language of political discourse. New government programs are touted as "investments," payments to government entities such as health alliances are listed as "premiums," and so on. Whether Clinton is really a "new democrat" and, if so, what that really means remain unanswered questions.

In his approach to ordering military intervention in Bosnia, in his policies toward Haiti, and in the difficulties he encountered in Somalia (Bolton, 1993), Clinton often said one thing and did another. Was this the cool strategic calculation of a tough-minded president, a reflection of indecision and ambivalence, or an attempt to accomplish goals without clearly examining the potential difficulties and costs (Wolfowitz, 1993)?

So, too, in many of Clinton's domestic policies similar questions have been raised. Clinton has backed away from a number of his domestic campaign promises. Moreover, he has compromised or abandoned major parts of his policies initiatives. Is this the reflection of a mature pragmatic leader settling for what is obtainable, or does it reflect deeper inhibitions or concerns? How do we explain the puzzling discrepancies between his talents and performance? How will the public, other political actors, and professional analyzers of his administration come to view and evaluate the Clinton presidency?

The Psychological Context of the Clinton Presidency

The answers to these questions ultimately rest on two related factors. The first depends on the psychology of the president himself, his character, thinking, judgment, vision, and leadership skills. The second depends on his ability to successfully resolve what I term the *basic public dilemma*. I define the basic public dilemma as a fundamental unresolved question concerning public psychology facing the president on taking office. It is not a specific question about public policy but rather the public's psychological connections to its institutions, leaders, and political process. This unresolved public concern underlies and frames more specific policy debates.

Franklin D. Roosevelt faced one such dilemma in 1932 in deciding how the government would respond to potentially major national economic and social dislocations. For Lyndon Johnson in 1964, the question was whether and how the government should be the implementor of major programs designed to further the civil rights of and economic opportunities for disadvantaged and politically marginal groups. For Gerald Ford, in 1974 after Richard Nixon, and for Jimmy Carter in 1976, after the Johnson, Nixon, and Ford presidencies, the basic public dilemma was whether they could accomplish their policy purposes honestly as well as competently. For Ronald Reagan in 1980, the question revolved around the restoration of public faith in the office of president after the flawed presidencies of Lyndon Johnson and Richard Nixon and, as the public perceived them, the well-intentioned but ineffectual presidencies of Gerald Ford and Jimmy Carter.

Some presidents appreciate the nature of this major public dilemma and respond successfully, as did Franklin Roosevelt and Ronald Reagan. Others realize the dilemma but lack the skills to respond successfully, as was the case with Jimmy Carter. Still others, such as Lyndon Johnson, appreciate the major question but become distracted by other issues and wind up being unsuccessful.

What is the major public dilemma that faces Bill Clinton's presidency? It is not Bosnia and it is not his policy toward Iraq or the former Soviet Union. It is not the problem of the deficit or trade or health care, as important as all these problems are. It is the dilemma of public trust in public policy. At base, this dilemma reflects a fundamental public question about whether government policies, even those that are constructive in intent, can be fair in formulation and successful in result.

Americans' belief in the competence and fairness of government has been repeatedly challenged since the Great Society programs begun by Lyndon Johnson in 1964. Policies of government intervention designed to redress economic and social imbalances, constructive and even laudable in intent, have often not realized their goals. Moreover, they have often resulted in unanticipated and unsatisfactory consequences. More recent government policies designed to let the market accomplish laudable social purposes have not been adequate to the task, as the persistence of problems of poverty, crime, and the environment attest.

Wilson McWilliams (1993, 194) argued that "the clearest message of 1992 was the majority's demand for active government engaged to relieve America's discontents and reclaim the future." Perhaps so. But this public aspiration has a number of more specific expectations connected with it.

Clinton campaigned on a personal platform that stressed government's ability to develop and implement public policies that are fair to groups across the political spectrum and not just those that have traditionally supported the Democratic party. He promised that his policies would solve old problems, while not creating a host of new ones. And he promised to do so in ways that the public would understand and support. In short, he promised, in David Osborne and Ted Gaebler's (1992) ambitious phrase, to "reinvent government."

We now have some indications of the Clinton administration's approaches to a number of social issues and public policies. What is not clear is whether and how these approaches will work. The consequences of the administration's actions in many areas will not become clear for years.

Beyond and perhaps underlying the consequences of particular policy initiatives lie the areas of leadership, character, and judgment. These refer not so much to the substance of actual policies but to the choices the president makes in designing policies, mobilizing support, orchestrating the policy process, and consolidating his political and policy legacy.

The stakes are high. How high is suggested by a preliminary analysis of the implications of the 1992 election by Peter Nardulli and Jon Dalanger (1993; see also Ladd, 1993). They examined three possible implications of that election: that the election was a "deviating" election, with continuing strong prospects for the Republican party; that the election was a critical realignment at the presidential level; or that the election continued the process of electorate "dealignment." They concluded that the election might have enduring electoral consequences but that they will be dependent in part on "perceptions of his success in office." These perceptions, they argued, "will depend on what he accomplishes. ... But they will also be informed by what he is expected to accomplish. Clinton has promised much, and many groups who have been outsiders during decades of Republican rule are expecting much from him. In addition, expectations will be fueled by speculation that his victory, which is sizable given the historical measures we have used, marks the beginning of a democratic realignment" (166). Clinton certainly brings to these tasks a forceful personal psychology and obvious political talents. Let us now turn to some assessments of his prospects.

Notes

This chapter is a revised version of the introduction to a panel entitled "The Psychology of the Clinton Presidency: First Appraisals," which was presented at the annual meeting of the American Political Science Association, Washington, D.C., September 2–5, 1993, and was subsequently further refined and expanded (Renshon, 1994).

1. Telephone interview with Linda R. Pine, chief archivist, University of Arkansas Library, December 7, 1993.

2. For a detailed documentation of the strong personal connections among the elites in various sectors of Arkansas, see Boyer's (1994) analysis of the interrelationships of the various actors involved in what has come to be known as the "Whitewater case." Also relevant to this point is a summary by Engelberg and Gerth (1994).

References

Allen, Charles Flynn (1991). "Governor William Jefferson Clinton: A Biography with a Special Focus on his Educational Contributions." Ph.D. diss., University of Mississippi.

Blumenthal, Sidney (1994). "The Education of a President." *The New Yorker,* January 24, 31–43.

Bolton, John (1993). "Wrong Turn in Somalia?" *Foreign Affairs* (January-February):56–66.

Boyer, Peter J. (1994). "The Bridges of Madison Guaranty." *The New Yorker,* January 17, 32–38.

Engelberg, Stephen, and Jeff Gerth (1994). "The Whitewater Case: Finding the Connections." *New York Times,* January 16, A12.

Greenstein, Fred I. (1982). *The Hidden-Hand Presidency: Eisenhower as Leader.* New York: Basic Books.

Herbert, Bob (1994). "The Truth Sculptor." *New York Times,* January 12, A21.

Ladd, Everett Carl (1993). "The 1992 Vote for President Clinton: Another Brittle Mandate?" *Political Science Quarterly* (Spring):1–28.

McWilliams, Wilson Carry (1993). "The Meaning of the Election." In *The Election of 1992,* ed. Gerald Pomper, 190–218. New York: Chatham.

Nardulli, Peter F., and Jon K. Dalanger (1993). "The Presidential Election of 1992 in Historical Perspective." In *America's Choice: The Election of 1992,* ed. William J. Crotty, 149–167. Guilford, Conn.: Dushkin.

Osborne, David, and Ted Gaebler (1992). *Reinventing Government.* Reading, Mass.: Addison-Wesley.

Peters, Charles (1994). "Whitewater, and Other Thin Ice." *New York Times,* January 12, A21.

Renshon, Stanley A. (1994). "The Psychological Context of the Clinton Presidency." *Political Psychology* 15, no. 2:331–336.

Wolfowitz, Paul (1993). "Clinton's First Year." *Foreign Affairs* (January-February):28–66.

PART I

*Presidential Psychology—
The 1992 Campaign:
What Did We Learn?*

2

How George Bush Lost
the Presidential Election of 1992

BETTY GLAD

The Campaign

At the beginning of the 1992 presidential campaign, George Bush had several advantages vis-à-vis the Democrats for reelection. He enjoyed a big lead in the polls. Bush's leadership of the allied coalition during the war against Iraq had propelled him to the highest level of popularity of his presidency. In March 1991 his approval rating in a CNN/*Time* poll was nearly 90 percent (Yankelovich et al., 1992). A survey published in the *Los Angeles Times* on March 9, 1991, found that 86 percent of respondents said that Bush had strong leadership qualities (Pomper, 1993, 41). Patriotism and pride in America's strength as a world power seemed to sweep the nation.

This overwhelming support for Bush led such big-name Democrats as Mario Cuomo, Bill Bradley, and Jay Rockefeller to decide not to enter the 1992 race. They saw entrance as a suicidal endeavor. Even after Bush's thyroid problems became public in May 1991, the Democrats failed to capitalize on this opening. Instead, leading Democrats fueled the media with debates over possible messages and strategies. By August 1991, with only six months until the beginning of the nomination season, Paul Tsongas was the only committed Democratic contender.

Eventually six major Democratic candidates entered the race—in addition to Tsongas, there were Bill Clinton, Tom Harkin, Bob Kerrey, Douglas Wilder, and Jerry Brown. But early in the season it was clear that there were two front-runners, Tsongas and Clinton. Neither man at the time seemed particularly formidable. Tsongas had no charisma, and many voters were concerned about his health problems. In January and February an array of politically damaging charges arose suggesting that Clinton had had an extramarital affair with Gennifer Flowers, that he had avoided the draft, and that he had smoked

11

marijuana while a student. These accusations raised serious questions within the electorate about his character and his trustworthiness. After the February 25 South Dakota primary, 32 percent of the voters said they were concerned about Clinton's character (Hitchings, 1992, 124). Exit polls from the South Dakota primary showed him falling 20 points after these allegations (Hitchings, 1992, 423).

In these circumstances, Bush's decision to rely on campaign strategies that had worked either for him or for other Republican leaders in the recent past seemed to make sense. First, he used an Oval Office strategy. Bush had a record that he thought he could run on. It included the victories in Panama and Iraq, the end of the Cold War, the cuts in the nuclear arsenals of the United States and the Soviet Union, the passage of the Clean Air and the Americans with Disabilities acts, and a deficit reduction plan (Podhoretz, 1993, 192). Also, focusing on the accomplishments and duties of the president had worked well in the past when a president had had a substantial lead in the polls (e.g., Richard Nixon in 1972 and Ronald Reagan in 1984). In a meeting with campaign aides at Camp David in August 1991, Bush decided to follow this policy, running on his record and using the same "feel-good" model for the campaign that had sent Reagan back to the White House in 1984. At that point in the administration, Bush was more than 10 points higher in the popularity polls than Reagan had been at the same point in his first term (Podhoretz, 1993, 192).

No real efforts were made to prepare for the reelection campaign until December 1991 (Germond and Witcover, 1993, 58). It was not until January 1992, when Bush was challenged by Patrick Buchanan in New Hampshire, that the president came out of the White House to meet voters personally on the campaign trail, and even then he did so for only a limited time. Later in the primary season when Buchanan had been removed as a real threat to Bush's nomination, Bush let Vice President Dan Quayle take over much of the campaigning. In the fall Bush continued to shy away from the campaign trail. It was not until after the last presidential debate on October 19 that he seemed to awaken and become an aggressive campaigner (Germond and Witcover, 1993, 484).

Second, he ran on his reputation as a foreign policy leader. In his first reelection campaign speech to the voters of New Hampshire on January 15, the president focused on his recent successes in the Gulf (Graubard, 1992). The next day he released a triumphant statement commemorating the first anniversary of the beginning of the Gulf War, calling the effort "a tremendous victory for the United States of America" (Bush, 1992b, 22).

Third, Bush chose to ignore the economy as much as possible and paper over difficulties he needed to address. In his State of the Union address in 1991, he saw only a "temporary interruption in America's economic growth" (Bush, 1991, 92). Throughout most of 1991, Bush voiced feelings that the economy was basically sound and improving and that there was no need for programs to stimulate growth. But in December 1991 the new White House chief of staff, John Sununu, did say that the country was in a recession (Rosenthal, 1991, 1). And during the first campaign trip to New Hampshire in January 1992, Bush did admit that the economy was in a "free fall." But then he insisted that the situation might not be that bad. "There are some fundamentals that are pretty darn good," he said (Bush, 1992c; Germond and Witcover, 1993, 291). As to specific proposals, he told voters to "stay tuned to the State of the Union address" to hear about his economic program (Germond and Witcover, 1993, 144). But when the January 28, 1992, address was aired, he emphasized foreign policy by discussing it first. When he did address domestic issues, his economic proposals were mostly warmed-over projects he had offered earlier in his presidency. Washington, he said, "must clear away the obstacles to growth: high taxes, high regulation, red-tape, and yes, wasteful government spending" (Bush, 1992a, 157). In June 1992, shortly after unemployment had jumped from 7.2 to 7.5 percent and the jobless rate had been reported to be the highest since August 1984, Bush said that he thought the economy was getting better (Bush, 1992d, 421).

Fourth, Bush also renewed his efforts, as he had more or less successfully in the past, to consolidate his position with those on the right of the Republican party. His relationship with them had always been problematic. Unlike Reagan, Bush was not a product of the conservative movement, as Republican consultant Charles Black noted (Germond and Witcover, 1993, 21). Indeed, in Bush's early career he had been progressive in several respects. As a member of the House of Representatives, he had disclosed his personal finances and had voted for a congressional ethics law, the amendment to permit eighteen-year-olds to vote, the ending of the draft, and the establishment of the Peace Corps (King, 1980, 57). After some flip flops he voted for the Civil Rights Act of 1968 (which provided for open housing for veterans). Moreover, he belonged to two foreign policy groups anathema to the right wing—the Council on Foreign Relations and the Trilateral Commission (Blumenthal, 1993, 54–55).[1] During the 1980 primary campaign, Bush opposed a constitutional amendment that would have overturned *Roe* v. *Wade,* the Supreme Court decision that had legalized abortion.

As Reagan's running mate in 1980, Bush moved to the right. He dropped his memberships in the Council on Foreign Relations and the Trilateral Commission. As vice president, he changed his mind on the abortion issue and said he favored a "human life amendment." In 1985 he met with evangelist Jim Bakker, and three Bush advisers were put on the payroll of Praise the Lord, Bakker's evangelical organization. In January 1986 Bush addressed a Jerry Falwell convention, noting that America "is in crying need of [Falwell's] moral visions" (Blumenthal, 1993, 69). Shortly after Reagan returned from the Moscow summit in the spring of 1988, Bush positioned himself to the right of the president regarding developments in the Soviet Union. "I don't agree that we know enough to say that there is a kind of fundamental change ... on the part of the Soviet system" (Blumenthal, 1993, 254).

As a presidential candidate in 1988, Bush chose the conservative Dan Quayle as his running mate and made the now famous "no new taxes" pledge. On foreign policy issues, Bush noted several times that the Cold War was not over (Blumenthal, 1993, 254). As president, he opted for a more distant, rigid, and confrontational relationship with the Democratic-led Congress, vetoing the Democratic civil rights bill as well as more than twenty-nine other bills (Pomper, 1993, 24). His nomination of Clarence Thomas to the U.S. Supreme Court was another effort to tilt the court further in a conservative direction.

Yet as president, Bush also took several actions that created frustrations in the right wing of his party. Many Reagan supporters felt that Bush's focus on a kinder, gentler America and emphasis on his appointees being held to a higher standard of ethics (Germond and Witcover, 1993, 24) implied invidious comparisons between the Bush and Reagan administrations. Several key Bush administration officials, including Chief of Staff John Sununu and Office of Management and Budget director Richard Darman, were not in attendance in the White House East Room on November 15, 1989, when the portraits of Ronald and Nancy Reagan were unveiled (Podhoretz, 1993, 145). Foreign policy militants were distressed when Bush provided only a weak condemnation of the People's Republic of China after the crackdown on prodemocracy demonstrations in Tiananmen Square and when he failed to take advantage of a coup attempt in Panama to oust Manuel Noriega from office (Germond and Witcover, 1993, 35, 42). Moreover, when Doug Wead, the White House conservative liaison person, complained about a gay rights group's invitation to the White House signing of a bill on hate crimes, he was fired. After Sununu, the man who had claimed to be the conservatives' "best friend in the White House," left his position as chief of staff, conservatives were trading stories about the disrespect with which he had treated them (Podhoretz, 1993, 94).

Most important, when Bush agreed to the budget deal of 1990, which included tax increases in an effort to reduce the federal deficit, he made no real attempt to justify this renunciation of his solemn 1988 campaign promise. The right wing reacted with great indignation. Ninety Republican members of the House of Representatives signed a letter to Bush saying that they were "stunned" by his announcement and declaring that a tax increase was unacceptable (Germond and Witcover, 1993, 42).

As a consequence of these actions, Bush during the 1992 presidential campaign had to once again repair his relations with the radical Right. Suggestions that he replace Quayle as the vice-presidential nominee were rejected. Shortly after the New Hampshire primary, Bush fired John E. Frohnmayer as chair of the National Endowment for the Arts (Germond and Witcover, 1993, 231). On the campaign trail, the Bush team used the conservative family values issue to secure his base with the Christian Right. The Republican party was portrayed as the bastion of traditional work values, while the Democrats were painted as liberals who were soft on crime, welfare, and other such issues. Thus, the election was characterized as a war between traditional values and a "cultural elite" that mocked families, religion, and patriotism. This emphasis on "traditional family values" would not only energize moral conservatives; it would also focus attention on Clinton's earlier marital problems.

Finally, the Republican campaign organization resorted to the kind of negative campaigning that had worked in 1988. Michael Dukakis's substantial lead after the Democratic convention had melted under such a barrage. The 1992 Republican campaign polls suggested that a similar campaign would work against Clinton. His record in Arkansas was not that well known, and charges of marital infidelity and the draft issue had raised substantial questions about his character.

Ignoring the conventional wisdom that it is best to leave personal attacks to campaign advertisements and other members of the campaign organization, President Bush, in the fall of 1992, spearheaded the attack. Sometimes Bush worked within the clearly acceptable range of critiques, going after his opponent's record. Thus, in late September the president toured Arkansas's border states, saying, "I have resisted the urge to focus on Governor Clinton's record. But I must tell you, I am very tired of the distortions, tired of the half truths. And the stakes are too high to let America be deceived by a negative campaign. So today I have to ... talk about my opponent's record ... in Arkansas. ... And that means explaining the Grand Canyon that separates his rhetoric from the reality of his record" (Germond and Witcover, 1993, 431).[2]

In several more bruising personal attacks, Bush demeaned the Clinton-Gore team and zeroed in on the character issue. He called Senator Al Gore "the ozone man" and compared Clinton's foreign policy experience with that of the Bush family dog, Millie (Germond and Witcover, 1993, 496). Bush hammered away at Clinton's explanation of his effort to avoid draft induction twenty-five years earlier and questioned his patriotism. A particularly strong accusation came on October 7 when on *Larry King Live* in a set of carefully guarded innuendoes, Bush suggested that Clinton had engaged in particularly suspicious acts when he traveled to the USSR as a student at Oxford. "*I don't want to tell you what I really think because I don't have the facts.* But to go to Moscow one year after Russia crushed Czechoslovakia, not to remember who you saw? ... You can remember who you saw in the airport in Oslo, but you can't remember who you saw in the airport in Moscow? I say level with the American people on the draft, whether you went to Moscow, how many demonstrations he led against his country from a foreign soil" (Rosenthal, 1992a, A1).

With less than seven weeks until election day, the president went all out on Clinton's draft record. In a radio interview with talk show host Rush Limbaugh, Bush blasted Clinton's "total failure to come clean with the American people" on the draft issue. Clinton's "fundamental difficulty is that he has not told the full truth, the whole truth, and nothing but the truth." Inaccurately, Bush charged that in a letter to Colonel Eugene Holmes, an army recruiter in Arkansas, Clinton had called the military "immoral" (Germond and Witcover, 1993, 430). In the third presidential debate, at Michigan State University, Bush again raised "this question about trust," charging that to please one group and then another, Clinton had shown a pattern that "is a dangerous thing to suggest would work for the Oval Office" (Germond and Witcover, 1993, 14).

Despite all these efforts, George Bush experienced a precipitous and steady decline in his approval ratings from his high standing during the Gulf War. Indeed, Bush sustained the greatest drop in presidential popularity ever recorded. His overall job performance had slipped from a nearly 90 percent positive ranking in March 1991 to 47 percent in December 1991, according to a January 16 *Washington Post* poll. By the eve of the Republican convention, he had received the lowest job approval rating of any president at a similar point in his presidency and the highest disapproval rating of any incumbent president seeking reelection (Gallup, 1992, 142).

In the end, Bush won 38 percent of the popular vote to Clinton's 43 percent and Perot's 19 percent. He lost the electoral college to Clinton by a vote of 370 to 168. He also dropped states that had been Republican since 1964: Vermont, New Hampshire, California, Montana, Colorado, New Mexico, Illinois, New Jersey, and Nevada. He also lost Georgia, a state that the Republican party had concentrated on and expected to win. Most of the industrial Midwest went to the Democrats and really sealed Bush's defeat. Clinton also won all six New England states. Bush managed to lose almost 30 percent of his 1988 voting base and joined the ranks of John Adams, William Howard Taft, Herbert Hoover, and Jimmy Carter in presidential coalition collapses (Pomper, 1993, 31). Bush did, however, win Texas, making Clinton the first president to win without the Lone Star State.

Independent candidate Ross Perot won no states. But he received from 25 to 30 percent of the vote in Maine, Utah, Alaska, Idaho, Kansas, Montana, Nevada, Oregon, and Wyoming. He won more of the popular vote than any other twentieth-century third-party independent candidate. Exit polls suggested that he pulled more from the Republicans (31 percent) than from the Democrats (26 percent), though his main appeal was to the independents (43 percent). Though he had reinforced Clinton's campaign earlier in the campaign season, at the end of the run he pulled almost evenly from the two other candidates. Perot supporters were split evenly between Bush and Clinton for their second choice (Hitchings, 1992, 825, 826).

The Loss: Structural Explanations

At the most basic level Bush's loss was due to changes in the political situation in which he operated and his failure to respond appropriately to those changes. First, George Bush's emphasis on his foreign policy credentials no longer had the appeal it had once had. He and other Republicans generally tried to take credit for "winning" the Cold War. But the disappearance of a formidable external enemy dictated that foreign policy would no longer command the attention of the American people as it had earlier. Moreover, public exultation over the U.S. victory in the Gulf War faded as it became apparent that Saddam Hussein would remain in power and continue to create problems. Even limited wars in which one side can claim a victory are apt to have ambiguous results. Public opinion polls in early 1992 showed that 63 percent of the American people believed that Bush had stopped too soon by declaring a cease-fire before Hussein was ousted or killed. An NBC News/*Wall Street Journal* report on January 11 showed that fewer than 60 percent of Americans believed that the Gulf War had been worth fighting (Hitchings, 1992, 23).

Second, the economy was getting worse, which often bodes ill for an incumbent president. The 1981 tax cuts had permanently unbalanced the federal budget, and the Republican refusal to raise taxes combined with the refusal of the Democratic-led Congress to support drastic program cuts created a situation in which no corrective actions could be taken. The ultimate consequence was an explosive increase in the federal deficit as a share of the gross national product and thus in federal debt. By 1992 the U.S. debt had quadrupled to more than $4 trillion. To compound Bush's difficulties, the United States was in a recession during the campaign. The unemployment rate jumped from 7.2 percent in April to 7.5 percent in May 1992, according to Labor Department figures released in June. These figures were the highest since August 1984 (Hitchings, 1992, 423). News stories compounded the problem. Reports on the downsizing of major corporations in response to major structural changes in the economy indicated that this time many white-collar people were being laid off. Even those who had jobs no longer felt safe.

Third, as a result of these developments, the electorate in 1992 had different concerns than it had had in 1988. The conservative moral values issue had less appeal than in 1988. A summary of polls in 1992 indicates that the electorate was not interested in the issues of adultery, abortion, racism, taxes, and family (Gallup, 1992). Other polls showed that Americans thought that the economy was in bad shape. In late November 1991, a *New York Times*/CBS poll showed that only 25 percent of the U.S. population approved of Bush's handling of the economy (Toner, 1991, A1).

Fourth, Bush's challenger for the Republican nomination, columnist Patrick Buchanan, undermined the president's credibility and widened the split within the Republican party. On the campaign trail in New Hampshire, for example, Buchanan argued that Bush "would put America's wealth and power at the service of some vague new world order. We put America first" (Germond and Witcover, 1993, 134–135). Buchanan also critiqued the president's mismanagement of the economy and his reneging on the 1988 promise of no new taxes. One television commercial showed a close-up of Bush's face saying, "Read my lips: No new taxes." Then a commentator noted, "It was not some liberal Democrat who declared, 'Read my lips: No new taxes,' then broke his word to cut a seedy back-room deal with the big spenders on Capitol Hill. It was not Teddy Kennedy who railed against a quota bill, then embraced its twin. It was not Congress alone who set off the greatest spending spree in 60 years, running up the largest deficits in modern history. ... No, that was done by men in whom we placed our confidence and our trust and who turned their backs and walked away from us" (Germond and Witcover, 1993, 135). An ad airing on February 26 accused Bush of condoning pornography by supporting the National Endowment for the Arts and showed part of a movie with leather-clad black homosexual men dancing that had received indirect funding from the endowment. An announcer said, "This so-called art has glorified homosexuality, exploited children and perverted the image of Jesus Christ" (Germond and Witcover, 1993, 233).

Buchanan was never a serious contender for the presidency. Several polls indicated that most of the people who voted for him were simply registering their discontent with Bush; they did not expect Buchanan to be president. In New Hampshire a relatively high unemployment rate seems to have contributed to the protest vote (Hitchings, 1992, 108). Even in Georgia, where the economy was relatively healthy, 81 percent of Buchanan's voters said that they had voted for him because they wanted to send a message to Bush; only 15 percent said that they thought Buchanan would make a good president (Hitchings, 1992, 149). Buchanan's candidacy, however, drove the president even further to the right, which undermined his ability to appeal to the center.

Fifth, the Democratic nominee in 1992 ran a much smarter campaign than Dukakis had in 1988. Bill Clinton made the economy his major issue. The issues of race, abortion, and class that had divided the Democratic party since 1964 were deliberately low-keyed by the Clinton campaign organization. Positive advertisements focused on Bill Clinton's commitment to "make America work." Negative attacks focused on Bush's failures with the economy but stayed on the safe side of the insult line. One commercial, for example, quoted the president as saying, "I am not prepared to say that we are in a recession." Then an announcer remarked, "If Bush doesn't understand the problem, then how can he solve it?" (Pomper, 1993, 99).

Clinton was also far better at damage control than Dukakis had ever been. An organization was created for that purpose, and it had computerized data banks that developed instant rebuttals to every Republican attack (or serious media critique). Press releases were assembled and faxed to journalists from campaign headquarters in an effort to end a detrimental news story before it went to press. If that was not possible, the charge and its rebuttal would appear in the same news cycle. If the press crew failed at this endeavor, then Clinton or Gore often responded directly (Pomper, 1993, 85).

Other major figures of the campaign also counterattacked. Hillary Rodham Clinton, for example, put the media on trial in a *Vanity Fair* interview when she referred to rumors about Bush allegedly having had an extramarital affair and claimed that "the establishment" had shielded Bush from any questions about it. Vice-presidential candidate Al Gore capitalized on the disclosure that the State Department had conducted a special search to find the Clinton passport files. "This is not a police state, George Bush," he shouted at one rally. In a written statement, Gore called the State Department records search a "startling abuse of power and a violation of our country's most basic principles" (Rosenthal, 1992c, B10). Clinton's communications director, George Stephanopoulos, called the Bush attack on Clinton's patriotism while on *Larry King Live* "a sad and pathetic ploy by a desperate politician. If he worried as much about what most Americans are going through in 1992 as he does about what Bill Clinton did in 1969, we'd all be in better shape" (Germond and Witcover, 1993, 434). Clinton himself stated that he was proud of his opposition to the Vietnam War but was not a big organizer of antiwar activities.

In the first debate in St. Louis on October 11, Clinton himself used George Bush's father against him. Responding to Bush's attack on Clinton's youthful demonstrations against the United States while abroad, Clinton countered, "When Joe McCarthy went around this country attacking people's patriotism, he was wrong, and a senator from Connecticut stood up to him named Prescott Bush. Your father was right to stand up to Joe McCarthy. You were wrong to attack my patriotism. I was opposed to the war, but I loved my country" (Hitchings, 1992, 765; Germond and Witcover, 1993, 475).

Finally, Ross Perot's independent candidacy for the presidency, announced two days before the New Hampshire primary, also had a detrimental effect on Bush's campaign. Perot's somber warnings during the primary season about the state of the entire country buttressed the Clinton message. Throughout the spring campaign he criticized the president's economic plan and the growth of the national debt. His announcement on the last day of the July Democratic convention that he was withdrawing from the race served to boost Clinton's campaign. Attributing this decision to a "revitalized" Democratic party, Perot reinforced the message that Clinton was in fact a different kind of Democrat. And though Perot declined to endorse Clinton or Bush, he noted that the Democratic party had "done a brilliant job, in my opinion, of coming back" (Hitchings, 1992, 517, 525).

When Perot reentered the race on October 1, he continued to focus on the bad state of the economy and on at least one occasion came to Clinton's rescue. In the first debate, right after Bush argued that his superior experience distinguished him from his rivals, Perot said, "I don't have any experience in running up a four-trillion-dollar debt. I don't have any experience in gridlock government." In the third debate, at Michigan State University on October 19, after Bush had hammered away at Clinton's character, Perot countered with the common-sense proposition that a person's actions as a young man were less relevant than his actions as an adult politician. Perot then went on to cite Bush's role as vice president in the decision to trade arms to Iran in exchange for the release of hostages in Lebanon.

In addition to reinforcing the Clinton message, Perot's presence in the campaign, particularly during the primary season, diverted the energies, money, and arrows of the Bush team. "The Republicans made a fatal mistake turning their howitzers on Ross Perot," Stephanopoulos said. "It gave us an opportunity to come up the middle" (Germond and Witcover, 1993, 354).

Ideological, Tactical, and Stylistic Factors

Some of Bush's campaign difficulties—the declining importance of foreign policy, certain economic problems, the Perot candidacy—were caused by complex factors beyond George Bush's control. But other problems were rooted in the ideological base from which Bush worked. He was simply being true to his own conservative values when he refused to recommend any major new economic plans to address the recession. As a conservative he was bound to the laissez-faire policies of the Republican party. Social reforms, as Bush suggested in an ABC interview, did not consist of "being able to match the highest bidder on federal money." His pitch as president for a kinder, gentler nation, as a friend of C. Boyden Gray noted in 1988, was mainly an appeal for personal generosity (Solomon, 1988, 2711). In terms of public policy, as one of his aides noted, his pitch involved such things as tax credits for day care, not some new bureaucracy or new spending (Dionne, 1989). As Kerry Mullins and Aaron Wildavsky (1992, 32) said, Bush was committed to an inclusive hierarchy in which all classes, races, religions, and interests would be integrated into a cohesive whole in which leaders would serve and followers would "grant them the authority due to their positions." Within this framework individuals would be free to compete for economic goods in a free market. Free enterprise zones, not an increase in the minimum wage, which would cut into employers' freedom of choice, were his remedy for economically distressed regions of the United States. Economic growth would be promoted by a reduction in taxes, not an increase in spending to boost consumer demands.

Other problems were the consequence of tactical mistakes. Bush had a tendency to overcorrect for his political problems. This was evident in his courting of the Right. By the time of the Super Tuesday primaries on March 10, Patrick Buchanan had failed to win more than 32 percent of the vote in any state; it was clear that his campaign was over, though he vowed to continue through the California primary. But the Bush team continued to see him as a major player and made concessions to him that hurt Bush with the political center he needed to win in November (Scheider, 1992, 668). In exchange for an endorsement of Bush at the Republican convention, the Bush team agreed to let Buchanan speak during prime time. Though a copy of the speech was faxed to the White House, campaign operatives Jim Lake and Bob Teeter simply scanned it to see if it contained a sufficiently enthusiastic endorsement of Bush. They completely overlooked the potentially negative effect of Buchanan's declaration that the election was a religious war being fought "for the soul of America" and his blasts against the Clinton team for endorsing homosexual rights, abortion on demand, women in combat, and policies "discriminating" against religious schools (Germond and Witcover, 1993, 410). At the convention, Marilyn Quayle presented herself as a different kind of baby-boomer. "I came of age in a time of turbulent social change. ... But, remember, not everyone demonstrated, dropped out, took drugs, joined in the sexual revolution, or dodged the draft. Not everyone believed that the family was so oppressive that women could only thrive apart from it." She was met with uproarious applause from fellow moralists.

These images that the moral Right had taken over the Republican party might have shored up Bush with the Right, but they dismayed Republican moderates at the convention and turned off middle-of-the-road Americans who would have to be brought aboard for a Republican majority to be reached in the general election. It is true that there was a short-term postconvention bounce for Bush (Germond and Witcover, 1993, 416). But by August 26 those gains had evaporated as the polls showed Bush at 30 percent approval as opposed to Clinton's 51 percent (Clymer, 1992, A1).

Stylistically, George Bush undermined his own campaign by his apparent complacency. He often appeared indecisive, unable to articulate what he sought from political office and what his policies would be. In October 1987, for example, when asked by *Newsweek* correspondent Margaret Garrard Warner why he entered politics, he roamed all over the field. "It's hard to describe. ... I got intrigued with it, I felt fascinated, believe in the country, in its strength, in helping people. You know, all the reasons people go into politics. Challenges and rewards" (Blumenthal, 1993, 71; cf. with equally vague statements in Bush and Gold, 1988, 192). As president, he had been slow to define what his policies toward the Soviet Union would be, and he was slow to remove top aides such as John Sununu and Samuel Skinner when they were a political liability. (James Baker did not become chief of staff until August 24, 1992.) During the 1992 campaign, as we have seen, he was slow in getting out of the White House and onto the campaign trail and slow and low-key in describing what he would do during a second term in office (Duffy and Goodgame, 1992).

Certainly, even as a conservative Bush could have handled the economic issues more forcefully than he did. His campaign staff warned him that he should pay more attention to the economy. In August 1991 Republican campaign adviser Mary Matalin argued at a Camp David meeting that Bush could not rest on his foreign policy laurels alone but would have to develop a domestic agenda for the reelection campaign. Later Bob Teeter, the campaign manager, warned Bush that because of the economy, his reelection was not a sure thing (Germond and Witcover, 1993, 58–59).

But Bush just could not see how this situation differed from past ones in which he had been successful (Germond and Witcover, 1993, 59–61). Throughout 1991, as we have seen, he downplayed economic issues in his political statements. He failed even to pay sufficient attention on the campaign trail to the modest reforms he had outlined in his January 1992 State of the Union speech. Nor did he ever attempt to explain as a matter of the government's principle why doing more would have been counterproductive (Solomon, 1992). His suggestion late in 1992 that if reelected, he would make Jim Baker his domestic czar suggested that Bush was so weak he could not perform the basic policy function of personally providing direction in the economic realm (Hitchings, 1992, 764).

Bush's complacency about the economy was compounded by certain reactions that suggested he was out of contact with the concerns of ordinary people. On February 4 in Orlando, Florida, he expressed astonishment when confronted with a mock-up of a supermarket checkout counter at the exhibition hall of the National Grocers Association convention. He could not believe the electronic devices used to detect check forgery or the electronic scanners that used bar codes for reordering and ease of checkout (Rosenthal, 1992b, A1, A19). (Many grocery stores had begun using scanners as early as 1972.)

Even more damaging was his response to a question at the Richmond debate in the fall about how the national debt had affected each candidate's life. Bush responded by mentioning the effect on interest rates. Then he concluded, "I love my grandchildren. … I want to think that they're going to be able to afford an education. I think that that's an important part of being a parent." When debate moderator Carole Simpson explained that the question was about the recession, not just the deficit, Bush described how he sought and heard from many people in the White House each day, how he went to an AME church and read in its bulletin about the difficulties families were having making ends meet. "But I don't think it's fair to say, 'You haven't had cancer, therefore you don't know what it is like' " (Germond and Witcover, 1993, 10). At this, Clinton campaign press spokesperson Dee Dee Myers exulted, "The campaign is over. George Bush is dead. He just killed himself." Then

Democratic campaign aides rushed to the press room to put that spin on Bush's remarks (Germond and Witcover, 1993, 9, 12–13).

Bush's credibility as a leader was undermined further by certain speech patterns. A patrician who liked to be liked, he tried too hard to look hip or ordinary or tough or to be a good ol' boy. Oftentimes the result was a series of non sequiturs. For example, after one of his health scares, Bush was asked if he intended to keep Quayle with him on the 1992 ticket, to which he responded, "Do you want that by hand or do you want it by word?" (Germond and Witcover, 1993, 393). In Dover, New Hampshire, he explained that, despite his burdens, he felt blessed. "Don't cry for me, Argentina" (Germond and Witcover, 1993, 144). Toward the end of the 1992 campaign at a rally at Macomb County Community College, he explained his calling Al Gore "ozone man" with, "You know why I call him ozone man? This guy is so far off in the environmental extreme, we'll be up to our necks in owls and out of work for every American. This guy's crazy. He is way out, far out. Far out, man!" (Germond and Witcover, 1993, 495). On Halloween at a rally in Burlington, Wisconsin, Bush warned that "if Clinton is elected, every day is going to be Halloween. Fright and Terror!" The same day at Oshkosh, he continued with, "Fright and terror! Witches and devils everywhere!" (Germond and Witcover, 1993, 502).

Psychological Factors

Shortly after his inaugural, it seemed that Bush might turn out to be an activist president. Maureen Dowd (1989, A1, A8) of the *New York Times* noted that Bush seemed to be "pulling items out of his political hope chest with dizzying speed, drawing dramatic distinctions between himself and Ronald Reagan." It was also evident that he clearly enjoyed his new job, showing visitors around the White House with "gleeful enthusiasm." He had an enormous capacity for friendship and play, writing hundreds of personal notes and entertaining scores of people. In choosing John Sununu as chief of staff, he chose a brusque individual who complemented his own amiable personality. Reports on his family suggested that he had the kind of anchoring that would enable him to be a man of judgment and balance. His sibling and his children were all loving, polite, and loyal to each other and good at family values (Safire, 1989, A25).

Yet, as it turned out, George Bush excelled only when he was leading the country in a team effort that could be understood in terms of traditional values. He had been impressed as a young man when Henry Stimson addressed the students at Phillips Andover Academy on the need to stand up to aggressors. The battle Bush led against Saddam Hussein can be understood in terms of his decision not to be a Chamberlain in dealing with another Hitler. Here Bush's personal contacts and skills had considerable currency, helping build the coalition that fought that war (Glad, Whicker, Phiffner, and Moore, 1993, 80).

Traditional norms, however, did not provide him with clear guidelines for dealing with the problems in the American economy that came to a head on his watch. Moreover, his procrastination on the campaign trail in 1992 was caused partly by the absence of traditional guidelines for him to follow so that he could both serve the country and satisfy the components of his electoral coalition. Nor did "traditional" Republican campaign tactics—an emphasis on foreign policy and social issues, a tilt to the right, an emphasis on feeling good and/or attacks on the personal qualities of his opponent—provide him with a campaign rhetoric and a strategy that would work in the electoral clime of 1992.

Several Republican leaders have noted some of these qualities. One high-level Reagan administration official who worked on Bush's 1988 campaign noted: "When faced with a conflict among ideas his tendency is not to try to get analytical leverage or to formulate the nature of the problem and the choice. ... His tendency is a political tendency. He tries to have it both ways" (Blumenthal, 1993, 52). A senior strategist of the Bush campaign called Bush a transitional figure (Blumenthal, 1993, 52).

George Bush's reliance on traditional norms also meant that his hyperactivity, with notable exceptions such as his management of the allied coalition during the war with Iraq, often lacked discipline and direction. *Newsweek,* for example, noted that his "frenetic activity often puts the emphasis on activity not action." Thus, on one day the previous week he had traveled twelve hours to give two ten-minute political speeches (DeFrank and McDaniel, 1989, 30).

Some of his stylistic mistakes on the campaign trail derived from the fact that, like many organization men, George Bush was not an intuitive person who could feel his way through complex situations. When he had to be political, he did what he felt was necessary, but he never quite got the subtleties of the act he had to perform. The problem was how to reconcile his own patrician past and taste for management with certain political necessities. He was willing, as he told journalist David Frost (Pomper, 1993, 85), to do whatever it took to be reelected. But if he showed himself as an upper-class, Yale-educated patrician, he would not be elected. So to make contact with common people, he talked the way he thought others talked. As Sidney Blumenthal (1993, 51, 53) noted, "He walked like a patrician; he looked like a patrician; he had the accents of a patrician; yet he did not really talk like one." "The use of the vernacular by the genteel," Blumenthal continued, "is always an effort to cover vast social distance."

Bush's "tough talk" is an example of the problems he had in negotiating that social distance. Early in his career, George Bush was widely perceived as a wimp—a puzzling view given his history as a combat pilot and World War II hero. This perception was rooted partly in his proclivity to avoid conflicts within the organizations in which he worked and partly in his patterns of speech. When he talked of getting into "deep doo doo," Bush sounded like a New England prep school boy.

Aggressive language was a way of countering that image. His remark after his debate with Geraldine Ferraro in 1984—that "we kicked ass" last night—was one such episode. His encounter with Dan Rather on January 25, 1988, over his role in the Iran-contra affair was another (Blumenthal, 1993, 75). A Bush media adviser, according to two commentators, stationed himself next to the camera where Bush could see him and held up key responses on a legal pad. Afterward, Bush reported to the aide that Rather was a "bastard" who had not been "able to lay a glove on me" (Blumenthal, 1993, 75).[3] The wimp charge was put to rest at this time by these devices.

Yet in both events Bush showed a tin ear. His statement about Ferraro was one that "no good ol' boy would likely make about a woman" (Blumenthal, 1993, 51). His comments after the Rather interview were equally inappropriate. Bush bragged privately that Rather was even more of a "pussy" than CBS interviewer Leslie Stahl (Orman, 1991, 9). But this statement carried highly inappropriate and sexist innuendoes that Bush very shortly thereafter had to correct. He claimed that he had called Rather a "pussycat" (Orman, 1991, 8).

Characterological Roots

At this point a few words on the sources of organizational loyalties should be noted. The reason executives conform to organizational norms may differ from individual to individual. For many people, as William Whyte Jr. noted in *The Organization Man* (1956, 14–59, 129, 141–156), which was published at a time when Bush was first building his economic base, conformity to organizational norms is a response to a need for belonging and togetherness in the capitalist structures of the day. Loyalty to the company, it was assumed, would be paid off in the company's loyalty to the individual who played by the rules.

The extent to which these rules are internalized, however, varies from person to person. For some individuals, conformity may be due to strategic considerations. In certain organizational and political contexts, going along may be the only way to get ahead. Some of these leaders, when they reach the top, may emerge with creative political agendas (Glad, 1991). But for many, conformity has deeply rooted psychological causes. People are generally afraid of the "godlike" in themselves, as Abraham Maslow (1968, 61–62) noted. To see and hear things on one's own are a condition of growth, but they are also dangerous. Independence of this sort can be seen in others as a challenge and can lead to feelings of isolation. People who hold authority figures in awe may additionally fear that such actions will bring down the wrath of these older, stronger men.

When George Bush first took office, several observers saw him as suddenly emerging from a cocoon. As Dowd (1992, 1) noted, the "64 year-old Mr. Bush has made his passage from faithful and sometimes fumbling lieutenant to self-assured leader with an ease that has amazed all but those close to him." A person appointed to his cabinet noted that "it's as though a great shadow has lifted" (Dowd, 1992, 1).

This transformation, as we have seen, did not occur. George Bush's conformity, it seems, was deeply rooted in his personality and history. In essence he found his security by operating within the frameworks he had inherited. Partly this conformity was based in his temperament. From the beginning, he wanted people close to him to like him. Even as an infant he was a friendly, sharing child. His nickname, "Have Half," came from his willingness to share his toys, food, and clothes with everybody. Moreover, he was inseparable from his older brother, Prescott Jr. Once when the family moved into a new house, his mother, after hearing a child psychologist speak, gave each boy his own room. Two months later the two boys came to their parents and told them what they wanted for Christmas: to go back to sharing the same room (Kilian, 1992, 36; Bush and Gold, 1988, 231). George was also so miserable when Prescott Jr. first started Greenwich Country Day School that their father arranged for George's early admission to that school, although he was quite small and less strong than his older classmates (Green, 1992, 12).

Bush's proclivities to "go along" were also due to familial and broader cultural factors. While finding pleasures with peers, young George faced awesome parental models, which would have made rebellion against them very difficult. Prescott Bush, at six feet four inches tall, was an imposing figure. He had made his fortune in a St. Louis hardware firm and then joined a prestigious Wall Street firm (Brown Brothers and Harriman and Company). He served as a captain in the army in World War I and attended Yale, where he excelled at sports and academics and was elected to the Skull and Bones, the most prestigious secret society on campus. He also believed in public service. Throughout George's childhood and early adult years, Prescott was the moderator of the Greenwich, Connecticut, town meeting and a top fund-raiser for the Republican party. During World War II he headed the United Service Organizations. He also served, at various times, as president of the U.S. Golf Association and on the board of Pan American Airways and CBS News (Green, 1992, 5). In 1952 he won a Senate seat, surmounting charges by Drew Pearson that he was "involved with Planned Parenthood" (Blumenthal, 1993, 57). A moderate Republican, he supported the Eisenhower internationalist foreign policy and spoke in favor of the censure of Senator Joseph McCarthy (R.–Wisc.). In 1960 Prescott Bush joined seven other Republicans and northern Democrats in an attempt to block a southern filibuster on a civil rights bill.

He was a "big guy, tough" is how Bush remembered his father as an adult (Frost in Blumenthal, 1993, 56). "It never occurred to me to differ. I mean, he was up here and I was this little guy down here" (Blumenthal, 1993, 56). Barbara Bush noted how even when she and her husband were adults, they tiptoed around Prescott Bush Sr. (Kilian, 1992, 35).

Bush's mother was also an impressive figure. Dorothy Bush provided a rich environment of friends, games, and vacations. According to George, she was also the most influential parent in terms of showing him how to relate to others (Bush and Gold, 1988, 26). She instructed all her children on morals, the need for modesty, and the importance of a polite demeanor, and she polished off their competitive edge in sports as she played tennis and ran foot races with them.

The downside of her attentiveness was an intrusiveness in monitoring her children's behavior. In accord with the Puritan values of her time, she attempted to curb their egos in ways now considered undermining. Once when a tender George explained that he had lost a tennis game because his game had been "off" that day, she retorted, "You don't have a game." She also insisted that he play right-handed tennis, even though he was left-handed (Green, 1992, 213). She continued to critique him in adulthood. She berated him for boasting of his war record in a campaign spiel (Green, 1992, 15–16). Bush himself recalled that she accused him of too much "braggadocio" in a news report on his campaign speeches. Even after he became vice president, she told him that "it didn't look right" for him to be reading something while the president was talking. When he explained that he was reading advance copies of the speech, she retorted that she did not see why that was necessary. "Just listen and you'll find out what he has to say." On another occasion she noted how thoughtful Ronald Reagan was of Nancy Reagan by remarking that Reagan never climbed off a plane ahead of his wife or walked ahead of her. Bush noted that "he got the message" (Bush and Gold, 1988, 26–27).[4]

Yet even though Bush was surrounded by disincentives to openly challenge the authorities of his early life, there were props giving him the energy to try meeting those high standards. His father was supportive and exulted in George's successes. According to Bush's sister, Nancy Ellis, Prescott Sr. once skipped a CBS board meeting so he could watch George play on Yale's championship baseball team (Green, 1992, 50). Moreover, he showed his affection for the children after they had left home. Whenever they returned home, "he would stand on the front porch waiting for us and then hug us all" (Green, 1992, 50–51).

The upper-class background in which Bush was reared reinforced the values he learned at home and provided support for the idea that he was destined for leadership. He was chauffeured to private Greenwich Day School as a child. At age twelve he attended the Phillips Academy in Andover, one of the country's largest and most prestigious all-male college preparatory schools. There he encountered a culture that emphasized discipline, service, and excellence in a wide variety of endeavors. Competition was encouraged, but "dirty play was unacceptable," as Fitzhugh Green (1992) noted.

Early successes reinforced the idea that he was born to lead. At Phillips Andover Academy Bush was elected president of the senior class and captain of the baseball and soccer teams, and he won the Johns Hopkins prize and a variety of other elected positions and awards (Green, 1992, 23). After Henry Stimson spoke to the boys of Hitler and Munich, Bush volunteered for the navy and became its youngest pilot and a war hero, winning the Distinguished Flying Cross for completing a mission over Chichi Jima (Bush and Gold, 1988, 39). At Yale he played first base and was elected captain of the varsity baseball team his senior year. He also won a Phi Beta Kappa key and was tapped for the Skull and Bones (Green, 1992, 46–47; Blumenthal, 1993, 57). At age twenty he married Barbara Pierce, a woman of his own social class, who served and supported him in the traditional ways. According to her own testimony, Barbara Bush had a certain awe of her husband. She was clearly convinced that the children needed a full-time mother, and she came to love her life as a politician's wife.[5]

George Bush was also able to differentiate himself from his father in some ways. His move to Texas was evidently an attempt to break from this overwhelming presence. As he noted in his autobiography, he did not "want anything pat and predictable" at that time in his life. Later Bush would boast that in Texas he was able to "make it on [his] own" (Blumenthal, 1993, 58). In his autobiography he noted that he started out in Texas on $3,000 he had saved while in the navy and that he and Barbara were determined to live on their own, to shape their own future. That was why he never went to his parents for seed money at this time (Bush and Gold, 1988, 23).

Yet a closer look at Bush's early career shows that his professional advances received early boosts from family members as well as later assistance from fatherlike patrons. As early as the beginning of his naval career, the navy waived its requirement that a man could not be admitted into flight training without two years of college. Bush appears to be the only person for whom this requirement was waived, thus making him the youngest pilot in the navy. His biographer "wonders" how this happened. When George Bush left for Texas, he was not completely on his own. His father, who was on the board of Dresser Industries, obtained a position for him in the executive training program of IDECO, a subsidiary of Dresser Industries. Several years later when Bush formed the Zapata Corporation, his uncle put up a large portion of the $500,000 in capital required. Eugene Meyer, owner of the *Washington Post,* an investing client of Brown Brothers and Harriman, Prescott Bush's legal firm, signed on for $50,000 (Green, 1992, 5, 228–229).

Bush received similar supports during his political career. Elected to the House of Representatives in 1966, he was the first freshman representative in sixty years to be placed on the powerful House Ways and Means Committee. Prescott Bush, who was leaving the Senate after a decade of service, asked chair Wilbur Mills (R.–Ark.) to do so. George Bush's decision to seek the Republican nomination for the Senate in 1970 was partly at the behest of President Nixon and other leaders of the Republican party. Nixon contributed $100,000 from a White House fund and Republican Senate Campaign Committee chair John Tower (Tex.) gave another $72,879 for the race—twice as much in party funds as for any other Senate candidate. President Nixon and Vice President Spiro Agnew and five Cabinet officers came to Texas to campaign for Bush. Nixon purportedly offered Bush a high-level appointment should he fail in the race. Certainly in December 1970, shortly after Bush lost that Senate race, Nixon pulled him to safety from possible political limbo, offering Bush the post of U.N. ambassador (Green, 1992, 112).

Once Bush had obtained a position, he operated within a framework of organizational values. He worked hard, adhered to organizational norms, and showed himself to be a team player, avoiding controversy. As a member of Congress, he was a congenial colleague and a hard worker. John Byrne (Wisc.), the ranking Republican on the House Ways and Means Committee, gave the following evaluation of Bush's work during that time: "He had a good reputation. He did his work. He did what was expected of him and probably gave a little more. But he wasn't trying to get into the limelight. ... George is a nice guy. You've got to start from that" (King, 1980, 6).

As U.N. ambassador from 1970 through 1973 and head of the American mission in China from 1974 through 1975, Bush had little room to maneuver. But he energetically pursued the foreign policies set by Henry Kissinger. Bush made a dogged, if unsuccessful, effort to support the U.S. dual China policy and was crushed when the Albania Resolution making the People's Republic of China the sole representative of China in the United Nations passed the General Assembly. In the midst of the debate his position was undermined when the news surfaced that Kissinger was engaged in secret talks in Beijing. Nixon and Kissinger were pursuing an opening to China without even informing the U.N. ambassador, a fact over which Bush showed no resentment in his memoirs (Blumenthal, 1993, 61; King, 1980, 69).

Even when Nixon offered Bush the chair of the Republican National Committee after the 1972 election, rather than one of the positions that he requested, Bush did what was asked of him. He wrote the president that he was "not at all enthralled" by the prospect but that he would do it (Blumenthal, 1993, 62). Because the Committee to Reelect the President had drained away the contributions of many Republican donors from the Republican National Committee, Bush had the unpleasant task of reducing the workforce he had inherited. He personally called in the people to be dismissed and explained to them as kindly and honestly as he could the reason for the cuts (Green, 1992,

130). As the Watergate scandal unraveled in 1973 and 1974, Bush traveled around the country in an effort to maintain morale in the party.

He also tried to avoid controversies with his close associates. He did this by seeking out posts that would not give him much responsibility. In 1974, when President Gerald Ford offered Bush his choice of an ambassadorship to France or to England, Bush told the astonished president he would prefer the position of chief of the American mission to Beijing. This choice was made despite Kissinger's statement to Bush that China policy would be made in Washington and that even his role of representation would be limited given the lack of full diplomatic recognition between the two countries (Green, 1992, 114, 144; Bush and Gold, 1988, 131).

As director of the Central Intelligence Agency (CIA), Bush showed skill as a manager, restored morale in the agency, and reassured a Congress disturbed by recent revelations of CIA wrongdoing that the CIA could be trusted under his management. Yet he dodged one of the most controversial problems facing the agency at the time. In response to critiques by conservative private citizens on the president's Foreign Intelligence Advisory Board that CIA estimates of Soviet military threat might be too sanguine, he appointed a nine-member committee headed by Richard Pipes of Harvard University to prepare an alternative estimate. The result was two very different estimates of the Soviet threat—that of the insiders' Committee A and that of the outsiders' Committee B. But Bush never made a clear choice between the two estimates. As a journalist from the *Washington Post* reported, "Bush had tiptoed successfully through this mine field, leaving everyone involved feeling unbruised. Both the career analysts on the A-Team and Pipes and his B-Team felt they had prevailed" (Green, 1992, 161). Yet Pipes also told some acquaintances that he just did not know what Bush's positions were. "I'm not sure that anyone knows" (Blumenthal, 1993, 64).

As vice president, Bush did not speak up in cabinet meetings and kept a politically neutral staff. Bush reported that he felt free to give whatever opinion he might have had to the president in their weekly private lunches together (Bush and Gold, 1988, 231).

He was also very sensitive to any appearance that he might be too ambitious or might be treading on his leader's prerogatives. When Reagan was shot in 1981, Bush was on a plane trip. He resisted the suggestion that after landing at Andrews Air Force Base he take a marine helicopter directly to the White House. Bush recalled his reasons for rejecting this suggestion: "It made sense, logistically and in other ways. But something about it didn't sit well with me. *The President in the hospital ... Marine Two dropping out of the sky, blades whirring, the Vice President stepping off the helicopter to take charge.* ... Good television, yes—but not the message I thought we needed to send to the country and the world" (Bush and Gold, 1988, 224).

Not only did Bush go along; he also seems to have been genuinely admiring of and loyal to those above him. Blumenthal noted that in the foreign policy arena, Bush was in the thrall of Kissinger: Bush liked to surround himself with other Kissinger acolytes and quoted the secretary of state at length (Blumenthal, 1993, 250–252). Certainly, his autobiography and the works of others suggested he did not mind not being informed of the opening to China, which undercut his efforts to defeat the single China policy of the U.N. General Assembly. Moreover, as chief of the American liaison mission, he did not seem to mind as he sat on the sidelines while Kissinger undertook negotiations with China's top political leadership (Blumenthal, 1993, 75).

Bush was also very loyal to President Nixon. As White House operative Chuck Colson wrote in 1971, "We should always consider using George Bush more often as a good speaker. ... He takes our line beautifully" (Blumenthal, 1993, 62). The day after the 1972 election, when Nixon told assistant John Ehrlichman to "eliminate the politicians" from his cabinet, he added, "Except George Bush. He'd do anything for the cause" (Blumenthal, 1993, 62). As chief of the Republican National Committee, Bush was a Nixon loyalist to the very end. He did not suggest that Nixon resign until August 7, after the Supreme Court had ordered the president to surrender the rest of the White House tapes. As the articles of impeachment were being voted on in Congress, Bush wrote Nixon:

> It is my considered judgment that you should now resign. I expect in your lonely embattled position this would seem to you as an act of disloyalty from one you have supported and helped in so many ways. My own view is that I would now ill serve a President whose massive accomplishments I will always respect and whose family I love, if I did not now give you my judgment. Until this moment resignation has been no answer at all, but given the impact of the latest development, and it will be a lasting one, I now firmly feel resignation is best for the country, best for this President. (King, 1980, 84–85)

Organization men, of course, may change when they achieve a top leadership role. Some creative leaders have gone along to reach the top and then surprised others with creative political agendas once they were in a position of authority (Glad, 1991). When Bush first took office, as we have seen, certain reporters thought he was about to make that shift from "faithful and sometimes fumbling lunatic out to be assured" (Dowd, 1989, A8).

Conformity to organizational norms has a cost, as Whyte (1956, 141–167) noted. Organizational men work extraordinarily hard, the demands for socialization become burdensome to them, and the continuing need to play a circumscribed role leads to feelings of emptiness. Loyalty, moreover, has its downside. Executives who rise to the top often maintain their ability to float to other organizations as it suits their careers (Whyte, 1956, 162–165).

George Bush evidently felt some of these strains. As a businessman in his early thirties he had worked eighteen hours a day and, according to his own recollections, was a chronic worrier. On a business trip to London his body broke down, a problem subsequently diagnosed in Texas as a bleeding ulcer. "All my life," Bush recalled, "I'd worked at channeling my emotions, trying not to let anger or frustration influence my thinking." Now he decided he also had to channel his energies. He was evidently successful along that line, as his ulcer healed completely and he never suffered a relapse (Bush and Gold, 1988, 12).

Yet other signs of strain emerged in his presidency. In early 1991 during the weeks before his atrial fibrillation, Bush was under a great amount of stress and was internalizing it, according to his close friends. The charge that he had arranged for the Iranian-held hostages not to be returned until after the 1980 election, the duties he personally shouldered overseeing the diplomatic side of Operations Desert Shield and Desert Storm, and the accusation that he had mishandled affairs with the Kurds of Iraq all placed him under greater than usual stress. The cause of his heart condition was Graves' disease, which creates an overactive thyroid and can be caused by bacteria and/or stress.

But Bush still did not let up. In January 1992 he played tennis despite signs that he had the flu, and he collapsed at a dinner with Japanese prime minister Kiichi Miyazawa. In March 1992 Bush's physician, Dr. Burton Lee, told the *Washington Post* that the president was not getting enough rest, that he was "tired," and that he was taking the tranquilizer Halcion as a sleeping aid on his foreign trips (Podhoretz, 1993, 188).[6]

Bush's passivity during the 1992 campaign seems to have been at base a reflection of the ambivalence he felt about his job as president. For a long time he had seen himself as a good president who was bound to win, as good people must. Until the end of the campaign, he repeatedly stressed that the polls were wrong and that the American people would honor his experience and let him "finish the job" (Jehl and Gerstenzang, 1992, A2). Yet though he did what was necessary to win office, he never really enjoyed the politicking that even a president has to do on the campaign trail.

His first public appearances after the election suggested that he was somewhat relieved that he no longer had to face the stress he had been under in his recent months as president. When he appeared before a small crowd at the Westin Galleria Hotel in Houston, two *Los Angeles Times* reporters (Jehl and Gerstenzang, 1992, A2) noted that "the lines that for months have etched his face in worry, anger and frustration were less apparent than his pride in family, friends and what he had accomplished."

What he seemed to prefer was doing something noncontroversial. As Bush noted in his session with the press at the Westin Galleria Hotel, the nation should "stand behind our new President," and he personally pledged himself to take all steps to "ensure the smooth transition of power" (Jehl and

Gerstenzang, 1992, A2). Some staff aides would later complain that Bush was overdoing it, committing himself to the "best transition ever"; they were not happy about that (Podhoretz, 1993, 233). But for most Americans, in these last official commitments he showed the grace and the skills that were his forte.

Notes

1. Yet Bush's political tendencies were somewhat mixed. He was never really a liberal Republican. He was endorsed by the Association for Constitutional Action, and as a member of the House of Representatives, he voted with the conservative coalition 83 percent of the time. In 1964 he endorsed Barry Goldwater, rather than Nelson Rockefeller, during the Republican primaries and opposed the 1964 Civil Rights Act. In 1968 Bush rejected the endorsement of the liberal Ripon Society (Blumenthal, 1993, 60).

2. Toward the end of October, the Bush people aired an ad that was called "Night of the Living Dead." It showed a buzzard sitting on a dead tree looking out over a wasteland while an announcer read dismal statistics about Clinton's record in Arkansas. In closing it said, "And now Bill Clinton wants to do for America what he has done for Arkansas. America can't take that risk" (Pomper, 1993, 98).

3. Friendship circles undoubtedly influenced his rise to the top. Fund-raisers for his presidential campaign included old high school friends. Administration officials such as treasury secretary Nicholas F. Brady and C. Boyden Gray were old family friends. James Baker III and commerce secretary Robert A. Mosbacher dated from his early days in Texas. He had known ten of the sixteen people in his cabinet for at least ten years. In his first nine months as president, he appointed a higher proportion of friends and supporters to ambassadorial posts than either Reagan or Carter had.

4. Dorothy Bush's admonitions that George avoid self-referent speech may account for some of his rhetorical proclivities as vice president. Peggy Noonan noted that he spoke "as though the use of the word I were somehow tacky and tasteless. He said things like, 'Went west, had a family'" (quoted in Podhoretz, 1993, 222). As president, according to Podhoretz, the dam holding back egocentric expressions seemed to burst. Bush "began talking about himself and never stopped. He lovingly interpreted his own feelings and motives" (Podhoretz, 1993, 222).

5. The early Barbara Bush had been somewhat more complex than the clearly self-affirming woman she was as first lady. Her relations with a beautiful and distant mother had never been close, and she had been overweight as a child. While in grade school, she led her friends into enterprises such as selecting one girl in their circle they would not speak to that day. Though she became a lovely, thin, and popular teenager, she still labored in the shadow of an older, beautiful sister. As a young housewife in Midlands, Texas, she admitted with considerable moral courage that she was sometimes "jealous of attractive young women out in a man's world." When George became director of the CIA, she suffered from "major" depression, in her own words, for about six months. Her problem, as she recalled, was partly that the children were all gone and partly that at Washington cocktail parties people moved away from her when they figured out she was "only" a housewife. Worse still, George could not talk about and

share his work with her as he had done while in China and at the United Nations. She and George gutted it out, she noted, and she was able to enjoy her friend again (Kilian, 1992, 3, 25–27, 54, 100).

6. When acting in response to a traditionally defined objective, however, that energy could become an asset. Bush's extremely high activity level at the beginning of his leadership of the coalition against Iraq could be attributed to his not-yet-diagnosed overactive thyroid. Abrams (1992) argued in a recent article that Bush's "thyroid storm" at this time could have contributed to his "overpersonalizing and overemotionalizing the crisis."

References

Abrams, H. L. (1992). "Desert Storm? or Thyroid Storm? An Inquiry." *Physicians for Social Responsibilities* (September).

Blumenthal, S. (1993). *Pledging Allegiance: The Last Campaign of the Cold War.* New York: HarperCollins.

Bush, G. (1991). "Address Before a Joint Session of the Congress on the State of the Union, Jan. 29, 1991." In *Weekly Compilation of Presidential Documents,* 90–95. Washington, D.C.: GPO.

_____ (1992a). "Address Before a Joint Session of the Congress on the State of the Union, Jan. 28, 1992." In *Weekly Compilation of Presidential Documents,* 156–163. Washington, D.C.: GPO.

_____ (1992b). "Address to the Community Leaders of Portsmouth, New Hampshire, Jan. 16, 1992." In *Weekly Compilation of Presidential Documents,* 22. Washington, D.C.: GPO.

_____ (1992c). "Campaign Address at Portsmouth, New Hampshire, Jan. 15, 1992." In *Weekly Compilation of Presidential Documents.* Washington, D.C.: GPO.

_____ (1992d). "Presidential Address, June 4, 1992." In *Weekly Compilation of Presidential Documents,* 421. Washington, D.C.: GPO.

Bush, G., and V. Gold (1988). *Looking Forward.* New York: Bantam.

Clymer, A. (1992). "Bush's Gains from Convention Nearly Evaporate in Latest Poll." *New York Times,* August 26, A1.

DeFrank, T., and A. McDaniel (1989). "This Is 'Ready on Day One'?" *Newsweek,* October 23, 30.

Dionne, E. J. Jr. (1989). "Which Way Does the New Breeze Blow?" *New York Times,* January 21, A1, A5.

Dowd, M. (1989). "Transformation of Bush: His Own Man." *New York Times,* January 20, A1, A8.

_____ (1992). *New York Times,* 1.

Duffy, M., and D. Goodgame (1992). *Marching in Place: The Status Quo Presidency of George Bush.* New York: Simon and Schuster.

Gallup, G. Jr. (1992). *The Gallup Poll: Public Opinion 1992.* Wilmington, Del.: Scholarly Resources.

Germond, J., and J. Witcover (1993). *Mad as Hell: Revolt at the Ballot Box.* New York: Warner.

Glad, B. (1991). "The Psychological Roots of Gorbachev's Performance as Leader of the Soviet Union." Paper presented at the International Society for Political Psychology Meeting, Helsinki, Finland, July.

Glad, B., M. L. Whicker, J. P. Phiffner, and R. A. Moore (1993). *The Presidency and the Persian Gulf War.* Westport, Conn.: Praeger.

Graubard, S. (1992). *Mr. Bush's War: Adventures in the Politics of Illusion.* New York: Hill and Wang.

Green, F. (1992). *George Bush: An Intimate Portrait.* New York: Hippocrene Books.

Hitchings, T. E. (1992). *Facts on File,* vol. 52, no. 2675. New York: Facts on File.

Jehl, D., and J. Gerstenzang (1992). "In Defeat, Bush Finds Some Relief from Grueling Year." *Los Angeles Times* (Washington ed.), November 4, A2.

Kilian, P. (1992). *Barbara Bush: A Biography.* New York: St. Martin's.

King, N. (1980). *George Bush: A Biography.* New York: Dodd, Mead.

Maslow, A. H. (1968). *Toward a Psychology of Being.* New York: Litton.

Mullins, K., and A. Wildavsky (1992). "The Procedural Presidency of George Bush." *Political Science Quarterly* 1:32.

Orman, J. (1991). "George Bush and the Macho Presidential Style." Address delivered at the Annual Meeting of the American Political Science Association, September, Washington, D.C.

Podhoretz, J. (1993). *Hell of a Ride: Backstage at the White House Follies, 1989–1993.* New York: Simon and Schuster.

Pomper, G. (1993). *The Election of 1992: Reports and Interpretations.* Chatham, N.J.: Chatham House.

Rosenthal, A. (1991). *New York Times,* 1.

_____ (1992a). "Bush Assails Clinton's Patriotism During Vietnam War Protest Era." *New York Times,* October 8, A1.

_____ (1992b). "Bush Encounters the Supermarket, Amazed." *New York Times,* February 5, A1, A19.

_____ (1992c). "Clinton's Embassy File Searched by High-Level State Dept. Order." *New York Times,* October 15, A1, A12.

Safire, W. (1989). "I'm Not Reagan." *New York Times,* January 23, A25.

Scheider, W. (1992). "Bush's Munich: Appeasing the Right?" *National Journal,* May 14, 1742–1746.

Solomon, B. (1988). "If Bush Is No. 1." *National Journal,* October 29, 2710–2713.

_____ (1992). "Bush's Passive Presidency ... or Don't Just Do Something." *National Journal,* November 14, 2628–2629.

Toner, R. (1991). "Casting Doubts: Economy Stinging Bush." *New York Times,* November 6, A1.

Whyte, W. H. Jr. (1956). *The Organization Man.* New York: Simon and Schuster.

Yankelovich, D. (1992). "Opinion Outlook." *National Journal,* June 6, 1376.

3

The Political Psychology
of the Ross Perot Phenomenon

JERROLD M. POST, M.D.

A Significant—and Unusual—
Third-Party Candidacy

For the most part, third-party candidacies have had little impact on U.S. presidential elections. But in the twentieth century, several elections stand out as exceptions to that general rule—the elections of 1912, 1924, 1948, and 1968.[1] To that small list we should now add the election of 1992, in which the third-party candidacy of Ross Perot had a dramatic impact. To emphasize the unusual nature of the Perot candidacy and the political psychology of the Ross Perot phenomenon, it is useful to place his third-party candidacy in the context of the other significant third-party candidacies of the twentieth century.

1912   As leader of the progressive wing of the Republican party, Theodore Roosevelt had won most of the delegates selected by direct primary, but the old guard conservative Republic machine that controlled the convention was determined to nominate William Howard Taft. Roosevelt withdrew and formed the Progressive party, dubbed the "Bull Moose" party. In the general election, Roosevelt defeated Taft, winning 29 percent of the popular vote to Taft's 25 percent. But the split of the Republican vote permitted Woodrow Wilson to win with 46 percent of the popular vote. That the Roosevelt third-party candidacy profoundly affected the outcome of the election cannot be doubted, arguably the most influential third-party candidacy in American history.

1924   A "progressive" Republican and founder of the Progressive movement, Senator Robert La Follette of Wisconsin campaigned for president in 1924 under the banner of the Progressive party. He won the endorsement of the American Federation of Labor and received nearly 5 million votes, 16.6 percent of the total cast.

1948   This election saw not one but two significant third parties—the "Dixiecrat" States' Rights candidacy of J. Strom Thurmond on the right and the Progressive party candidacy of Henry A. Wallace on the left. Although each received only 2.4 percent of the popular vote, Thurmond did amass 39 votes in the electoral college. Samuel Lubell (1952) argued that these third-party candidacies may have contributed to Harry Truman's election upset by consolidating the public perception of Truman as a centrist, what Walter Lippmann (1955) subsequently called "the vital center."

1968   This election occurred at the height of the Vietnam War. Hubert Humphrey waited too long to distance himself from the policies of Lyndon Johnson, and Richard Nixon achieved a hairbreadth victory, winning 43.4 percent of the popular vote to Humphrey's 42.7 percent. But the American Independent party candidacy of southern conservative Democrat George Wallace assuredly played a major role. Wallace amassed 13.5 percent of the popular vote, winning 46 votes in the electoral college.

The third-party candidacy of Ross Perot was one of the most unusual aspects of the unusual 1992 presidential campaign. He received 18.9 percent of the popular vote, among third-party candidates second only to the 29 percent total received by Teddy Roosevelt. As did Roosevelt's candidacy, Perot's candidacy had a major impact on the conduct of the 1992 general election. Morgan (1993) argued that the extremity of the Perot candidacy may have shaped a public perception of Bill Clinton as occupying the vital center and hence contributed to his victory.

Like Woodrow Wilson and Richard Nixon, both of whom were elected with a minority of the popular vote (46 percent and 43 percent, respectively), Bill Clinton was elected with a minority (43 percent) of the popular vote, a consequence of Perot's third-party intervention. But unlike Theodore Roosevelt, George Wallace, and John Anderson, each of whom represented disaffected factions of their party, Ross Perot's candidacy represented a genuine third-party movement, encompassing disaffected voters from both major parties. And unlike most third-party movements, which fade at the moment of defeat, the Perot phenomenon continues to have an impact on national political dynamics.

The Perot Phenomenon as a Charismatic Movement

A remarkable aspect of the Perot phenomenon was the diversity of his grass-roots support—conservative Republicans, liberal Democrats, entrepreneurs, hard hats, each seeing in Perot someone who understood them and would fight for them. He gained 22 percent of first-time voters, and 15 percent of his voters would not have voted if he had not run. As the grassroots movement for Ross Perot grew and gained power, it had many of the earmarks of charismatic movements.

Charisma is not the property of individuals. It is a system, a lock-and-key fit between leaders with particular personality qualities and ideal-hungry followers that occurs at moments of historical crisis (Post, 1986). Sometimes the political followers are so wounded, their yearning for a leader who will provide strong and confident leadership and rescue them so palpable, that they create a leader in their desired image. In these charismatic leader-follower relationships, the followers perceive the leader as superhuman, blindly believe the leader's statements, unconditionally comply with his or her directives for action, and give that leader unqualified emotional commitment (Wilner, 1984).

At these moments of historical crisis in a wounded nation, followers who temporarily need a hero join the ranks of true believers. An interesting contemporary example of a highly idealized leader created out of a nation's pain is Corazon Aquino of the Philippines, who inspired the "people power" movement. Her followers treated her with almost reverential awe, convinced she would rescue them from their plight. Were it not for the corrupt government of Ferdinand Marcos, who had long before lost touch with the person on the street, the "Cory" phenomenon could not have occurred.

The crippled presidency of Jimmy Carter gave us Ronald Reagan. The wounded American public had such a hunger for a strong, confident, wise leader who would protect it from gas lines and repair the humiliating wound of America held hostage by Iran that his followers endowed him with heroic, larger-than-life qualities. He was above criticism, beyond reproach. His followers actively ignored data that disconfirmed their idealization of Reagan, thus contributing to his image as the "Teflon" president.

By the same token, the perception of the failed national leadership of George Bush, especially in terms of the country's economic plight, left the nation with a palpable hunger for a strong, confident president who could provide the nation with effective leadership and lead the United States out of its economic doldrums and restore its rightful place in the world. There was a need for a rescuer. And despite Bill Clinton's economic policy expertise, he was unable to fit that need, for his candidacy was initially wounded by revelations concerning his extramarital affair with Gennifer Flowers and his antiwar activities during the Vietnam War. Clinton was not perceived to be the man of exemplary character for which the nation yearned. The hunger persisted.

It was this leadership vacuum that Ross Perot filled, this hunger for a strong leader with the answers to the country's economic ills that Perot satisfied. Perot had tapped into a vast pool of dissatisfied voters. A *Newsweek* poll in June 1992 indicated that the major reason (52 percent) given by Perot supporters for their preference was dislike of other candidates. When Perot repeatedly indicated that his campaign was not a matter of personal ambition, but was instead a response to the people's needs, he did not realize the profundity of that statement.

As with Reagan, failed presidential leadership and national malaise created such a need for a rescuer that Perot was endowed with heroic qualities. As with Reagan, Perot had the very same Teflon quality. There was such a strong need for a straight-talking, capable leader with integrity that the numerous media stories casting doubt on his image were systematically ignored or discounted. Perot was seen as a committed patriot, yet he tried to cut short his four-year service commitment after his education at the U.S. Naval Academy, complaining in a letter to his representative that life aboard ship was "full of swearing and drunken tales of promiscuity." He was seen as an outsider, yet it was widely reported that he regularly employed insider influence to gain preferential treatment for his business interests. These stories would have had Bill Clinton, the "Velcro" candidate to whom every accusation stuck, the focus of widespread criticism and merciless pounding by the press, but Perot shrugged them off, and his followers did not notice.

One of the most compelling aspects of the Perot appeal was the powerful following he attracted despite the absence of any clearly delineated positions on the central issues. In fact, it was Perot's substantive ambiguity, which gained him the name the "Rorschach candidate," that permitted (and still permits) such widely divergent followers to gather under his leadership mantle, projecting onto his "substance-free" ambiguity whatever they wished to see. They were not only actively uninterested in his positions but also became angry when probing questions were asked of their hero. They did not wish to know, for this would rip off the veil and might reveal their hero's feet of clay.

If Perot was—and remains—ambiguous about substantive details, there was no ambiguity about the image he projected of leadership with a capital *L*. Perot did strike a mythic chord for many who saw the Texan as epitomizing the lonesome cowboy hero, a modern-day Gary Cooper in *High Noon*. Perot's crusade against long odds to get his name on the ballot of all fifty states appealed to Americans' admiration for the lonely hero willing to take on the system. Although Perot was not a spellbinding orator in the tradition of Martin Luther King Jr., he had a gift for one-liners and pungent metaphors ideally suited to the age of sound-bite communication.

The charismatic Winston Churchill was the source of Perot's favorite saying: "Never give in; never give in; never, never, never, never give in." The feisty combativeness and determination in this aphorism were what Perot conveyed to his followers.

Even though such an uncompromising attitude could be problematic in the world of transactional politics, as it was in the boardroom of General Motors (GM), this wartime commander mentality was extremely attractive for a nation perceived to be at war. It was this sense of command that so energized his followers. Perot conveyed certainty, strength, vitality, and optimism—key qualities of leaders sought by ideal-hungry followers, qualities that the polity apparently did not find in either George Bush or Bill Clinton.

This idealization of Ross Perot suggests that elements of the charismatic leader-follower chemistry were present. The image he projected of a strong, confident leader met the needs of a populace desperate to be led at this critical moment in American history, when long-cherished values and the nation's position in the world appeared to be under siege and a wartime commander was in demand. With outside enemies vanquished, Americans were faced with the disquieting prospect of turning within. Perot was responding to this disquietude, implicitly promising that he had the answers, the personal leadership qualities to restore the faltering confidence of this once-proud nation.

In charismatic movements, the magnitude of the idealization is the measure of the disillusion that inevitably follows. The sense of conviction and assuredness Churchill conveyed provided a rallying point for Great Britain and the Western alliance during their darkest hours. When the crisis passed and the need for his dramatic wartime leadership evaporated, how quickly the British people demystified the previously revered Churchill, focused on his leadership faults, and cast him out of office. When the Perot idealization would be succeeded by disillusion was a question of consuming concern for both the Bush and Clinton camps.

During the spring of 1992, support ebbed and disillusioned followers left his camp. Nevertheless, significant support continued, and the mythic Perot continued to attract followers disillusioned with contemporary leadership and seeking a strong, clear-thinking leader with the answers to America's problems. This committed followership continued to revere the mythic Ross Perot and actively ignored information about his life and career that would debunk the mythic image.

The Reality of Ross Perot's Life and Career

Who is Ross Perot? What is the reality that his followers initially did not wish to confront, the reality that when confronted led many to become disaffected and defect from his camp?

As exemplified in the self-deprecating remark just quoted, in which he likened himself to a stray dog of uncertain pedigree, Perot has fostered the image of himself as the very embodiment of the Horatio Alger myth, a man of very humble origins who rose to become a billionaire by dint of hard work. In fact, his father, Ross Perot, was a successful cotton broker, and Perot grew up in comfortable middle-class circumstances—certainly a striking contrast to Bill Clinton's formative years, which were extremely difficult.

A shadow did hang over the Perot family that endowed the circumstances of Perot's birth with dark meaning and colored his formative years. The first-born son, Ross Jr., died at age two. The emotionally stricken family decided to have another child, and the future presidential candidate was born shortly thereafter and given the name Ray. According to Perot, his father never really recovered from the loss, and at age twelve Ray Perot changed his name to Ross Jr. (Wright, 1993).

The firstborn son is often the bearer of the family's hopes and dreams, as was Joseph Kennedy Jr. for his father, Joe Kennedy. And that son's death can leave a terrible void behind. The Kennedy family myth was that Joseph Kennedy aspired to have his firstborn son become president and that when Joe Jr. died the mantle was passed to the second oldest brother, Jack Kennedy. But Jack Kennedy was an adult when his older brother died in World War II.

When the firstborn son dies in childhood, the family wound is deep. The son born after such a loss has a very special burden and is often endowed by the family with special qualities, the so-called replacement child. Ataturk was born after three successive stillbirths. Volkan and Itzkowitz (1984) suggested that these very special circumstances led his family to treat him as a special gift from heaven, the basis for his profoundly narcissistic character.

Ray (Wright, 1992) was conceived to fill the void left by the death of the firstborn son and father's namesake. His birth must have been very special indeed. That Ray Perot felt constrained to assume the name Ross Jr. when he was twelve suggests an acceptance of the role of replacement child, the bearer of his father's hopes and dreams, the family savior. Ross would become the perfect son to salve his father's pain, which became the underpinnings of his fierce drive to achieve and receive recognition.

Indeed, he was driven to succeed from early on. His early education was at a private school, where he did extremely well. He approached Boy Scouts with single-minded determination, earning the rank of Eagle Scout within fifteen months of joining, a singular achievement. In a meeting with Ross Perot's mother, Perot's scout master said that he did not know what to do with the boy because he was so driven. Perot's mother responded that she would not ask her son to slow down.

Perot has emphasized his father's frugality, despite the family's comfortable economic circumstances, citing the fact that his father drove the same Dodge for twenty years. In shaping the Perot legend, he has referred to his own hard-working industriousness, placing it in the context of the Texas cowboy. He likes telling a story that he delivered papers from horseback, but in Tod Mason's (1992) unauthorized biography, this fact is refuted by Perot's childhood pals, who stated that Perot used a bicycle like everybody else, one derisively calling the newspaper boy on horseback story "bullshit." After the publication of the book, Perot harassed these friends until they agreed to confirm his story.

In Texas the high school football star is a demigod. But Perot's physique led him to choose tennis instead. It has been suggested that Perot's resentment of the adulation of the football stars was one reason he proposed that football players could not play without passing grades when he was active within the Texas education system.

Perot won an appointment to the U.S. Naval Academy, where he continued his academic success. He very much enjoyed his academy years and came to admire the navy and its traditions. Those years made a lasting impression on him, as reflected in his predilection for hiring former naval academy people, his preference for dress codes and short hair, and his managerial style.

But the navy was the scene of his first failure, for he was demoted in his first assignment after the academy, reportedly for having what was characterized as "a peculiarly rigid willfulness" (Blumenthal, 1992). Shortly after this demotion, Perot attempted to get out of his navy commitment. Ross Perot has given four reasons for wanting a release from active duty.

1. He stated that he was under the impression that he had only a two-year commitment. He rationalized that he had only a two-year commitment because the United States was not at war and that the four-year commitment occurred only in times of war.

2. He was outraged by the navy promotion system. He felt that the "sit and wait for your turn" promotion system penalized those with initiative and was therefore disadvantageous to him (this is almost the identical reason that he left International Business Machines [IBM], where he stated that the IBM quota system was a disadvantage to the go-getter).

3. He was outraged by the lax morals of his first captain.

4. He was upset that the life aboard ship was "full of swearing and drunken tales of promiscuity." This final—and most absurd—reason was conveyed by Perot in a letter he wrote to his Congressman asking for his release.

The desire to get out of his navy commitment after a personal setback was prototypical of his manner of dealing with reversals of fortune, a pattern that was to repeat itself throughout his life and career. He did not take personal responsibility for his own failure but rather attempted to blame others, diverting attention, externalizing. He blamed his captain, his other shipmates, even the navy. This event can be seen as foreshadowing the manner in which he dropped out of the presidential race in July 1992 in the face of serious difficulties with his campaign and falling popularity in the polls; he blamed Republican dirty tricks.

While in the navy, Perot had met a visiting IBM executive. On leaving the navy, he contacted that executive and obtained employment with IBM as a salesperson. Bringing his hard-driving personal style to his work, Perot was extremely successful, so successful, he maintained, that IBM instituted a quota system for its entire sales force. Perot felt that the quota system penalized initiative. He often filled the quota early in the year, which meant that if he worked anymore, he would not get paid.

Perot sought additional work with other companies. One of those projects was as a computer analyst with Texas Blue Cross. Perot realized from his experiences at IBM and Texas Blue Cross that data management was an industry of the future, and he conceived of selling unused computer space in one company's mainframe to another company.

Chafing at the restraint of working within the IBM sales bureaucracy, Perot decided to go to IBM with his idea for large-scale data management. He came to this decision at his usual barbershop when he read a quote by Thoreau that changed his life: "The mass of men lead lives of quiet desperation."

But IBM rejected the concept, so with Mitch Hart, another naval academy graduate, Perot left IBM and on his thirty-second birthday, June 27, 1962, started Electronic Data Systems (EDS) with $1,000 in capital. His board of directors consisted of his wife, his mother, and his sister. EDS's first contract was with Texas Blue Cross. There were several questionable aspects to this contract. This huge contract was given to an unproven company without any competitive bid. The contract was awarded to Perot even though he was working for Texas Blue Cross at the time. In effect, Perot supervised his own contract at Texas Blue Cross for the next year. Overnight Perot became a millionaire on the strength of this one contract.

Perot ran EDS like a paramilitary organization (Blumenthal, 1992). Even his two closest aides, Mort Meyerson and Tom Luce, were expected to call him "Sir" in meetings. Most of the new people hired, especially at the beginning when EDS was still small, were ex-military. Each group of new hires was given a military nickname, such as the "Dirty Dozen." Patterned after the IBM dress code, the office uniform consisted of white shirt, dark suit, and black shoes. Long hair was not permitted, and facial hair was verboten. Extra work without overtime pay was expected as a sign of loyalty. Adultery was grounds for dismissal. Lie detector tests were given regularly. Perot never shied from directly calling EDS managers, even junior ones, personally to find out how they were doing. Perot denies the autocratic work environment that has been described by former EDS employees, but two court cases seem to support them. EDS was ordered by federal courts to reinstate an employee who had been fired for wearing a beard in 1983. A second suit involved employee Bobby Joe King, who was fired from EDS in March 1986 after he told his supervisor that he had been hospitalized for acquired immunodeficiency syndrome (AIDS)–related pneumonia.

With a secure financial base at EDS, Perot pursued a public role and actively courted political leaders. Both in developing and forwarding the interests of EDS, Perot worked the system to a fare-thee-well.

The Consummate Insider and Lobbyist

Throughout the campaign and since the election, Perot has consistently portrayed himself as the populist outsider, attacking special interests and lobbyists and declaring the importance of "returning the country to the people." During the NAFTA debate with Vice President Al Gore, Perot derisively criticized the lobbying efforts of the administration and called the government a prisoner of lobbyists. When Gore called attention to Perot's lobbying, Perot stumbled and professed ignorance. For in truth Perot's financial success in significant part has derived from adroit playing of the system, including heavy lobbying. Thus, such righteous accusations were hypocritical to the extreme. His political contributions and lobbying activities have been detailed by Mason (1992).

- 1968: Perot did not financially contribute to the Nixon campaign but did lend it a company plane and seven employees.
- 1969: Perot spent $1 million on newspaper ads and a half-hour TV spot to drum up support for Nixon's Vietnam policy.
- 1970: Perot pledged, but did not give, $250,000 for congressional Republicans. EDS employees gave $229,000 to the Nixon reelection effort.
- 1971: Perot gave $200,000 to the Nixon reelection campaign.
- 1972: Perot sought assistance from the White House to gain tax deductions for the employees he had lent to the 1968 campaign.
- 1972: Through top EDS executives, Perot channeled $100,000 to the campaign of House Ways and Means Committee Chair Wilbur Mills, whose committee would play a major role in future health insurance plans.
- 1974: Perot came under investigation by the Department of Health, Education, and Welfare concerning his control of about 90 percent of the subcontracts for processing Medicare data during the previous five years. In that year Perot gave $56,000 to the electoral campaigns of the members of the Senate and House committees with jurisdiction over Medicare (Rocawich, 1992).

- 1975: Representative Phil Landrum (D–Ga.) introduced an apparently innocuous amendment into a tax bill that would have given Perot a $15 million capital-loss tax break. Ten members, out of twelve, of the Ways and Means Committee voted to give him the break, but it was later snuffed out in conference. Perot had contributed more than $27,000 to twelve members of the committee.

- 1986: When Perot founded Perot Systems to compete with EDS, he used his influence within the Reagan administration to arrange a sole-source contract to streamline the U.S. Postal Service that would have given Perot fifty cents for each dollar saved. The deal was rescinded by Congress.

- 1987: The Perot family had built Alliance Airport, an executive jetport in Fort Worth, using federal, state, and local funds worth some $150 million. Perot and his son purchased some sixteen thousand acres surrounding the airport and an industrial park. The family employed lobbyists, including the son of Jamie Whitten (D–Miss.), chair of the House Appropriations Committee, and contributed more than $50,000 to prominent legislators, including Speaker of the House Jim Wright (D–Tex.), Senator Lloyd Bentsen (D.–Tex.), and Vice President George Bush to expand the jetport to a full commercial airport facility. The airport was given to the city, but because of the associated properties will reportedly bring $1 billion in profits to the Perot family.

- 1992: According to Common Cause, Perot has given $90,000 to both parties (Carlson, 1992).

- Since 1980, Perot and his family have given some $175,000 to candidates running for federal office.

To say the least, this is not the record of an outsider. Yet somehow Perot has managed to persuade his followers that he is a virtuous and untainted outsider, entitled to criticize the money interests.

Perot in the Public Arena

Perot became active in the educational system and the drug war in Texas. His plans to improve the educational system were radical, but many believed his assessment of what was wrong with the system to be accurate and his proposed solutions correct.

When he did make an apparently public-spirited offer, there was often something in it for him as well. As head of the Texas Drug Commission in 1981, he offered to purchase a Caribbean island so that the Drug Enforcement Agency could develop a sting operation. The precondition for the purchase was that Perot would get to keep the proceeds from the smugglers' assets.

Perot also became active in national politics during his time with EDS and was a major financial supporter of Richard Nixon. Both in the business world and in the public arena, Perot has often been contemptuous of leadership and convinced that he has the answers. At times he has acted as the ultimate arbiter, as if he is a law unto himself. He conducted his own personal investigation of the CIA over Irangate.

Perot has a history of attempting huge projects and failing. I have already discussed his projects involving education and drug enforcement in Texas. Even though his solutions to these problems were lauded, he met with little administrative success.

His foray into Wall Street is instructive, demonstrating again his supreme belief in his own abilities. EDS purchased Du Pont Glore Forgan (a Wall Street brokerage house owned by the Du Pont family) in 1971. The reason for the purchase, according to Perot, was to save Wall Street. The project was doomed to failure. Wall Street was having a difficult time in 1971, and Perot felt that all it needed was a strong managerial hand. Perot lectured Wall Street concerning its substandard business practices, suggesting he and EDS might be the antidote to Wall Street's illness. He assigned Mort Meyerson to run the Du Pont campaign, the goal being to remake Du Pont and Wall Street in the image of EDS. Perot attempted to impose the same work ethic at Du Pont that he had enforced at EDS. Du Pont personnel were to cut their long hair, shave their beards, dress in a businesslike manner, and behave professionally. In addition, Perot stated that he wanted to change the language of Wall Street. He felt that terms such as "cage" were not conducive to good business and told Du Pont staff that it would take the lead in changing such language. This is historically Perot's method. Scorning incremental change, he advocates radical solutions that antagonize the very people he claims he is trying to help.

Another business venture that provides insight into Perot's leadership occurred in 1980. Bradford National Corporation won the Texas Medicaid contract in 1980. Its bid was between $40 and $50 million less than EDS's. Perot saw this loss as a personal challenge and affront. He raged at his staff, demanding to know how another company could come into his backyard and steal what was his. With Ken Riedlinger, Perot then started a no-holds-barred campaign against Bradford. Perot argued that anything that he did in this campaign was justified by the general good it would ultimately do for the public. Joseph Monge, the former chair of Bradford, recalled that when the company beat out EDS for the Texas Medicare contract, he started to receive harassing, threatening, maligning phone calls wherever he went. Other members of the Bradford board were getting these calls as well. The phone calls went on for about a year, until Bradford lost the contract. EDS sent investigators all over

New York, Bradford's home state. They interviewed ex-workers, clients, state officials, and even neighbors of the Bradford board members in an attempt to dig up dirt on Bradford. Perot believed Bradford was a "thieving band" that had stolen EDS's Texas Medicaid contract from its rightful owner. An outraged Perot, using his formidable political influence, lobbied Governor William Clements, Attorney General Mark White, and the Texas human rights commissioners to reconsider. As a result, EDS won back the Texas Medicare contract without a competitive bid. When asked why he had not entered the bidding, the chairman of the rival firm Computer Services Corporation, intimidated and frustrated, threw up his hands as he asked, "What's the use?"

The GM purchase of EDS in 1984 epitomizes both the positives and negatives of Ross Perot's leadership. The positives are his direct and personal managerial style, his desire to correct wrongs, his great sales ability, his drive, and, particularly, his formidable capacity to identify and diagnose problems. His negatives are his autocratic and rigid managerial style, his inability to accept gradual change, his inability to request outside help, his personally aggressive style, his predilection for using the press to air publicly disputes with management, and his trouble with outside authority figures who disagree with him. EDS when it was Perot's company developed a style of business that did not allow others to participate in decisions. When EDS won a contract, everybody in the company who did data management and would be dealing with EDS had to submit to the EDS method. That meant everything that went with EDS was purchased with the company—salary, dress code, conduct, and so forth.

When GM acquired EDS for $2.5 billion, Perot still wanted to be autonomously in charge of EDS and resented attempts by GM chair Roger Smith to influence or direct his leadership of EDS. (Smith was laboring under the assumption that because GM owned EDS, it should answer to GM.) As a consequence of this clash of personalities, Perot demanded that EDS be maintained as a separate entity within GM. Smith agreed to much of Perot's demands because with the purchase of EDS Perot became one of the biggest holders of GM stock and a member of the board.

From his vantage point on the board, Perot became aware of the problems with the GM managerial system and immediately became convinced radical changes were necessary. He passed out to GM board members one of his favorite books, *Leadership Secrets of Attila the Hun*. Unable to persuade the board majority of the need for these changes, he became an active adversary. He went public, holding press conferences to give voice to his caustic criticism of GM management. When Perot attacked in the boardroom and the pressroom, GM became defensive, and the relationship between EDS and GM became confrontational. GM could not deal with Perot and finally bought out his shares for $750 million. This is another case where Perot seemed unable to work within the system unless it complied with all his dictates. He did not understand how large bureaucracies work, he lacked the ability to compromise or effectively persuade, and he became embroiled in a highly personalized power struggle.

Demands Loyalty, Vindictive

In Perot's view of the world the other side is always wrong. While free, indeed quick, to criticize others, Perot is extremely sensitive to criticism, a vulnerability in the rough world of politics. Perot attacks the person who angers, disagrees with, or criticizes him. Although Perot says he does not like "yes-men," he tends to equate disagreement with disloyalty. Perot places high value on loyalty to him and can turn against senior associates when he interprets their constructive disagreements or different paths as treason.

There are many examples of Perot's vindictiveness:

- When Reagan distanced himself from Perot because of Perot's stand on soldiers who were missing in action (MIA) in Southeast Asia, Perot reneged on a promised $2 million for the Reagan library.
- When GM bought EDS, Perot began Perot Systems. He offered all the old EDS staff members jobs. Many of them decided to stay with GM, including Paul Chiapparone, one of the EDS workers rescued from Iran. EDSers had a party for Chiapparone a little time later, and Perot refused to go to the party, calling Chiapparone a traitor.
- Perot financed an attempt by Oliver North to get back a kidnapped CIA bureau chief in Lebanon. Perot provided $200,000 up front, and another $1 million later, to the terrorists for the return of the hostage. The terrorists took the money and ran. Perot blamed North and later initiated a personal investigation of North's conduct as well as of CIA agents and military involvement in Irangate.[2]
- Perot relieved longtime associate Ken Riedlinger of his duties because of Riedlinger's handling of GM. Riedlinger shortly thereafter obtained a high-level position with Ford. Perot threatened to sue Riedlinger because it was reported, erroneously, that Riedlinger's position was going to be systems management. Riedlinger is reported to have called Dallas and told Perot that he knew where "all the skeletons" were. Perot took no further action against Riedlinger.

A Penchant for Conspiratorial Thinking

Throughout his career Perot has demonstrated a psychological attraction to conspiracies. He has shown a readiness to believe in conspiracies, government and otherwise, and has lent his financial backing to uncovering and countering them. In times of stress, he has believed himself to be the target of conspiracies.

Perot, an extremely suspicious man, has bought into some far-fetched conspiracy theories brought to him by individuals of questionable reputations on the basis of the slimmest evidence. He has been characterized by political writer Sidney Blumenthal (1992) as "a MacArthur Foundation for conspiracy-spinners." Scott Barnes, whose reputation for self-serving activities and dishonesty was widespread, for years had told tales of a cover-up of MIAs in Vietnam. Perot became obsessed with this mission, would see the slightest evidence as confirmatory and major negative findings as trumped up. His was a conclusion of conspiracy in search of evidence. By 1973 he had organized, with substantial financial backing, his own mercenary group to seek out MIAs in Vietnam and Laos. When Reagan reopened the issue in 1983, Perot organized and financed a group of mercenaries for a foray into Laos in search of MIAs. (In all of this, he sees himself as above the law, manifesting contempt for the system and considering himself the possessor of the truth.) Trying to effect his cooperation, Vice President Bush showed Perot documents indicating that the government's thoroughgoing search for evidence of MIAs had not produced significant findings. Finally, Bush was directed by President Reagan to ask Perot to stop interfering with government efforts to resolve the MIA controversy. Bush's attempts to call off Perot's private involvement made the vice president a lifelong enemy. According to Bush, "It's a case of shoot the messenger. When I was vice president, Reagan wanted him to butt out of the P.O.W. thing. I basically told Ross to get out. I ordered him out. I said, 'Thank you very much, but we don't want you mucking around in this issue'" (*Vanity Fair*, 1992). According to a Bush adviser, "Perot went batshit and has never forgiven him" (*Vanity Fair*, 1992). (In fact, Perot was so angered by Bush's MIA "failure" that he contacted Michael Dukakis's political staff in 1988 and offered to share his negative critique of the vice president [Carlson, 1992]).

Perot himself traveled to Vietnam, where he represented himself as a "negotiator." In 1986, still totally convinced, he testified before a congressional hearing chaired by Stephen Solarz (D–N.Y.) that he had new witnesses on the MIAs but failed to produce a single name. His 1987 trips to Vietnam in search of information about MIAs raised concerns in the State Department that he was violating the Logan Act, which bars private citizens from conducting diplomacy.

But, more important, when under pressure Perot sees himself as the center of conspiracies. When he dropped out of the race in July 1992, he cited a conspiracy. He indicated that he had proof that an attempt was being made to produce fake photographs showing his daughter, who was about to be married, as a lesbian. Leslie Stahl of CBS prompted his dismissive anger when during an interview she tried to pursue the facts behind these allegations; he walked off the set. The allegations prompted presidential spokesperson Marlin Fitzwater, in a televised news conference on ABC *Evening News,* to call Perot "a delusional paranoid who hears voices." That falling popularity preceded Perot's allegations is instructive. It is preferable to be persecuted than to be ignored.

There are two possible explanations for these conspiratorial allegations: Either Perot believes them, or he does not. If the former is true, a tendency to imagine himself as the victim of conspiracies when he is under pressure is an alarming characteristic for a presidential aspirant. If the latter is the case, and he throws out these accusations to deflect blame away from himself, this, too, is of concern. Having vested faith in him, Perot's followers were bitterly disappointed by his sudden decision to leave the campaign in the face of difficulties. Perhaps the conspiratorial allegations were an attempt to blunt their anger.

Another example of a bizarre paranoid allegation occurred during the NAFTA campaign. The Justice Department became aware of assassination threats directed at Perot. Perot explained these by asserting that his leadership of the anti-NAFTA forces was threatening to Mexican drug kingpins. When the trade barriers with Mexico were removed, they hoped to smuggle cocaine and other drugs into the United States in lettuce and other vegetables. Because Perot was thwarting their plans, they were conspiring to assassinate him.

Obsession with Security

Perot is obsessed with security. He has a predeliction for hiring former military and ran EDS along paramilitary lines, fearing leaks and operating on the "need to know principle." His houses are well defended, and he has a sizable security and investigative staff. At campaign headquarters in Texas the volunteer and hired staffers liked to call the regular Dallas Perot people the "white shirts." The campaign staff was separated from Perot and contacted him through his personal staff. Republican political strategist Ed Rollins said that he had worked on many campaigns where he did not know what the candidate was going to say, but never on one where he did not know where the candidate was. When Rollins first went to Dallas, he was aware that Perot had had him investigated.

The Dallas campaign headquarters had a series of electronic keys, and each key determined how far into headquarters a person could go. Paper shredders were placed next to each desk. Signs were posted cautioning workers to destroy papers. No loose papers were allowed on desk tops. Liz Maas, a campaign director, was told that the daily updated phone lists should be destroyed at the end of each day. When Rollins was fired from the campaign, Perot's security staff closed the building and would not allow anybody access to the computers. Staff members attempted to confiscate Rollins's computer files and fired everybody they were not sure of.

Perot's obsession with security and control of information has led to a complex relationship with the press. Many reporters enjoy interviewing Perot because he is usually open, has an engaging personality, and tells good stories. Perot likes using the press to air his opinions. The problem is that Perot wants to have control over what the press writes. As he told Ken Follett, the author of *Wings of Eagles,* what matters is the lesson, not the facts. Whenever anybody associated with him gives an interview or quote to the press, he later contacts this person and tells him or her what he or she should have said. Perot often rages when the media find out about something he did not want them to know. He spends hours tracking down sources of negative stories concerning him.

Virginia Governor Douglas Wilder was taken off the short list for Perot's vice-presidential running mate when somebody from Wilder's staff told the paper that Wilder was on the short list. Perot asked rhetorically, If Wilder could not control his own staff, then how could he be vice president? Perot blamed Rollins and advertising executive Hal Riney, his media adviser, for all the bad press that forced him out of the election, claiming that he had not gotten any bad press before those two joined his campaign. Perot charged that Rollins must have been a plant by Bush to discredit him. When Rollins's deputy Charlie Leonard left the Perot campaign, he was requested to sign a confidentiality agreement according to which he

> agree[d] to refrain from making any disparaging remarks or negative comments, either publicly or privately, directly or indirectly, regarding Ross Perot, his campaign for President, the [Perot Petition Committee]. ... In addition, you agree not to disclose any information to which you have been privy that I or the PPC consider confidential, including: information about strategy or tactics; budget information; issues information; information about the Vice-Presidential selection process or selection; conversations, interactions and anecdotes derived from meetings with Ross Perot, Tom Luce, Mort Meyerson, Jim Squires, Hamilton Jordan, or other PPC personnel; or the personality or management style of Ross Perot. (*Vanity Fair,* 1992)

As the press tried to penetrate the fog of generalities and became increasingly aggressive in press conferences and interviews, Perot responded angrily when he could not control interviews. ABC reporter Cokey Roberts told of his preemptory anger when she tried to pursue a point not on his agenda, saying he would have brought his charts (the specifics of his economic program) if he had known that was what she wanted to talk about. When she reminded him that they had agreed this would be an open-ended interview, he angrily interrupted her. He later called to calm the roiled waters, but when she indicated she thought he had been rude, he angrily hung up.

The Sudden Dropout in the Face of Difficulties

As his standing in the polls began to fall, and the failure to define issues came increasingly under attack, in early June Perot brought two high-powered political advisers into his campaign—Republican political strategist Ed Rollins, who had run Ronald Reagan's 1984 campaign and had been dubbed "the king of three spin doctors," and Democratic strategist Hamilton Jordan, who had helped elect Jimmy Carter. But despite promises of support, Perot was unwilling to let these professionals conduct their profession, and his autocratic management style totally frustrated Rollins and Jordan. Characterized by financial advisers as "throwing nickels around like manhole covers," Perot was aghast at the cost of producing TV political commercials and told media adviser Hal Riney that he would not spend more than $5,000 for a commercial. He would not let Rollins and Jordan send out advance teams, he disrupted the press operation, and he would not let them write campaign speeches. The most dramatic and disastrous example of his continuing personal control of the campaign occurred in an address he personally drafted to the critically important National Association for the Advancement of Colored People, a speech he had not shown to anyone on his staff. In this speech, he referred to "You people," which produced a firestorm of protest and accusations of racism from the African-American community, accusations that Perot never understood.

On July 10 Rollins wrote a succinct memo to Perot telling him he had three choices: to run a proper presidential campaign; to continue the way he was going, in which case he did not need Rollins and Jordan; or to quit (Vanity Fair, 1992). On July 13 Perot's number two, Mort Meyerson, told Rollins and Jordan that "you professionals need to go." At the time of Rollins's discharge, Meyerson repeated a suspicion he and Perot had entertained that Rollins was a spy sent in by the Bush campaign. "We thought this might be a conspiracy. We thought you were here to blow this campaign up, that you were sent here by Bush. We came to the conclusion that you had given up so much that unless the C.I.A. was paying you some exorbitant some of money …"

On July 16, in the face of the unraveling of his campaign, Perot abruptly announced his decision to drop out of the race. Although he initially cited as his reason for withdrawing the "revitalization of the Democratic party" and his wish to avoid throwing the election into the House of Representatives, he also made dark reference to Republican dirty tricks, including the faked photograph depicting his daughter as a lesbian.

In fact, there is reason to believe that probings by the press into family matters may well have contributed to his decision to drop out. A story was about to break that Perot had a private detective investigate his daughter Nancy's boyfriend, a Vanderbilt professor who was Jewish. Perot is reported to have exclaimed to his friends, "You don't think I'd let my daughter marry a Jew?" (Rocawich, 1992).

Some Republican officials opined that his decision to drop out was occasioned by his having accomplished his primary mission—to get revenge on George Bush. Having surpassed Bush in the polls and believing he had fatally wounded the president, according to this theory Perot had accomplished his vindictive mission and could now drop out.

Perot's language in an interview following the announcement of his decision to drop out of the race is instructive. Often the denied feeling reveals the true one. Indicating that getting out "was the morally responsible thing to do," Perot stated, "I just wanted to do the right thing. I don't have a power drive, an ego drive. ... I don't need to be king of the earth" (*Newsweek,* July 27, 1992).

It is interesting to observe that Perot purchased his childhood home and restored it to its original stature, which meant disassembling the bricks and rotating them. This was done because a contractor told him that once bricks are painted, they cannot be returned to their original color. This preparation of a future shrine was not the work of a man without a considerable ego. Out of his league in the rough and tumble of politics, feeling a situation out of control, his considerable ego wounded by his fall in popularity and the shambles of his campaign, Perot quit rather than face further humiliation.

The Return of the Dropout

Perot's precipitous decision produced a flood of protest from his followers, many of whom felt embittered. And it produced a tidal wave of negative media stories about his quixotic and disruptive campaign. Perot was probably both defensive concerning his followers and stung by the media criticism. More important, he almost certainly missed the spotlight of national attention. Having reveled in being at the very center of national attention, he must have been stung by the relative obscurity that attended his no longer being a candidate. Moreover, many were unswerving in their continuing support and called for his return. "Their candidate had called it quits without even issuing a platform. And still they loved him and believed in him" (*Educational Digest,* 1992, 26). And as suddenly as he had dropped out, the prodigal candidate returned.

Remarkably, considering the quixotic manner in which he dropped out, Perot retained significant support. Only now it was so late in the game that the question no longer was, "Who is Ross Perot?" Rather the question was, "What will be the impact of Perot's resumption of his candidacy on the campaign?" With a blitz of expensive infomercials in the last weeks of the campaign, and significant success in the presidential debates, Perot had a major impact on the election, winning 18.9 percent of the popular vote.

This exposure to national prominence had a profound impact on Ross Perot, and unlike previous third-party candidates, he has continued his self-appointed role as spokesperson for the American people. From his position as president of United We Stand, he regularly criticizes the establishment.

Perot continues to appeal to many disaffected voters with conventional politics, who see a dearth of leadership among Democrats and Republicans alike. He has been a nettlesome burr under the saddle of President Clinton, especially as the president attempted to mobilize support for NAFTA, but Perot's play for Republican support concerns Republicans as well. Both establishment Republicans and Democrats have been reluctant to attack Perot, fearful of alienating his considerable following.

Perot was outspoken in his opposition to NAFTA, referring in his characteristically pungent way to "the giant sucking sound" of jobs going to Mexico as a consequence of the trade agreement. Democrats and Republicans alike were wary of crossing Perot until Jimmy Carter had the courage during the NAFTA campaign to denounce him as a demagogue. Noting his disregard for the truth, during a televised discussion by political journalists, George Will called Perot "an intellectual sociopath." When the Justice Department revealed it had learned of an assassination plot targeted at Perot, Perot gave an explanation reminiscent of the bizarre faked photograph accusation.

Struggling for votes, the Clinton team made the high-risk decision to challenge Perot to a debate on NAFTA. The debate with Vice President Al Gore was a watershed event, for prior to the debate the media and politicians alike had handled Perot with kid gloves, being reluctant to criticize, reluctant to pursue inconsistencies. Now he was fair game, and criticism of Perot was scathing from politicians and media alike. The debate, televised on Cable Network News (CNN), did not have a large national audience. The importance was its impact on opinion makers. Indeed, his performance in the debate led many pundits to write Perot's political obituaries.

But reports of his demise are probably premature. Although many of his formerly uncritical admirers have dropped from the ranks, the hunger for a strong hero with straight answers and clear solutions persists. Perot's enjoyment of his public role, his capacity to attract media attention, his vast resources, and the core of followers who distrust Washington and find his promise of simple solutions to the nation's problems attractive all suggest that the Ross Perot phenomenon will continue. "It's just that simple."

Notes

1. The John Anderson candidacy in 1980 had initially created a great deal of enthusiasm, but when the final ballots were cast, he won only 6.6 percent of the popular vote. His third-party candidacy was not considered to have had a major impact on the course of the general election. Like Theodore Roosevelt, a disaffected Republican,

Anderson, a disaffected Democrat, drew the bulk of his support from his own party ranks.

2. Blumenthal observed that Perot, despite his ultimately feeling betrayed by North, was intrigued by the concept advanced by North of acting covertly through private channels in order to avoid government oversight.

References

Blumenthal, S. (1992). *The New Republic,* June 15.

Carlson, M. (1992). *Time,* May 25.

Educational Digest (1992). P. 26.

Lippmann, W. (1955). *Essays in the Public Philosophy.* Boston: Little, Brown.

Lubell, S. (1952). *The Future of American Politics.* New York: Harper.

Mason, T. (1992). *Perot: An Unauthorized Biography.* Business One Irwin.

Morgan, F. (1993). Personal communication.

Newsweek (1992). June 15.

Newsweek (1992). July 27.

Post, J. (1986). "Narcissism and the Charismatic Leader-Follower Relationship." *Political Psychology* 7, no. 4.

Rocawich, L. (1992). *The Progressive* (November).

Vanity Fair (October 1992).

Volkan, V., and N. Itzkowitz (1984). *The Immortal Ataturk: A Psychobiography.* Chicago: University of Chicago Press.

Wilner, A. (1984). *The Spellbinders: Charismatic Political Leadership.* New Haven: Yale University Press.

Wright, L. (1992). *New York Times Magazine.*

4

Character, Judgment, and Political Leadership: Promise, Problems, and Prospects of the Clinton Presidency

STANLEY A. RENSHON

In this chapter I frame some basic questions about the psychology of the emerging Clinton presidency. Toward that end, I develop a psychological and, more specifically, a psychoanalytically informed analysis of President Bill Clinton's character, political leadership, and presidential behavior.[1] Relying on several complementary data sources, I first briefly outline some basic elements of his character and psychology as they emerged in the presidential campaign of 1992 and the first year of his presidency.[2] I then briefly discuss some associated psychological traits and trace their impact on Clinton's approach to the presidency. I conclude by suggesting some dilemmas for Clinton's presidency and its ultimate success (in the areas of leadership, judgment, and public policy) that flow from these characteristics.

Presidential Psychology and Performance: Bill Clinton and the Dilemma of Ambition

A psychologically framed analysis of any president must begin with three basic questions: (1) What are the major, defining elements of this president's character and psychology; (2) what theory or theories help us make sense of these core elements and the psychological characteristics associated with them; and (3) what specific implications do these core and associated psychological elements hold for specific aspects of presidential performance? In the past, political psychologists who studied the psychology of presidents were primarily concerned about psychological deficits, such as a lack of political skills or the wish to acquire power to overcome low self-esteem (Lasswell, 1948). James

57

Barber's (1992) theory of presidential character represented a conceptual advance precisely because it went beyond concerns with low self-esteem and lack of political skills. However, without understanding the specific psychological functions that activity and a strong commitment to it play in a president's psychology, we cannot be sanguine about either the purpose or results of high levels of activity. Pleasure in the pursuit and exercise of power is no guarantee that it will be used ethically, responsibly, or successfully (producing beneficial policy results).

Nor is having a president in office who expends enormous energy pursuing power, enjoys using it, and has enormous confidence in his capacities (and intentions) necessarily an unmixed blessing. Harold Lasswell (1948, 39) and Barber (1992, 9, 80–83) both worried that "political men" would amass and use political power against the public's interest to overcome low estimates of self. These scholars did not consider the possibility (or its implications) that a highly able president might amass and use power to validate *high* estimates of himself.

Bill Clinton: Active-Positive, Active-Passive, or Hybrid?

In Clinton we appear to have an important test case of Barber's and other political psychologists' assumptions about the psychology of presidential ambition and achievement. Barber argued that a president's activity level and his feelings about it (positive or negative) are keys to his character. A president who is very active and feels good about it would be an active-positive president—in Barber's view, the character type most fitted for the role of president. At first glance there seems little doubt where we would put Bill Clinton in Barber's typology. Clearly, on initial impression, we would think to place Clinton in the active-positive category. But there is evidence that this initial impression might be mistaken.

Clinton is a man who has at his disposal enormous energy. There are many indications of Clinton's high activity level. Historically, there are numerous accounts of Clinton's high level of activity beginning with his high school years (Levin, 1992, 30–32) and extending through his college, Oxford, and Yale Law School years.

This pace has continued. Consider this recent description of Clinton's frenetic campaign schedule during the presidential campaign. Senator David Pryor (D.–Ark.) (1992, xx), a good friend, noted, "His enormous energy ... his schedule defied human tolerance. ... On February 17, the day before the New Hampshire primary vote, he made 17 stops over the state. At 11:30 that night, schedule completed, he asked, 'Isn't there a bowling alley that's open all night? We need to shake some hands.'"

One difficulty with Barber's theory, however, and with Clinton's placement in it, is that it does not adequately distinguish between levels and causes of activity. Both Harry Truman and John Kennedy were active-positive presidents according to Barber, but Clinton's level of activity (the twelve- to eighteen-hour days) seems closer to the driven investments of energy of active-negative Lyndon Johnson than to the activity of either Kennedy or Truman. Clinton has characterized himself as "almost compulsively overactive" (in Moore, 1992, 35).

What of the other continuum of Barber's typology: the enjoyment and satisfaction that the president derives from his activity? Here again, on first glance we might well conclude that Clinton enjoys a number of aspects of the pursuit and exercise of power. Yet in a recent interview published in *Rolling Stone*, a very different picture emerges. At first, Clinton's responses seem typically active-positive (Wenner and Greider, 1993, 40):

> Wenner: Are you having fun?
> Clinton: You bet. I like it very much. Not every hour of every day is fun. The country is going through a period of change. ...
> Wenner: But are you having fun in this job?
> Clinton: I genuinely enjoy it.

But at the end of the interview, one interviewer tells Clinton of a call he received from a young person invited to the inaugural as part of Clinton's "Faces of Hope." The interviewer tells Clinton that this young man is very dejected and disappointed with Clinton's performance. The interviewer passes on to Clinton a question from the young man: "Ask him what he's willing to stand up for and die on."

The second reporter then describes the exchange as follows (Wenner and Greider, 1993, 81):

> Wenner: The president, standing a foot away from Greider, turned and glared at him. Clinton's face reddened, and his voice rose to a furious pitch, as he delivered a scalding rebuke—an angry emotional encounter, the kind of which few have ever witnessed.
> Clinton: But that's the press's fault, too, damn it. I have fought more damn battles here for more things than any president in the last twenty years ... and have not gotten one damn bit of credit for it from the knee-jerk liberal press, and I am sick and tired of it and you can put that in the damn article. I have fought and fought and fought and fought. I get up here every day, and I work till late at night on everything from national service to the budget to the crime bill and all this stuff, and you guys take it and you say, "Fine, go on to something else, what else can I hit him about?" So if you convince them I don't have any conviction, that's fine, but it's a damn lie. It's a lie.
> Look what I did. I said the wealthy would have to pay their fair share, and look what we did to the tax system. ... [Clinton then mentions another accomplishment.] Did I get any credit for it, from you or anyone else? Do I care if I get credit? No.

> Do I care that man has a false impression of me because of the way this adminis-
> tration has been covered? ... I have fought my guts out for that guy and if he
> doesn't know it, it's not all my fault. And you get no credit around here for
> fighting and bleeding. ... And if you hold me to an impossible standard and
> never give us any credit ... that's exactly what will happen, guys like that will
> think like that. But it ain't all my fault, because we have fought our guts out for
> 'em.

In this exchange Bill Clinton sounds more like Richard Nixon than John
Kennedy. The whole exchange has a definite active-negative cast to it and appears to contradict the earlier assertions of how much Clinton is enjoying his
role. The sense of being "done in" in spite of good deeds; of receiving no acknowledgment for hard, indeed almost herculean, efforts ("fighting my guts
out," "fighting and bleeding"); and of being held to "an impossible standard" (in a sense, being set up by others' failures) are all consistent with the
bitter sense of futility ("No matter how much I do, it's never good enough")
that pervades active-negative character types.

Which is the real Bill Clinton? One possibility is that the first ("I like my
job") is the real one and that the second ("I can't get any acknowledgment
for my immense and good efforts") is a temporary outburst of frustration.
Another possibility is that the reverse is true: that the angry, frustrated Bill
Clinton who is rarely seen (but, as I argue later in this chapter, is not completely absent from public view) is the real one and that the active-positive Bill
Clinton is in some respects how he would like to feel and be seen.

We cannot dismiss this idea out of hand in this age of the strategic manipulation of presidential character by staff and, on occasion, by the president himself. It is well to recall that when President Jimmy Carter met James David
Barber, he said he had read Barber's book and wanted to be an active-positive
president. A presidential candidate who mounted an extraordinary plan
(Kelly, 1992c) to market a new persona to the public to answer its doubts
about him during the campaign is not beyond reading and using Barber.

The real test of active-positives is not how they feel when things are going
well. After all, even Richard Nixon in a pre-Watergate interview seemed to be
relaxed and enjoying his presidential role. The real test is how they respond
when things are not going their way.

Nevertheless, it seems premature to make a definite statement at this point.
Clinton may represent one of the hybrid types or special variations that Barber
mentioned. Or the original theory may not be sufficiently able to distinguish
certain complexities of character enactment or to fully anticipate the capacity
for "masked active-negatives" to exist. Psychologists have long known that
the persona does not always reflect the real person. Therefore, active-positive
character elements may coexist with, and more likely be built on top of, an active-negative character core. In other words, the first might be the core; the
second, the superstructure.

The Role of Ambition in Presidential Psychology

The origin of the energy that is crucial to Barber's character typology is not fully accounted for in his theory. In Barber's view, active-positives are motivated by achievement and mastery; active-negatives, by the compensatory acquisition of power. A core psychological element has been left out of this formulation, however, and that is ambition.

Heinz Kohut (1971, 1977) reminded us that ambition, the sibling of what he called "healthy narcissism," is, along with ideals and the talent to achieve them, one foundation of a well-realized life. Without ambition there is no achievement, and without achievement there is little basis for consolidated self-regard. This being the case, the neglect of this core motivational element carries with it substantial theoretical and explanatory costs.

In the particular case of Bill Clinton, his ambition seems clear and manifest. There appears to be a close relationship between his high levels of energy and his ambition. It therefore would be difficult to consider his presidential psychology without examining this core element.

In Kohut's theory, ambition, even substantial ambition per se, is not problematic. On the contrary, for Kohut a substantial lack of ambition would connote a developmental arrest. As long as childhood grandiosity, which is the foundation of ambition, is gradually and successfully modulated by empathetically attuned others and "optimally frustrating" experiences, ambition does not run the risk of careening out of control and interfering with judgment and behavior (Kohut, 1971, 8–9, 107). What can make ambition problematic is its relationship to other characterological elements, such as one's view of and confidence in oneself or one's relationship to others. In short, we must look to a constellation of characterological elements, rather than a single one, to help us distinguish between productive and problematic ambition. What are these other essential elements? How particularly do they come together for Bill Clinton and with what implications for his presidency? I now turn to these questions.

The Basic Element of Presidential Psychology and Performance: Character

Character represents one's integrated pattern of responding to three basic life spheres or domains. The first is the domain of purposeful initiative, action, and capacity. This is the sphere of ambition. The basic concerns in this domain are the desire and ability to invest oneself for the accomplishment of one's immediate and life purposes.

The second basic character domain is the identity sphere. It is anchored by the level of consolidated self-esteem. Ordinarily, a consolidated sense of self-esteem is associated with a view of oneself (self-perception) as basically a "good enough" (Winnicott, 1965) person, a person whose values, skills, aspirations, and accomplishments measure up to generally accepted standards. These two elements in turn (and ambition as well) are related to the vision of the person one wishes to become. One's self-aspirations reflect the mixture of ambitions, talents, and values that help shape life pursuits.

The third domain concerns one's basic stance toward relationships with others and the function(s) that such relationships serve in one's psychology. This is the relational sphere. In this sphere are arrayed the continuum of interpersonal relationships and the psychology that shapes each. They range from antagonistic, unfriendly relationships at one pole, through various kinds of friendships, to intimate relationships anchoring the other pole.

The basic framework for psychological functioning that flows from these basic core psychological elements constitutes character. These elements represent one's approach to the most basic cornerstones of human experience and existence. They are the psychological foundation on which the superstructure of personality develops. Because they are so central and because they are so intertwined with the personality traits one develops, they are connected both individually and collectively with any president's stance toward his role and capacity for effective performance.[3] Thus, character shapes performance but does not determine it.

Character has a developmental history. The child shapes the adult, but the adult is not synonymous with the child. In addressing the role of character in presidential psychology, we must therefore address some aspects of its development. Because an extensive analysis of Clinton's developmental history is premature, I focus on the phenomenological and dynamic levels of analysis here.

Three Foundations of Character: A Political Psychology Profile of President Clinton

What are the three major core elements of Bill Clinton's character and psychology that correspond to the preceding formulation? I suggest they are (1) his substantial level of ambition, (2) his immense self-confidence coupled with a somewhat idealized view of himself, and (3) his strong need for validation. Each of these individually and the three collectively shape Clinton's approach to his presidency.

The Ambition Sphere (Purposeful Initiative, Action, and Capacity)

There can be little mistaking Bill Clinton's substantial ambition (that word here in the purely descriptive sense). His path from Hope, Arkansas, to Washington, D.C., is a chronicle of and testament to his personal and political ambitions. The realization of ambition, however, requires talent and skills. They are its means. Without ambition, talent and skill are empty vessels for accomplishing purposes. Therefore, no account of successfully realized ambition can dispense with a consideration of them. The successful integration of these two different but related levels of psychological functioning represents a developmental achievement. In examining Bill Clinton, we can discern at least three such skills/talents. One is primarily cognitive and the other two primarily motivational. They are (1) high-level cognitive capacities, (2) an ability to invest himself in work, and (3) an intense commitment to accomplishment.

Clinton's cognitive capacities are clear. They are reflected in part in his successful record as a student at Hot Springs High School, Georgetown, and Yale Law School and as a Rhodes scholar and a professional practitioner of public policy and its details during his twelve years as governor. These capacities were often on display during his candidacy and continue to be evident in his presidency.

He is able to answer questions on diverse policy topics with an array of information and a sophisticated appreciation of the issues involved. He clearly has the ability to master a great deal of information and has developed meaningful categories in which to organize it. (I leave aside for the moment the question of whether these categories reflect deep or creative integration of this information in ways that point toward the successful resolution of policy dilemmas.)

The second and third characteristics, his ability to invest himself in activity and his commitment to accomplishment, are reflected not only in the history of his academic and political career but also in the many other activities he was involved with while pursuing his education and his career. In addition to compiling a strong academic record in high school, Clinton was a member and/or president of a number of school organizations. Indeed, Robert Levin (1992, 30) reported that Clinton was president of so many of his high school activity clubs that the principal of Hot Springs High School, Jonnie Mae Mackey, limited the number of organizations that a student could join, "or Bill would have been president of them all."

In these activities Clinton was an invested participant. For example, he not only played in the high school band but also made the all-state band, a recognition of talent but also of practice and commitment. Carolyn Staley (1993, 36), a high school friend with whom Clinton practiced for a state music competition, recalled that "we met several times a week at my house to perfect his solo. We never sat around and chatted. The rehearsals were intense. Bill was always serious about his performances and worked hard to win first place."

Clinton's highly competitive nature is another aspect of this intense desire to accomplish that deserves mention in connection with ambition. As Staley recalled (quoted in Allen, 1991, 12), "He had to be the class leader, he had to be the best in the band. He had to be the best in his class—in ... grades. And he wanted to be in the top ... in anything that put him in the forefront of any course."

There is some evidence this characteristic persists. President Clinton is an avid golfer. And his playing partners say, "He is very competitive, always keeping careful score" (Berke, 1993b, A1). His competitiveness can also be seen in his determination to achieve his policy goals.

The Identity Sphere (Self-Esteem, Self-Perception, and Self-Aspirations)

The second basic element of one's character, the identity sphere, is anchored by one's level of consolidated self-esteem and by the frequently (but not always strongly) associated view that one holds of oneself. A consolidated sense of self-esteem is a developmental achievement, but it is at the same time a foundation of character. When a strong sense of self-esteem is coupled with a strongly positive view of oneself, one result is a substantial level of personal confidence.

There is much evidence to support the view that Clinton has developed extremely high levels of self-confidence. Rudy Moore Jr. (1993, 92; italics added), Clinton's campaign manager during his first run for governor and also his chief of staff during Clinton's first term, recalled that Clinton "always had *boundless confidence* in his ability to forge a consensus and work out *any problem*." Clinton is also willing to talk publicly, at length, without notes, on a range of subjects. He is one of the most verbal presidents in modern history. Few modern presidents have felt so secure talking at length in a variety of settings.

What developmental experiences help account for this characterological element? Clinton's high level of self-confidence is, I think, a result of an appreciation of his own skills and his own history of generally successful accomplishment. He is intelligent, articulate, outgoing, and determined. These personal skills are the vehicles of his success and the foundation of his high self-confidence. Moreover, these skills were developed over the many years of his political apprenticeship (which stretches back into adolescence). Apprenticeship experiences in high school, college, postgraduate studies (Rhodes scholarship and law school), and state and national political work were instrumental both in refining his skills and cementing his ultimate confidence in them. It is this combination that fuels and supports his determination.

The other element of this character domain, his view of himself, is essential to understanding Clinton's psychology. Clinton entertains few doubts about his abilities, his accomplishments, or himself and his motives more generally. In his responses to the press and others who raised questions about him during the campaign and the first months of his presidency, he painted a picture of himself as a man of conviction, determination, integrity, and principle. He sees himself as fair, open, honest, and genuinely interested in and responsive to others' points of view and concerns. He attributes to himself the most sincere and best of motives. He sees acknowledged errors as basically correct efforts gone temporarily awry, misunderstandings that would disappear or be mitigated on further investigation or else be attributable to naïveté and inexperience. The latter is, of course, another way of assigning oneself good intentions.

I do not list these characteristics because I believe them to be wholly untrue. Rather, I note them because they reflect a strong component of *self-idealization*. Most people wish to think well of themselves. However, Bill Clinton appears to have come to believe the *best* of himself and to either avoid or discount evidence from his own behavior that all is not as he believes it to be. When confronted by discrepancies between his real behavior and his view of it, as was done by the press during the campaign and first months of the presidency, Clinton responds with denial, exculpatory explanations, often long answers that do not always deal directly with the point, and, when all else fails, unconcealed frustration and anger.

During the campaign and the first year in office, there were many examples of Clinton engaging in contradictory behavior (see "The Wish to Have It Both Ways" later in this chapter). However, one of the most striking recent pieces of evidence along these lines is contained in the *Rolling Stone* interview. In it, the interviewers ask why Clinton allowed the CIA to publicly present Congress with a very unflattering profile of Jean-Bertrand Aristide, whose return to Haiti to govern that country Clinton supported (Wenner and Greider, 1993, 81; italics added):

> Greider: But can't you direct the CIA either to shut up or support your policy? In another administration, the director of the agency would have been gone by that evening if he had done that to the president.
>
> Clinton: The director didn't exactly do that. The guy who expressed that opinion—or at least revealed the research on which it was based—was a career employee. He did that work in a previous administration under a previous director. Under the rules of Congress, when someone is called to testify and asked their personal opinion, they have to give it.
>
> Greider: Yea, but the CIA, come on. They're the last agency to believe in free speech.
>
> Clinton: All I'm saying is, consider the flip side. What if the story is, today the president suppressed information from the CIA ... information that [North Carolina Senator] Jesse Helms knew about because he's been on the committee.
>
> Greider: He had you either way.
>
> Clinton: He knew he had me either way. He knew I'd been given this information when I became president. ... So what was I to do? Try to jam it? Eventually it would have come out. ... So I reasoned so that since I knew it was out there before I took office, and it was a matter of fact, and Congress had a legal right to know it, that rather than gagging this guy or playing games with him, the best thing to do was to let it happen. ...

Wenner: *What's the most important thing you've learned about yourself since you've become president?*

Clinton: *All the old rules are still the ones that count. I feel better every night when I go home if I've done what I think is right.*

There are many interesting aspects to this exchange. The president spends most of his time explaining that he did not suppress an unfavorable report because he could not since others already knew of it. He also appears to be arguing that he had no choice. We can view Clinton's answer as simply an illustration of "hardball politics" or a good grasp of "political reality." However, it also reflects a strong element of expediency: The ethical calculus expressed appears very responsive, not to what is right, but to how his action would look in the morning papers.

Another striking aspect of this exchange is Clinton's response when he is asked what most important thing about himself he has learned in the presidency. He does not in fact answer the question, does not reveal any new self-knowledge. Instead, he discusses the importance of traditional virtues, which presumably he has reaffirmed in his behavior as president, and then adds that he can sleep better knowing he has done what he thinks is right. Clinton shows no indication that the two sets of statements, one immediately following the other, might somehow be related. Is political expediency, however finely calculated, one of the traditional virtues that Clinton has reaffirmed? Is that what he means when he feels more able to sleep well at night having "done what I think is right"?

One important and related consequence of Clinton's enormous accomplishment coupled with his self-idealization is a belief in his own essential goodness and *correctness*. It is a sense that he has about himself, about what he does, and about what he wishes to accomplish. The importance of maintaining this view of himself is, I believe, at the heart of the third basic core element of his character, his interpersonal relations, which are organized around his need for validation.

The Relational Sphere (Interpersonal Relations)

The third basic dimension of character is one's stance toward interpersonal relations. Some time ago psychoanalyst Karen Horney (1945) suggested that as a result of early experience, people develop an interpersonal style in which they move toward, away from, or against people. In the first style, one reaches out to others, gaining psychologically from relationships. In the second style, one moves away from relationships either because they are less important than other needs (such as those for autonomy or solitude [Storr, 1990]) or because they have been a source of disappointments. In the third style, one wants contact but engages with others in a way that ensures distance, not intimacy or friendship.

Each of these general orientations is accompanied by specific constellations of personal needs and interpersonal skills. We carry others within us through memory and experience, and they influence not only how we approach them but also what we want and expect from them (self-object functions, as Kohut [1971] termed them). Others can serve to affirm, threaten, or bolster us. And we vary in turn with regard to the interpersonal skills (empathy, outgoingness, verbal facility) we bring to the world of relationships.

At first glance, Clinton's interpersonal style is a movement toward people. Many have noted Clinton's empathy and natural friendliness, and to a substantial degree (with some caveats to be noted) these characterizations appear accurate. Clinton exhibited these characteristics at an early age, which suggests that they are linked to the loss of his father and his mother's decision to leave him with his grandparents in Hope, rather than to his upbringing with an alcoholic stepfather (Wright, 1993, 28).

Much has also been written about Clinton's difficulty in saying no (e.g., Cliff, 1993) and his eagerness to please (e.g., Klein, 1993). Both are often attributed to "Clinton's well-known need to be liked." Indeed, the brief biography of Clinton that appeared on the front page of the *New York Times* on the day of his election (Kelly, 1992a) was entitled, "A Man Who Wants to Be Liked, and Is."

However, I believe this analysis to be mistaken. At least two theoretical and factual difficulties stand in the way of this argument. First, there is the issue, already noted, of Clinton's very strong sense of self-confidence. Ordinarily, the need to be liked is not associated with such high levels of personal confidence. Second, the idea of a need to be liked does not fully address Clinton's frequently observed tendency toward public and private displays of anger. When told (erroneously) during the nomination campaign that Jesse Jackson had come out in support of a party rival, Clinton, who was not aware that he was speaking near an open microphone, angrily denounced Jackson as a "back-stabber" (Berke, 1992, A14). When news reporters followed the president-elect onto a golf course, he lost his temper, cursed them, and complained to the manager of the club (Kelly, 1992b). When asked about the decision process that resulted in the nomination of Ruth Bader Ginsburg to the Supreme Court, Clinton (1993, 1082) angrily rejected the question and abruptly terminated the news conference, saying, "I have long since given up the thought that I could disabuse some of you from turning any substantive decision into anything but political process. How you could ask a question like that after the statement she just made is beyond me. Good-bye. Thank you."

Gwen Ifel noted (1993, 4) that Clinton "has trouble concealing his exasperation when things do not go his way." It is possible, of course, that some of this anger is strategic. However, by this time there have been enough public instances (including the *Rolling Stone* interview) and enough reports of Clinton's anger in private to suggest that it is more than strategy.

Nor in the area of anger does the need to be liked theory address another psychological component of Clinton's political style: his tendency to build up and then lash out against institutions or groups that oppose his policies. The press is one example of such a group, but there are others, including "lobbyists," "special interests," "profiteering drug companies," "greedy doctors," "muscle-bound" labor unions, and so on. Presidents, like others, can be known by and benefit from having certain kinds of enemies. However, for a man who is said to have such a strong need to be liked, the list is rather long and inclusive, and the characterizations are often somewhat harsh. Moreover, Clinton's tendency to develop enemies, even if partially for political purposes, runs counter to another important theme that he has often publicly expressed: the need to bring Americans together and stop practicing the "politics of division." I think the central emotional issue for Clinton, rather than a need to be liked, is a strong need to be validated, and this need is the key to understanding the third key element of character, his stance toward others.

The need for validation is reflected in one's efforts to be acknowledged for the specific ambition, skills, and accomplishments that are central to one's view of oneself. It is important that these specific aspects of oneself be met with appreciation and acknowledgment from important others. Validation and self-regard are closely connected under normal circumstances but are even more critically joined in cases such as Clinton's, where self-regard and idealization are firmly entwined.

The concept of validation is a useful key to understanding Clinton's response to criticism. Few people like criticism and in this Clinton is no exception. One difficulty in analyzing Clinton's response to criticism is that he promised a great deal. Therefore, in some respects criticisms of his accomplishments (criticism of his behavior) tend to raise the issue of whether he promised too much because he was too ambitious, too willing to say anything to get elected, and so on (criticisms of Clinton as an individual). And every president, especially one elected with a plurality, may feel the political need to defend his record. However, I believe that Clinton is particularly sensitive to several kinds of criticisms, all related to his own view of himself.

One very sensitive area concerns Clinton's view of himself as a man of accomplishments. The acknowledgment that he is doing things is very important to Clinton. He briefly considers criticism that he is doing too much and then summarily rejects it. Criticism that he is not doing needed things results in extensive lists of how many more things he has done than his predecessors and how well this compares to presidents such as Franklin Roosevelt, with whom Clinton wishes to be identified and with whom he does personally identify (Blumenthal, 1993b; Samuelson, 1993). If he cannot receive validations from others on these important grounds, he validates himself.

A second area of criticism that appears to directly affect him comprises questions about his own view of himself as a good person. Charges that he had been less than forthcoming about his marital difficulties, the draft, and other matters during the campaign led Clinton to complain that he was being un-fairly and inappropriately targeted by the press, and he reacted with anger. As president he has reacted the same way when questions are raised about his leadership style. At one point in the campaign, he cried out in response to more critical questions that he had considered all the questions raised about him and come to the conclusion "It's not me!"

Clinton appears to subscribe to the view that if people who disagree with him know the facts as he sees and understands them and appreciate the sincer-ity and strength of his convictions, their opposition will fade. In some cases, his barrage of facts and loquaciousness has its effects (but it is not always clear that this is so because the person has been persuaded or exhausted). Clinton has always been an articulate leader, a skill that he has effectively developed over the years. However, when his articulateness does not work, Clinton has a tendency to be angered by the failure of others to be convinced.

Structural Implications of Character: Character-Based Personality Traits

Character forms the foundation and basis of a person's overall psychological functioning. But the configuration of the three basic character elements is also generally associated with the development of a stable set of psychological ori-entations, which I term *character-based personality traits.* These are the stable characteristics that spring from the ways in which the three basic character ele-ments have come together. These traits develop out of character but are not synonymous with it.

How are these personality traits to be understood in the overall psychologi-cal structure of the individual? Every individual can be located along a contin-uum of personality traits. Some traits play relatively minor roles in an individ-ual's psychological structure. Others have much more centrality in overall psychological functioning. The concern of the analyst is to identify the latter traits, which are potentially more important in understanding the person's ap-proach to experience and behavior.

We can discern several important character-based personality traits in Clin-ton. They originate in his strong ambition, strong sense of personal confi-dence, high self-regard coupled with a strong degree of self-idealization, and an orientation toward people designed to, among other things, secure contin-ued validation for his somewhat idealized view of himself. In the analysis that follows I examine these personality traits and draw some implications for Clin-ton's approach to political leadership and the presidency.

Persistence

Persistence refers to the capacity to consistently and systematically pursue one's goals in the face of adversity. Psychologically, it reflects a capacity to tolerate disappointments, frustrations, and setbacks to one's plans and not be deterred from continuing the attempts to achieve them. Persistence is a good example of a character-based personality trait because it is related to, not the same as, character. The capacity to persist is a partial function of the strength of one's desire to achieve one's purposes (ambition). The higher one's ambition is, the more likely one is to continue trying to realize it. Persistence is also related to self-esteem. The greater one's self-esteem is, the more capacity one has to persist.

However, persistence owes its development to psychological and experiential elements less based in character. It is, for example, related to the range and level of one's capacities and skills. The more developed one's skills are, the more personal resources one has to bring to bear on achieving one's goals. Persistence also depends on the level of self-confidence one has as well as on one's past level of success (these two are related). And the capacity for persistence is related to the emotional and (often) material support of others in times of need.

The evidence appears to bear out the observation that Clinton is both determined and resilient. We know that he has suffered a number of serious setbacks from which he has recovered and from which he has gone on to new achievements. Many of these occurred in the political arena and date back to his high school days. The "Comeback Kid" persona that Clinton used so effectively after coming in second in New Hampshire and elsewhere has a real developmental basis. Clinton himself views his determination as a political asset (Blumenthal, 1994, 33, 43), which it is. However, we can also question why he is often in the position of having to recover. Are there some elements or consequences of Clinton's character that continue to get him into personal and political trouble?

Achievement

The combination of intense ambition and strong self-confidence leads Clinton to be very directed toward achievement, but achievement of a particular type. Because of the intense nature of Clinton's ambition and his equally high self-regard, modest attempts at achievement are not sufficient. His achievement is self-defined at extremely high levels of attempted accomplishment. Nor are the formulation and successful implementation of some major policy initiatives enough. "Many" may even be too few given Clinton's definition of policy success.

Need to Be Appreciated

The need for validation requires that one be appreciated. In this circumstance, a president may come to feel that the public has to know all he is doing. This is one reason that Clinton finds it very hard to be a "hidden-hand" president. He is and most likely will continue to be a most public president.

Clinton is a man with strong analytic capacities and a mastery of facts that comes from decades of immersion in these policy areas, and he wants us to know this. He is a man who believes strongly in his abilities to solve the public's problems and wants others to know and appreciate what he is doing. This characteristic is reflected in his personal and public association with the development of his policies as well as their implementation. One striking illustration of these tendencies was seen during the economic conference staged by the administration in December 1992. "Professor" Clinton demonstrated at length his grasp of policy detail, putting his intelligence on display in a setting structured to be supportive of ideas he had presented during the campaign. Sidney Blumenthal (1994, 34) characterized the conference as "one last campaign stop, a sterile event conducted in the absence of conflict." This characteristic can also be seen in Clinton's willingness to speak in public at length about so many things—in many cases more than is needed and sometimes more than can be educationally absorbed.

This tendency to inundate the public with his technical knowledge may have a political as well as a personal payoff for Clinton. Certainly the demonstration of policy knowledge is an asset to a president interested in policy leadership. So, too, educating the public is an important part of effective political leadership in a democracy. However, it is also true that information can confuse as well as enlighten. Too much information or too specific a formulation of information may disguise purpose as well as reveal it.

The Primacy of Interpersonal Relations

Clinton is a man for whom interpersonal relations and "chemistry" are critical, but his relationships to others are more complex than has generally been acknowledged. Clinton is by many accounts a charming, gregarious, and friendly man. Unlike Gary Hart and Richard Nixon, two men with a tendency toward interpersonal isolation, Clinton is the center of and surrounded by a group of admiring friends. Given Clinton's concern with validation and his interpersonal skills, this is not surprising.

The Friends of Bill (FOB) is a network that Clinton began developing early. It has reached proportions that are almost without precedent in the modern presidency. For the most part, these friends are extremely supportive of the man and his accomplishments. In a number of cases, there are strong tendencies toward uncritical idealization (see, e.g., Levin, 1992; and a number of the recollections in Dumas, 1993).

Clearly there is something in Clinton that many find attractive. He is outgoing and conveys the sense that he cares. He has been compared to an "empath," a species on a popular television show whose special power is being in attunement with the emotions of others. This may be so. However, there are several reasons to suggest that this characterization is somewhat broad and may well be overdrawn. One reason is that the characterization of Clinton as an empath makes no attempt to distinguish between real and strategic empathy and the relative mix of each in a particular individual.

Strategic empathy can be usefully distinguished from empathetic attunement. Its primary purpose is advantage rather than understanding. Thus, one motivational source of strategic empathy is to get something from others that they might not otherwise offer. Strategic empathy in this instance is a sophisticated form of manipulation for direct personal gain. One who makes use of this form sees others essentially as objects whose primary function is to service one's wants or needs. There is little real consideration of others since to do so might interfere with their use. Another motivational source is the attempt to receive validation or approval from others. Here empathy is put in the service of knowing what others want so that one can be appreciated for providing it. The primary motivation in this instance is not so much to take as it is to give for the purpose of receiving.

At a theoretical level it may be prudent to explore these dimensions of strategic empathy in connection with Clinton. Such an exploration does not begin with the assumption that he is manipulative, only that the view of Clinton as being selflessly attuned to others may be somewhat idealized. One reason for exploring this area more closely is that there are clearly areas where Clinton's empathetic attunement does not extend. One of those was on view in his ill-fated attempt to reverse by presidential edict a ban on openly gay men and lesbian women serving in the armed forces. I am not addressing here the wisdom or the ultimate correctness of that policy. I am only pointing out that there were an array of feelings held by those who had concerns about such a policy. Clinton may have been aware of these feelings, but he never suggested during his campaign or before the controversy broke that he had considered them and discussed the reasons he found them unpersuasive. He appears not to have given them much thought. Congressional and Pentagon opposition essentially forced Clinton to consider these other points of view seriously enough to integrate them into his policy design. He himself appears to have accepted that some of these concerns, such as the issues of group cohesion and close quarters, were legitimate matters on which people might hold different views.

Another reason to examine this area more closely comes from Clinton's well-documented tendency to convey the impression to each party that he talks with that he understands and is in touch with its views (even if the views of the parties are in strong opposition). A corollary assumption, which Clinton does nothing to dispel, is that he is in agreement with each party's views and will act on that agreement. These tendencies came up several times in the recollections of those who worked for Clinton as governor. Stephen Smith

(1993, 14; italics added; see also Moore, 1993, 92), a friend, political adviser, and assistant to Governor Clinton, noted that "many times I saw groups that got a full and fair hearing subsequently feel betrayed by a lack of support for favorable action on their request because they assumed that the absence of 'no' meant 'yes.' That happened partially because supplicants for support are always more inclined to hear what they wanted to hear and partially because *they were not explicitly or immediately told what they did not want to hear.*"

The Wish to Have It Both Ways

I have noted in discussing Clinton's idealized view of himself that he often seems unaware of the discrepancies between what he says and what he does. This myopia was apparent several times during the campaign and on a number of occasions after he assumed office. For example, Clinton is for public education, but he sends his child to an exclusive private school (Friedman, 1993). He is "prochoice" in education, but only within the public school system. This seems to suggest that a more wide-ranging choice is alright for his family but not for other families. He may feel there is good reason for his choices but is not willing to extend to others the same opportunity.

There are also discrepancies in his speech and action concerning ethics. Clinton has spoken of his commitment to setting a high moral tone for his administration and to following a tough standard of ethics. Yet the administration skirted the lobby law by inviting big contributors to the Democratic party to a "breakfast with president." This plan was dropped only after word of it became public (Ifel, 1993a). The president has also consistently decried the pernicious role of lobbyists. Nevertheless, he visited a large fund-raising dinner for lobbyists but would not allow the press to take pictures of him doing so. When criticism of this "stealth visit" mounted, Clinton promised to be more open in the future ("Clinton Pledges Open Fund-Raisers," 1993, A22).

There is an element in Clinton of not wishing to, or perhaps thinking that he does not have to, make the ordinary choices that individuals and presidents do. Whether this attitude comes from a sense of not wanting to be limited in any way personally or politically (itself a characteristic of interest to psychologically minded analysts as a possible manifestation of grandiosity), or whether it comes from a sense of being special and therefore entitled to operate differently, or whether it comes from both is not yet clear. But further examination would shed light on Clinton's character.

Substantial But Self-Protecting and Calculated Risk-Taking

The combination of strong ambition and high self-confidence pushes Clinton toward substantial risk-taking, but he does so in a calculated, rather than a reckless, manner. Clinton had enough self-confidence to risk public defeat running for the presidency against a then-popular president. However, this risk was not reckless given the circumstances.

We do not yet know the basis of Clinton's personal and political calculations in this matter. It is possible that Clinton's polling information suggested George Bush's vulnerability and that he decided on this basis to make the run. But in doing so, he was also hedging his political bets. He was, after all, still a sitting governor. And his calculations might well have included the belief that a strong run against Bush, even if unsuccessful, would have made him a front-runner in 1996, especially as there was no strong Republican contender (such as a widely respected vice president) on the immediate horizon.

More recently, we have seen his willingness to take large political risks in regard to his economic package, NAFTA, and his health care package. Yet each of these shows a mix of ambition and self-protective hedging. For example, the budget package passed in August 1993 called for increased government spending first (that is, during his first term in office) and cuts in government spending to reduce the deficit in 1996 and later (that is after his first term and possible stand for reelection). Similarly, the health care program now before Congress calls for major and extensive changes and is based on projections of savings that will not be seen for some years after it is enacted. In other words, the program's results, for better or worse, will not be clear for some years.

Some Implications of Presidential Psychology: Bill Clinton's Approach to Political Leadership

Presidential style is the president's approach to dealing with the responsibilities of his office. It is defined not only by what the president chooses to emphasize (see Barber, 1992, 5 for one view of style defined in this way) but also by how he approaches and carries out his presidential responsibilities. The roots of presidential style lie in character, personality, beliefs, and skills. Its results can be seen in the world of presidential action. What can we say of Clinton's style at this point?

An Episodic, Discontinuous Presidency

There has already been some evidence of the discontinuous, episodic nature of the Clinton presidency. There have been some impressive accomplishments but also some serious setbacks, some of the administration's own making. Among the pieces of evidence for this characterization are the confusions of the administration's first months in office, including the frustrating and frustrated search for an attorney general and other appointments; policy reversal and retreats; momentum gathered by excellent speeches such as the president's address to Congress on health care, which was then dissipated as no actual policy was presented; and so on.

The high level of policy ambition that characterizes this administration means that often the administration must cope with many, perhaps too many, policy initiatives at the same time. Clinton at one point acknowledged this difficulty but then backtracked in favor of continuing the fast, self-imposed pace. That Clinton so firmly believes in the necessity and correctness of his policy undertakings leads him to action. But this very same set of beliefs may run his many purposes into trouble.

First, the machinery of policy deliberation and public understanding may be unable to sustain such a pace. A lack of understanding and comfort with those policies is one result. Second, the president's conviction that all these policy initiatives must be accomplished quickly raises the concern that there will be too little time for consultation, public education, and policy refinement. Third, the consistent introduction of new initiatives, coupled with the almost continuous refinement of the old ones as they meet opposition from one source or another, means that it is difficult to keep track (for the public, Congress, and the administration) and follow through.

The fast pace of Clinton's policy initiatives is one strategy for accomplishing rapid social and political change, but in the past Clinton has paid a price for that strategy. During his first term as governor, the pace of this social and policy agenda in Arkansas cost him reelection.

An Intensely Personal and Political Presidency

I have noted the importance of interpersonal relations to Clinton. In what ways does this emphasis influence Clinton's approach to presidential leadership? At this point, several hypotheses can be put forward. One is that Clinton's need for validation is very closely connected to his intensely personal style of leadership. His is and will be a very personal presidency. We can see this quality in the importance that Clinton attributes to "chemistry" in interviewing potential high appointees and his surrounding himself with close personal friends (from the FOB network). We can also see this quality in Clinton's love of campaigning itself. Like other presidents, he seems to thrive on close personal contact with friendly crowds. However, unlike other presidents, he is willing to adapt the "permanent campaign" as one tool of policy mobilization.

Clinton's is also likely to be a very political presidency. The combination of a large controversial social and policy agenda, a determination to accomplish it, and a style that emphasizes relentless efforts to win people over augurs a presidency in which the public will be consistently lobbied for support of a continuing series of presidential initiatives.

An Ideologically Ambiguous Presidency

In answer to the question "Who am I?" Clinton's response has been to say that he is an amalgam. He is a Democrat, but a new kind of Democrat. He is for government programs, but only if they work. He accepts the use of force, but only if it is consistent with American ideals. There are many other examples of this tendency.

It is possible that Clinton truly believes that he can reconcile these traditional opposites. In trying to bridge these alternatives, Clinton is following the path of several former presidents, among them Richard Nixon and Jimmy Carter, who resisted attempts at political or ideological labeling. And there is no doubt that the attempt to do so serves a political purpose as well. However, some of Clinton's social and public policies reflect the traditional policies of the Democratic party. Programs such as the stimulus package and large new government initiatives in a variety of areas (health, a national student service program, and others) seem largely in keeping with the traditional Democratic party focus of activist, interventionist government. In addition, Clinton has been extremely sensitive to traditional Democratic party constituency politics. There have been programs and policies for labor, minorities, gays and lesbians, women, and so forth. Clinton may be a new Democrat in his mind, but in some important ways he resembles an old one.

Clinton has occasionally been willing to say no to some groups traditionally associated with the Democratic party. He supported NAFTA in spite of opposition from some labor unions. However, he has much more frequently supported labor's agenda. He has canceled the ban against air traffic controllers instituted by Ronald Reagan (Bradsher, 1993a), and he has supported legislation barring companies from replacing union personnel on strike (Kilborn, 1993), rescinded an order requiring federal contractors to post notices informing nonunion members they were not obliged to join unions or to allow unions to use money collected from them in lieu of dues for union activities (Kelly, 1993b), and reversed an order prohibiting federal agencies and contractors from requiring that workers on government projects be members of a union (Kelly, 1993b). The question may not be whether Clinton is a new Democrat but whether his version of being a new Democrat is really that significantly different from being an old one.

Some Complications of Presidential Psychology: Some Dilemmas of Clinton's Presidency

Every president has three mandates. He must address policy issues, make decisions, and invest some effort in carrying them through. The first requires us to focus on the president's approach to resolving policy dilemmas. The second points us toward the president's understanding of the issues involved and his judgments about resolving them. And the third points us to how a president mobilizes, orchestrates, and consolidates support for his policy decisions. Let us now turn briefly to some potential dilemmas of Clinton's presidential psychology and political style in each of these three areas, beginning with political leadership.

Political Leadership

Clinton has experienced setbacks, but his experience suggests and he believes that planning, the application of intelligence, and sheer determination will eventually accomplish his goals. Clinton is not used to losing or suffering permanent setbacks; there is always another way to be tried and another day to succeed. His level of energy coupled with his sense of policy correctness and determination suggests a strategy of coming back repeatedly to accomplish his purposes until opponents either tire or despair. The problem with this approach is that it may also exhaust public understanding and patience. It may prove effective in the short term in getting policies passed, but it runs the risk of not providing a firm foundation for public acceptance. In that sense, this approach may not successfully resolve the basic public dilemma that Clinton faces.

There is also in Clinton a willingness to shade meaning and be less than forthright. This came up during the presidential campaign in his evasive answers regarding the draft, Gennifer Flowers, and the marijuana controversies. Not surprisingly, this trait has surfaced in his presidency. We can note a tendency in this administration to play fairly loosely with its budget figures and estimates. We can argue, however, that previous administrations also did so, but this argument misses an important point: Clinton campaigned against politics as usual, one aspect of which was to not fully inform the public. Other presidents have paid a price for this strategy, and it has had a damaging effect on the nation's support of government programs.

We can also see these nuances in this administration's very strong concern with appearances. For example, Clinton has presented himself to the public as having a close and loving relationship with his wife. Yet his campaign produced a memorandum detailing the ways they should act in public (contrary to how they had acted toward each other in public previously) to convey this image (Kelly, 1992c, A1). It suggested "events where Bill and Hillary can go on dates with American people" and the arranging of such events as "Bill and Hillary surprise Hillary on Mother's Day."

There also appears to be a tendency to claim more for the results of Clinton's policies than are warranted. Given that trust and policy competence are such important issues for this administration, these tendencies are unfortunate. The July 1993 economic summit in Tokyo provides a public case in point. The ambiguously worded agreement reached by President Clinton and Japanese prime minister Kiichi Miyazawa at the G-7 summit was hailed by the administration as a "major breakthrough" (Apple, 1993). In fact, it was an agreement to hold future talks about trade and appears to have been brought about by the administration's retreat from its publicly stated position of having Japan agree to specific levels of reduction in its trade surplus with the United States (Sanger, 1993; Pollack, 1993). By February 1994 the "breakthrough" based on "mutual understanding" had in fact resulted in a total impasse and renewed threats of a trade war (Ifel, 1994).

Judgment and Decisionmaking

Clinton's strong intelligence and his mastery of policy detail coupled with his selection of advisers on the basis of chemistry (which can be translated as "They get along with me and I with them") run the risk of giving too much weight in the decision process to concurrence. By all accounts Clinton dominates his staff policy meetings. Blumenthal (1993a, 37) noted that Clinton has "surrounded himself with deferential advisors who are either without national experience or much younger." Who is knowledgeable enough, strong enough, and secure enough in his or her own position to tell Bill Clinton when he is wrong? Al Gore has emerged as one person who does so on occasion, but one person is not enough, and apparently Gore does not press his points too insistently (Berke, 1994).

There is also the issue of the effects of Clinton's strong sense of competence and high self-confidence on his judgment. He runs the danger of shading off into overconfidence. One striking example of this occurred in an interview he gave ("Excerpts from an Interview," 1993, 10A; italics added) before his inauguration regarding the possibility of a new relationship with Saddam Hussein. Clinton's comments on the matter reflect a remarkable self-assurance about his ability to change Hussein and his pattern of behavior: "*I think that if he were sitting here on the couch I would further the change in his behavior.* You know if he spent half the time, just a half, or even a third of the time worrying about the welfare of his people that he spends worrying about where to place his SAM [surface-to-air] missiles and whether he can aggravate Bush by violating the cease-fire agreement, what he's going to do with the people who don't agree with him in the South and in Iraq, I think he'd be a stronger leader and be in a lot better shape over the long run."

President Clinton appears to believe that he can personally bring about this change and that he can do so by persuading Hussein that he would be a better leader and in a better situation if he followed Clinton's advice. The expectation that people can be won over by words is an understandable and plausible premise given Clinton's experience in the presidential election, but it is a potentially dangerous misapplication in this context.

There is an element of naïveté in these beliefs. It is to be found in the belief that Clinton would be able to overcome, indeed reverse, the character patterns that have been evident in Hussein's adult career and behavior and do so by appealing to what Clinton sees as Hussein's long-run interests. The confidence that Clinton expresses in his ability to bring about such a change is a potential source of difficulty. The potential error of judgment that may await President Clinton is not that he will discount Hussein's shrewdness but that he will overestimate his own potential impact.

Resolving Policy Dilemmas

Clinton's high levels of ambition and self-confidence lead him to generate policy initiatives that are sweeping in their scope and complexity. His health care program is a good example of this, as was his initial economic program. The complexity and scope of these initiatives mean that Clinton is willing to take a large policy gamble—namely, that the untried policies that he proposes will in fact work the way he says they will, that they will not result in other damaging public consequences, and that they will work in a way that is fair.

Given the scale of Clinton's policy aspirations, he frequently falls short of them. However, large ambitions that produce modest results do not appear to be what Clinton has in mind for himself or his presidency. The attempt to achieve a lot and settle for substantially less is one possible strategy of policy leadership. However, it has costs.

Using a "maximizing" strategy to achieve "satisficing" policy objectives raises at least three issues. First, constructing ambitious, complex policy architecture runs the risk of creating policy structures that will prove to be unworkable. Such an outcome would cast further doubt on government's ability to solve social problems. Second, such large-scale policy architecture and concerns about its workability run the risk of increasing public anxiety. Third, complex large-scale policies generally offer numerous targets for critics. More modest proposals present less numerous targets for concern and disagreement.

In the policy arena there are numerous examples of Clinton's "yes and" approach, which is the policy equivalent of wishing to have it both ways. These examples include his stands on defense ("I'm for maintaining a strong defense and cutting it dramatically") and trade ("I'm for free trade, but we must protect vital industries" [Bradsher, 1993b]). It is not clear whether this approach is a function of cognitive complexity, political opportunism, an inability to make and be bound by the inevitable limits of decisions, or some of all three. It is possible that Clinton believes that he has developed a special and unique synthesis of these opposites. However, it is also possible that Clinton may have convinced himself of more than is possible or real.

There are many reasons that presidents may choose to try having it both ways. One reason is that such an approach gives them political flexibility in dealing with problems of mobilizing their constituents. Another is that it may also give them policy flexibility as they attempt to orchestrate their policy initiatives. It may also be used as a gauge to ascertain responses to one side or another of an issue or to reassure every side that the president is considering its particular point of view. I have already noted that Clinton used this approach to political decisionmaking as governor of Arkansas.

However, like other patterns of chosen political behavior, this one may also reflect psychological elements operating for the president. A yes and view of policy may reflect a certain disinclination to be bound by the need to choose, which is to say an ability to recognize and accept limits. Certainly this is one psychological lesson that Clinton could have drawn from his own experience of successful accomplishment and overcoming of barriers.

A yes and approach to policy issues may also reflect the very high and (idealized) standards that define his level of "satisfactory accomplishment." When one has an extremely strong sense of self-confidence, possesses a somewhat idealized view of oneself, and has committed oneself to large goals, modest accomplishments may be experienced psychologically as substandard performance. Clinton's yes and seems clearly reflective of his ambitious policy aspirations.

It remains to be seen, given Clinton's dislike of limits and traditional policy categories, whether his policies will really integrate alternative policy ideals in a constructive way. It may be that his policies will ultimately be seen as adapting a "split the difference" approach in which he adapts the symbol and substance of both liberal and conservative approaches to policy issues and attempts to combine them without really integrating them.

Selling Public Policies

The Clinton presidency coincides with, and has made extensive use of, the development of an extremely sophisticated public lobbying apparatus. While decrying special interests and lobbyists, the administration has made extensive use of the same machinery and tactics in support of its own view of the public interest. Policy issues and positions are fully pretested with multiple focus groups, while words and phrases are honed and others deleted. The results are marketed with sophisticated public relations strategies that include the systematic convening of selected members of the "ordinary public" to present the most effective but not necessarily the most representative aspects of the policies that are to be "sold." The president's economic stimulus package, his health care proposals (Kelly, 1993a), and even his inaugural (Berke, 1993a) were carefully scripted public events designed and carried through for political purposes.

All presidents must to some degree "sell" their policies. But the student of political leadership must remain alert to the distinction between "selling" and educating. This is a particularly important distinction for Clinton to be aware of given his promise to "reinvent government" and the lingering problem of trust with which he began his presidency. To the extent that trust in government policies is the major public dilemma facing President Clinton, his now-recurring suggestion that major savings will help finance his new programs is a pattern that raises concern. In announcing his new health care proposals, Clinton suggested savings were the means of funding them. In announcing his new welfare reforms, he put forward unspecified large savings as the method of funding. New and dramatic savings were said to be one result of his reinventing government initiative. However, a study by the Congressional Budget Office suggested that the real savings from such a program would be substantially less than those projected by the Clinton administration (Reischauer, 1993).

All administrations must educate the public regarding new policies and build support for them. Traditional democratic theory assumed that there was a relationship between the two. There seems, however, to be an emphasis in the Clinton administration on selling its policies, as opposed to educating people on the merits and limitations of the alternatives chosen and the rationale for having done so. This is policy implementation by focus group, and it does not augur well for Clinton's attempt to resolve the basic public dilemma.

The hype surrounding the health care proposal and the hype accompanying NAFTA are only two large cases in point. Clinton's ambition to accomplish coupled with his belief that he knows what should be done and his determination to do it sometimes leads to cutting corners. Leadership consists of real public education, not selling policies by using big concepts such as "security" that are not really representative of the range of consequences that Clinton's proposals will entail.

The appointment of David Gergen as one of Clinton's major advisers may be viewed in this context. Many have suggested that Gergen's appointment represents a "turn toward the center." However, Gergen's chief talents and past responsibilities have been in the area of presidential public relations (Blumenthal, 1993a). He has felt comfortable serving a range of ideologically diverse presidents and has committed himself in each instance to getting that leader's views across to the public and serving his policy and public relations purposes. Gergen should not be expected to counter the tendency in the Clinton administration to sell, as opposed to educate, the public on policy, Rather, Gergen is likely to make that effort more professional and effective.

And herein lie the potential irony and perhaps tragedy of Clinton's character and presidency. He is a man of tremendous intelligence and enormous accomplishments (including his willingness to take on tough policy problems). These by themselves would be a lot. Yet Clinton has not appeared satisfied with his real accomplishments and seems to want to make them what they are not likely to be: full, no-cost solutions to difficult, perhaps intractable problems. Given the public's concern with its ability to trust government to do what is right, Clinton must be very careful that he, the "Man from Hope," does not come to be seen as the Man from Hype.

Notes

This chapter was prepared for delivery at a conference held at the City University of New York Graduate Center. This chapter refines and further develops themes first presented in a paper at the annual meeting of the American Political Science Association, Washington, D.C., September 2–5, 1993, on the psychology of the Clinton presidency and subsequently published elsewhere (Renshon, 1994). I wish to thank Fred I. Greenstein, Margaret G. Hermann, Bruce Mazlish, Jerrold M. Post, Peter Suedfeld, and Ann E. Zemaitis for comments on an earlier draft of this chapter. I am especially indebted to Alexander L. George for his many valuable observations and questions on a number of points.

1. At least since Freud's problematic analysis of Woodrow Wilson, it has been clear that the analyst's own political preferences and views can play an important and distorting role in assessing psychological suitability if care is not taken. This can happen because the analyst either admires, dislikes, or has some other set of feelings about his or her subject. I therefore want to preface my analysis by clearly stating my stance toward Clinton. The analyst, especially one who makes use of and is trained in psychoanalytic psychology, has a particular obligation to be clear in these matters. No analyst can avoid personal responses to the materials used to construct an analysis, but he or she can try to be as explicit as possible. In that explicitness lies at least a partial solution to unintended or, worse, systematic bias.

I voted for Bill Clinton, but did so on balance. His expressed philosophy of government, which balanced government initiatives to redress inequalities with individual responsibilities, came closest to my own personal political views. Nonetheless, as I observed the presidential campaign, transition, and first months of the administration, I could not help being struck by the mix of enormous political skills and potentially troubling tendencies. It is this mix and the implications of Clinton's basic psychology for his presidential performance and success that frame one of the most important sets of questions about this presidency.

In the end, of course, the analyst's stance toward his or her subject, examined or not, must stand the scrutiny of others. Do the frames of analysis put forward appear to cover the most important aspects of what needs to be explained psychologically? Is the evidence adduced for putting forward those categories of analysis persuasive? And finally, are the implications drawn regarding these characteristics found in the real world of the president's actual behavior? These questions, not the correctness of the analyst's personal views, are what must ultimately be primary.

2. A major purpose of this chapter is to specify behavioral clusters and begin to theoretically account for them (cf. Greenstein's [1969] discussion of the phenomenological and dynamic levels of analysis). In this I follow the process described by the Georges (1956, 317–320) in describing their method for approaching Woodrow Wilson. It consisted of an interplay among an immersion in the basic behavioral data, tentative exploration, and use of appropriate psychological theory. The analyst first attempts to become thoroughly familiar with the basic behavioral data and the questions that emerge from them. He or she then examines these data in the context of the psychological theory or theories that appear to best explain them. Often in that process, the theory must be modified to fit the specific and often complex patterns found in an individual life.

The Georges were aided in their search by the existence of and their access to a great deal of published and unpublished data about their subject. Much of this kind of data—personal letters, diaries, and so on—are not available to researchers at this point, and so a first step must be the gathering and analysis of publicly available materials.

To do this, I depend in part on multiple, cross-checked news accounts of the events; multiple, cross-checked biographical accounts; and the words of Bill Clinton himself. Each of these is used in a specific way for a limited purpose, with recognition of each method's advantages and limitations.

For example, the news and other journalistic accounts are primarily used as a documentation of the major facts around a particular event, such as a presidential candidate making a particular pledge or a particular event taking place within a certain sequence of events. The accounts themselves are for the most part concerned with describing the events and the circumstances surrounding them. Our detailed knowledge of both is necessarily limited, so news accounts can be used only with appreciation and acknowledgment of their limitations.

News accounts provide at least five kinds of important information for the analyst. First, they can be used to establish the basic existence of an event. Second, the nature of the event and its place in a sequence of events can often provide an analyst with important information with which to help construct an understanding of the meaning of the events. Third, by following such accounts over time, the analyst can use later accounts and *outcomes* to cross-check the validity of earlier accounts. Fourth, news accounts can help establish some of the circumstances surrounding an event. These details, although most likely incomplete, do help deepen appreciation of the context. Fifth, news accounts can convey some sense of an actor's understandings of these events as reflected in his or her public discussions or actions.

Of course, news accounts, even when cross-checked, have limitations that must be kept in mind. First, reporters may report events accurately but miss important aspects of an event either because they were not evident at the time because the reporters did not have access to all that went on, or because they simply did not appreciate the implications of what they were reporting. Second, reporters often piece together their understanding of events in the form of a "story," and this subtext can be shaped both by a reporter's attitudes or view and by decisions (strategic or unconscious) of the person(s) on whom the reporter relies. For these reasons, events data must be *one* of a number of data sources that an analyst uses.

Another important source of data for psychologically informed events and case analysis is the stated understanding and experience of the events by the individual. Therefore, a key source of supplementary evidence to accounts of events themselves is the transcribed words of Clinton himself. The formal speeches and spontaneous words of candidates and presidents provide important and revealing information. I have made extensive use of *The Weekly Compilation of Presidential Documents,* which gives verbatim accounts of *most* (but not all) of the president's speeches, news conferences, statements, exchanges with reporters, interviews with news media, and other forms of public communication. I have supplemented these with transcripts of other interviews and remarks not contained in the *Weekly Compilation.*

We must appreciate and take into account the fact that the individuals involved in such events have private understandings or motivations that they do not reveal (and possibly are not aware of). This does not, however, require us to discard as unimportant their publicly stated views. The public statements of presidents may actually reflect what candidates or presidents really think (a point that is often lost sight of in discussions of methodology surrounding case studies). These statements also provide a useful starting point for comparing what is said with what is done, itself an important source of analytical information.

What a president says in a variety of contexts can also be quite useful in revealing what the president wishes to convey to others about his views and himself. Therefore, an important source of information for this analysis is the unstructured (but not necessarily unrehearsed) interviews, press conferences, and other spontaneously recorded transactions that are a part of every campaign and presidency.

Each of these sources of information has its limitations. Formal speeches are good reflections of what candidates or presidents may wish to project or may themselves wish to believe. However, such speeches do not necessarily reflect the sometimes conflicting views that may underlie the formal presentation or the political or personal calculations that resolved them.

So, too, unstructured interviews, while in some ways more revealing of the candidate, are often not completely spontaneous. It is a fact of political life that candidates and presidents spend much time behind the scenes considering how they should approach or respond to public issues or events. Lastly, the amount of uncalculated information that is reflected in the give-and-take of a question-and-answer format depends in large part on the nature of the format. General questions from supportive or for other reasons uncritical audiences allow a candidate or president more opportunity to respond in preselected ways than a real debate does.

In the end, a researcher must rely on a confluence of evidence from several sources, depending wholly on no single one. It is likely that fuller knowledge of circumstances will emerge in time, and this may in turn modify an analysis tentatively based on the circumstances, understandings, and motivations involved in the actions and events that the original accounts described. Nevertheless, the actions that are described herein are part of an ongoing series of events. The substantial history of these preceding events and the analyses of them therefore provide an additional theoretical foundation on which to rest these analyses.

At the same time that the research process described above was being undertaken, Bob Woodward, a reporter for the *Washington Post,* was independently examining the Clinton presidency, using the vehicle of repeated anonymous interviews with key members of the administration. His book (1994), published as this work was going to press, presents a detailed *description* of events surrounding the development and passage of the Clinton administration's first budget. In many respects, his descriptions of what occurred inside the administration are consonant with the theoretical observations made in this chapter, a case of two independent and different approaches to an overlapping set of examined circumstances supporting each other.

3. I have more fully developed this theory of character and its relationship to presidential performance elsewhere (Renshon, "Psychological Assessment," forthcoming). I do not address here the question of the development of character and its potential for change over the course of life. Readers interested in this specific question are referred elsewhere (Renshon, 1989).

References

Allen, Charles Flynn (1991). "Governor William Jefferson Clinton: A Biography with a Special Focus on His Educational Contributions." Ph.D. diss., University of Mississippi.

Apple, R. W. Jr. (1993). "7 Nations' Leaders Open Tokyo Talks; Expectations Low." *New York Times*, July 8, A1.

Barber, James David (1992). *Presidential Character: Predicting Performance in the White House*. 4th ed. Englewood Cliffs, N.J.: Prentice-Hall.

Berke, Richard L. (1992). "Easing Friction, Clinton Meets with Jackson." *New York Times*, November 23, A14.

———— (1993a). "An Inauguration Designed to Play to the Cameras." *New York Times*, January 18, A11.

———— (1993b). "Politicians Find Jogging with Clinton Is No Stroll in the Park." *New York Times*, July 26, A1.

———— (1994). "Al Gore: Good Scout." *New York Times Magazine*, February 20, 29–35, 44, 54, 57, 62.

Blumenthal, Sidney (1993a). "Letter from Washington: Dave." *The New Yorker*, June 28, 36–41.

———— (1993b). "Letter from Washington: Rendezvousing with Destiny." *The New Yorker*, March 8, 38–44.

———— (1994). "Letter from Washington: The Education of a President." *The New Yorker*, January 24, 31–43.

Bradsher, Keith (1993a). "Controllers Ban Lifted by Clinton." *New York Times*, August 13, A17.

———— (1993b). "For Clinton, 'Managed Trade' Is Emerging as a Policy Option." *New York Times*, March 30, A1.

Cliff, Eleanor (1993). "Playing Hardball." *Newsweek*, April 19, 24.

Clinton, William J. (1993). "Remarks on the Nomination of Ruth Bader Ginsburg to Be a Supreme Court Associate Justice." *Weekly Compilation of Presidential Documents*, 1075. Washington, D.C.: GPO, June 23.

"Clinton Pledges Open Fund-Raisers" (1993). *New York Times*, October 13, 22A.

Dumas, Ernest (ed.) (1993). *The Clintons of Arkansas: An Introduction by Those Who Know Them Best*. Fayetteville: University of Arkansas Press.

"Excerpts from an Interview with President-Elect Clinton After the Air Strikes" (1993). *New York Times*, January 14, 10A.

Friedman, Thomas L. (1993). "Clintons Pick Private School in Capital for Their Daughter." *New York Times*, January 6, A1.

George, Alexander L., and Juilette George (1956). *Woodrow Wilson and Colonel House*. New York: Dover.

Greenstein, Fred I. (1969). *Personality and Politics*. Chicago: Markham.

Horney, Karen (1945). *Our Inner Conflicts*. New York: Norton.

Ifel, Gwen (1993a). "Democrats Drop Donor's Session with President." *New York Times*, May 2, A1.

———— (1993b). "Globe Trotting Clinton Faces Trip's Side Effects." *New York Times*, July 9, A8.

_____ (1994). "Clinton and Japan Chief Say Trade Talks Fail; U.S. Threatens Action." *New York Times,* February 12, A1.

Kelly, Michael (1992a). "A Man Who Wants to Be Liked, and Is: William Jefferson Blythe Clinton." *New York Times,* November 4, A1.

_____ (1992b). "After 13 Months, Clinton Relaxes." *New York Times,* November 8, B28.

_____ (1992c). "The Making of the First Family: A Blueprint." *New York Times,* November 14, A1.

_____ (1993a). "Hillary Clinton's Health Panel Invites Ideas from the Invited." *New York Times,* March 13, A7.

_____ (1993b). "President Moves in Favor of Labor." *New York Times,* February 3, A17.

Kilborn, Peter T. (1993). "Buoyed But Wary, Union Chiefs Gather." *New York Times,* February 15, C4.

Klein, Joe (1993). "Slow Motion." *Newsweek,* May 24, 16.

Kohut, Heinz (1971). *The Analysis of the Self.* New York: International Universities Press.

_____ (1977). *The Restoration of the Self.* New York: International Universities Press.

Lasswell, Harold D. (1948). *Power and Personality.* New York: Norton.

Levin, Robert E. (1992). *Bill Clinton: The Inside Story.* New York: SPI Books.

Moore, Jim, with Rick Ihde (1992). *Clinton: Young Man in a Hurry.* Fort Worth, Tex.: Summit Group.

Moore, Rudy Jr. (1993). "They're Killing Me Out There." In *The Clintons of Arkansas: An Introduction by Those Who Know Them Best,* ed. Ernest Dumas, 85–94. Fayetteville: University of Arkansas Press.

Pollack, Andrew (1993). "U.S. Appears to Retreat from Setting Targets to Increase Japan's Imports." *New York Times,* July 10, A4.

Pryor, David (1992). "Introduction" to *Bill Clinton: The Inside Story,* by Robert E. Levin, xvii–xxi. New York: SPI Books.

Reischauer, Richard D. (1993). "Letter from the Director of the Congressional Budget Office to Majority Leader Richard Gephart [with 11-page analysis of CBO estimates of H.R. 3400, Government Reform and Savings Act of 1993]." Washington, D.C.: Congressional Budget Office, November 15.

Renshon, Stanley A. (1989). "Psychological Perspectives on Adult Development and the Political Socialization of Leaders." In *Political Learning in Adulthood: A Sourcebook of Theory and Research,* ed. Roberta I. Sigel, 203–264. Chicago: University of Chicago Press.

_____ (1994). "A Preliminary Assessment of the Clinton Presidency: Character, Leadership and Performance." *Political Psychology* 15, no. 2: 375–394.

_____ (forthcoming). *The Psychological Assessment of Presidential Candidates.*

Samuelson, Robert J. (1993). "Clinton as Roosevelt." *Newsweek,* May 24, 49.

Sanger, David E. (1993). "Clinton Achieves Trade Framework in Japanese Pact." *New York Times,* July 10, 1.

Smith, Stephen A. (1993). "Compromise, Consensus, and Consistency." In *The Clintons of Arkansas: An Introduction by Those Who Know Them Best,* ed. Ernest Dumas, 1–16. Fayetteville: University of Arkansas Press.

Staley, Carolyn (1993). "The Music of Friendship." In *The Clintons of Arkansas: An Introduction by Those Who Know Them Best*, ed. Ernest Dumas, 34–41. Fayetteville: University of Arkansas Press.

Storr, Anthony (1990). *Solitude*. New York: Free Press.

Wenner, Jann S., and William Greider (1993). "President Clinton: The *Rolling Stone* Interview." *Rolling Stone*, December 9, 42–45, 80–81.

Winnicott, Donald W. (1965). *The Maturational Process and the Facilitating Environment*. New York: International Universities Press.

Woodward, Bob (1994). *The Agenda: Inside the Clinton White House*. New York: Simon and Schuster.

Wright, George Jr. (1993). "Everyone's Friend." In *The Clintons of Arkansas: An Introduction by Those Who Know Them Best*, ed. Ernest Dumas, 28–29. Fayetteville: University of Arkansas Press.

PART II

*Public Psychology—
Leadership Style*

5

The Cueless Public:
Bill Clinton Meets the New
American Voter in Campaign '92

W. LANCE BENNETT

"He wore cheap sunglasses. He blew the saxophone. He explained that he really wanted to inhale; he just didn't know how."[1] Is this the description of a fallen Hollywood star trying to stage a TV comeback after a scandal? No, it is the opening of a news story on the 1992 election campaign. The actor, of course, is Bill Clinton, who appeared on the Arsenio Hall show as part of an elaborate direct-to-the-people media campaign to reconstruct his ailing character before the voting public. It turned out that a plurality of that public suspended their usual levels of disbelief to follow the "Comeback Kid," as his media strategists promoted him, through scores of talk shows, electronic town halls, and madcap bus trips across the heartland. In the end, the prize of victory was his.

While Clinton was building his tenuous electronic relationship with the mass public, another improbable candidate by the name of Ross Perot was managing to sell himself as a billionaire populist to another 19 percent of a clearly destabilized electorate. Pursuing a different strategy within the same electronic media, Perot's string of talk show appearances and infomercials may not have won him the presidency, but the $35 million that Perot spent on television appeals was regarded as so successful a means of getting public attention that *Advertising Age* magazine crowned Perot the "Adman of the Year" for 1992.[2] (The Perot persuasion style became a model for commercial advertisers, who immediately cloned Perot scenarios for dozens of ad campaigns.)

It was George Bush who felt the sting of the new voter psychology most painfully, if only because he engaged with it most ineptly. By all accounts, the incumbent president took for granted that the effects of his masterful psychological campaign of 1988 were still in place, and he thus resisted a replay in 1992. It was widely known that the patrician Bush had found the construction of his 1988 campaign persona distasteful, from his focus group makeover as a tough-guy character whose attacks helped pin the "wimp" label on hapless liberal opponent Michael Dukakis, to the droning negative backdrop of Willie Horton and revolving door prison ads. It is easy to imagine how Bush was tempted to think this tawdry business could be avoided in 1992. First, he may have succumbed to the euphoric assumption that the people truly loved him when his public approval ratings hit recorded highs near 90 percent following the U.S. and allied victory in the Gulf War of 1991. The temptation to run a traditional campaign "on his record" must have been even greater after the pundits pronounced him unbeatable just a year before the election.

As it turned out, however, George Bush experienced the greatest recorded public approval free fall in history. He lost the election with a campaign that missed the great lesson of his own victory in 1988: The psychology of the American public had changed in fundamental ways. When he "went negative" with a vengeance in the closing weeks of the 1992 election, he seemed perplexed that the attacks were not having the effect that they had had in 1988. And it was not until the last desperate days of the campaign that Bush finally agreed to an appearance on MTV, an electronic venue he had dismissed earlier as "a teenybopper network." Not surprisingly, Bush finished a poor third in the youth vote. In fact, his ragged campaign organization failed in its attempts to reach so many groups that the candidate finally canceled his daily poll briefings in the last week of the campaign.

The campaign that clearly learned the lessons of 1988 was the Clinton team. It saw that there was a new psychology forming in the electorate and that simplistic formulas such as "going negative" did not fully grasp it. Negative appeals and personal attacks did not produce stable opinions. To the contrary, majorities in the polls in 1988 reported that they hated the negative psychology. The effectiveness of that strategy had to do almost entirely with the failure of the Dukakis campaign to alleviate the doubts that those attacks planted in the minds of voters.

The 1992 campaign demonstrated that responsiveness, intimacy (no matter how contrived), and continual reassurance were the keys that unlocked the hold of negativity (as well as the keys to understanding the underlying public psychology). There is much evidence for this proposition in the Clinton campaign. It is doubtful that any modern candidate suffered more negative press than Clinton did in 1992. He overcame so many seemingly fatal media blows that he earned the nicknames "Robocop" and "Terminator" from the same press pack that inflicted those wounds. Among those who put the mystique of negativity to rest was Pat Buchanan's media consultant, Ian Weinschel, who said of Clinton's comebacks from repeated character attacks, "I've never seen anybody come back from being attacked in that fashion. It's like going through a car crash with no seat belts and then going through the window and hitting a wall and walking away. It's absolutely astounding."[3] How did Clinton deflect so much negativity and go on to win the election? What was the basis of his appeal to a cynical public?

The Changing American Voter

This is more that just a story about Bill Clinton; it is a story about profound changes in the electoral process that have shaken the very foundations of voter psychology. What has happened to the American voter? How do changes in the electoral process account for changed voter dispositions? What are the consequences of these changes for the relationship between citizens and leaders in the American democracy? In the microcosm of Bill Clinton's election we find signs of an institutional breakdown in the psychological ties that once bound citizens to parties, candidates, and, in turn, to each other in the American polity. Elections still go on, and voters still vote, but the psychology of the public political experience has become devoid of the stable cues and identifications that once allowed individual citizens to feel part of solid political groups such as parties and to have confidence in leaders. In other words, we are witnessing the deterioration of the psychological ties that once gave private citizens stable public identities.

This destabilization of voter psychology means that it is not an easy time to be a politician. The rules of the political game are changing. Public wrath against government can turn today's hero into tomorrow's fool. We have entered what might be called the "age of political independents": increasingly independent voters who seem to prefer independent politicians who make their own ways without emphasizing party allegiance or the virtues of government. Public hostility is directed not only toward politicians but also toward the media sources that convey political information. The result is an electoral system in considerable disarray, with politicians, the press, and the public all coming in for their share of blame for the situation, as indicated in these remarks made by Senator Jay Rockefeller (D.–W. Va.) to a group of reporters: "Voters … are angry with politicians like me. And they're angry with you in the media. Well, let me tell you something. The voters are no bargains, either."[4]

The perspective adopted in this chapter is that the electorate is not somehow outside the governing process looking in, but is an integral part of a system of relations that includes parties, candidates, campaign practices, the communications media, and voters all adjusting to changes in society and government. Specific changes in parties, campaign procedures, and communication technologies have affected public psychology and therefore how candidates appeal to that psychology in their efforts to get themselves elected. In this view, various manifestations of psychological distress in the electorate—from wild mood swings in approval ratings, to term limits, to the Ross Perot phenomenon—are systemic. In other words, we are talking about a mass psychological reaction to broader structural conditions that affect how people think and feel politically. Whether or not this public anger is well founded is really beside the point. The more important issue is to recognize and understand the underlying psychology of the electorate and to assess its impact on political campaigning in general and on Bill Clinton's election in particular.

In this climate of anger, suspicion, and restlessness, politicians must continually work up new strategies to keep themselves on the good side of the public, as the Clinton campaign illustrates so vividly. In the current electoral environment, candidates must manufacture short-term images and feed them back continually to skeptical voters in as intimate a style as electronic media permit. (The master of this psychology was Ronald Reagan, as explained in Jamieson 1988.) What matters most is that isolated individuals sense that a candidate understands their questions of the moment and is making an ongoing effort to answer them. In the end, the relevance of the questions or the quality of the answers may be less important than the psychological experience of fragmented individuals feeling somehow connected on a daily basis to a highly personalized (if distant) political figure.

The key to the new electoral communication is continual polling, focus group research, and the production of short-term marketing strategies to maintain this extremely tenuous psychological bond. This new imperative for candidates (and, once elected, for leaders) to continually reinvent themselves is the result of a widespread loss of faith in the holy trinity of the old voter psychology: party, issues, and character.

The New Psychology of Mass Politics

Changes in the electoral process over several decades have undermined the psychological cue system of *party, issues, and candidate character* that has long provided the foundation of voter choice and has therefore set the strategic guidelines for traditional campaigning (Campbell, Converse, Miller, and Stokes, 1960). As with most historic changes, there continue to be substantial ghosts from the old order that persist as vague and familiar outlines in the new historical context, leading some conservative analysts to proclaim that the American voter is, in fact, "unchanging" (Smith, 1989). Indeed, there is evidence that voters continue to use party identification above all other psychological linkages with the electoral environment in making their choices. However, this must be evaluated in the context of severely diminished levels of party identification that highlight the chaos, not the continuity, of contemporary elections.

In other words, the old psychological cue structure of party, issues, and character may remain as the leading information categories that voters continue trying to use. However, a growing body of evidence shows that the salience of all three information categories has been substantially diminished as voters increasingly shun party affiliation, regard election issues with increasing suspicion, and find that the contrived nature of marketing-driven campaigning offers few satisfying insights into the character of candidates. A brief overview of these changes illustrates how they have affected both the conduct of elections and the kinds of political problems that elected leaders face after they take office. (A more extensive analysis of the decline of these cue systems is available in Bennett, 1992.)

Party. Not only has party identification declined in the electorate from the peak levels recorded in the 1950s and 1960s, but something resembling a culture of political independence has also emerged to turn shifting voter loyalties into something of a virtue. Even if there was some clear meaning to the idea of a "radical middle" in American politics, the inability of parties to win and hold the loyalties of stable voter blocks at different levels of government leaves little incentive for elected members of those parties to worry about a governing agenda beyond the narrow promises required for personal reelection. The resulting personalization of politics (both the decline of candidate loyalty to party and the increasingly individualized appeals to voters) has destabilized both elections and governing.

Issues. Perhaps the breakdown of parties and party voting would not be a bad development if it corresponded to a higher level of issue voting and serious policy debate in elections. However, the long-term view suggests that much of what passed for issue discourse in American elections was tied to traditional party stands on social and economic policy matters. The issue discourse in recent elections has been constructed largely through marketing research aimed at winning short-term support among key voter blocks. As a result, there continue to be discussions about matters that candidates represent as issues, but neither the media nor voters take most of those issues very seriously. As Everett Ladd noted in his analysis of these trends, the candidates increasingly talk about "problems" that marketing research reveals to be on voters' minds. However, Ladd concluded that these "problems aren't necessarily issues. A problem becomes an issue only when voters see the parties differing in their approach to it or their capacity to solve it."[5] Although the 1992 election produced higher levels of voter issue satisfaction than other recent contests, the reason must be attributed to the artifact of the third-party candidacy of Ross Perot. Indeed, given the ill-fated decision of George Bush to run largely on his record, and the Clinton campaign's droning insistence on "The Economy, Stupid," a Perot-less 1992 race would probably have satisfied few voters on the issue dimension.

Character. The increasing construction of candidate images through marketing techniques has produced an increasingly wary electorate. The great loss is that credible leadership cues as primary considerations about character may be driven out of elections. To begin with, campaign strategies generally avoid the kinds of risky stands on principle through which candidates might display genuine leadership. In addition, the very process of constructing a political image may be so distasteful to strong political personalities that serious leaders are discouraged from seeking higher levels of public office, where they are increasingly advised to try being whatever their image managers tell them to be. There has been much speculation in the press that the departure of a number of promising politicians from government in recent years can be attributed to this combination of a breakdown in parties, a fragmentation of policy issue agendas, and the political risks of expressing oneself openly in public. Thus, the resulting character cues that are available to voters are likely to become heavily discounted in the choice process. Indeed, the reason for voters to make these deep character discounts may be quite well founded if the campaign process itself is driving those with more serious leadership skills out of electoral politics.

In short, the traditional foundations of voter psychology have crumbled. Even though fragments of the old order remain, they are unable to support satisfying or stable political choices in the modern electorate. Voters still receive cues, of course—and they probably receive them in greater sheer volume than ever before. However, the psychological cue system underlying contemporary voting choice involves appeals that are manufactured for short-term effects: aimed at the voter psychology of the moment, addressing diffuse problems rather than substantial issues, and aimed at the ongoing manufacture and renewal of short-term identification with untrustworthy politicians. The result of substituting these short-term individual appeals for more enduring, socially integrative political references is that the nature of both campaigning and governing is changing.

In the view of CNN pollster and political analyst William Schneider, Washington is increasingly a town of individual political entrepreneurs who rely less on parties for their political support than on their own media images, along with the popularity of visible politicians such as the president. When the president appears to be losing in the news, nobody wants to be associated with him or his programs, and the real power of the presidency goes down. When the president appears to be winning, everyone wants a piece of the media action, and the real power of everyone who jumped into the television spotlight—most of all the president—goes up. And so when Bill Clinton was heralded in the media for engineering a victory in Congress on the controversial North American Free Trade Agreement, even his archenemies, such as Georgia Republican Newt Gingrich, jumped into the media power circle, complimenting the president on his leadership.

Thus, the changing reference system on which mass psychology rests may be changing the nature of political power in American politics. And the reverse is surely true as well, with contemporary public psychology emerging not from mere moods or whims in the electorate but from structural changes in the electoral process itself—changes that span more than two decades. Although the main point of this analysis is to understand how the 1992 Clinton campaign appealed to this public psychology, it is worth reviewing the main underlying changes that produced it. (A more detailed explanation of these points is also available in Bennett, 1992.) In brief, three major trends are driving the electoral quest for the often elusive short-term approval that defines the psychological relations between candidates and voters (and later in office, between leaders and followers):

- A historic decline of the parties began with the alliance between the Democratic party and the civil rights movement, which drove a wedge into the conservative southern wing of the party, and continued with the subsequent conflict over Vietnam policies, which drove a wedge into the party's left wing. The Republicans failed to capitalize on a possible voter realignment with the Watergate scandal. A Republican realignment was further limited by a right-wing insurgency in the party that saw Ronald Reagan reach maximum sales potential for what turned out to be an ideological agenda of less than universal appeal. The result has been a notable party "dealignment," with independents and weak party identifiers increasingly holding the keys to electoral success.

- The resulting quest for fickle and more independent voters has moved marketing techniques to the center of elections, further undermining the credibility of issue positions and campaign promises in the eyes of many voters.

- Unable to convince voters of the benefits of supporting increasingly fragmented parties, or backing increasingly suspicious issue positions, candidates turn to the manufacture of character and attacks on opponents as the stock-in-trade of the contemporary campaign. As a result, media-savvy voters do not look so much for signs of true character as for short-term reassurance of their doubts about the fault lines they detect in the electronic images that bombard them.

The irony of this syndrome is that grossly distorted advertising and negative attacks may be effective, as they were in 1988, but not because voters like them or even find them credible. In an electoral environment deprived of familiar party cues, believable issues, or credible characters, voters must make the best sense they can out of the information offered to them, even when that information is distasteful, negative, shallow, or fanciful (Farah and Klein, 1989). As a result, electoral communication—and much of the public discourse between elections these days—is dominated by short-term emotional arousal and doubt-reduction strategies.

To carry this maxim beyond the electoral arena, we can point to a similar "short-term reinforcement" communication psychology as the genius of Ronald Reagan's "great communicator" mystique. His communications team worked on a symbolic presentation for nearly every day of the presidency. His chief pollster created a cognitive map of the public based not on enduring meanings but on symbols that fit the public mood of the moment. Reagan's advertising chief, Richard Wirthlin, converted these images into a continuing psychological campaign that eventually won him *Advertising Age* magazine's "Advertising Man of the Year" award for 1989, not for selling a product but for selling the president.[6] And the team of Michael Deaver and David Gergen worked in the trenches to carry out daily press strategy (Hertsgaard, 1988). When Clinton woke up to the fact that the same psychology that he battled every day on the campaign trail in 1992 continued to dog him as president, he hired David Gergen to manage White House communications with the public.

In light of this new voter psychology, as noted earlier, the great mistake of the Dukakis campaign in 1988 was the candidate's palpable failure to respond to the questions that the Bush attacks raised in voters' minds. By contrast, Clinton was at the ready to answer the steady flow of personal attacks, both from Bush and, more generally, from the press pack, on an almost daily basis throughout the 1992 campaign. Even as polls showed that voters were not interested in the character issue in 1992, and longed for more discussion of the policy issues, the continual preoccupation of the Clinton campaign was how to address the nagging doubts about its candidate that continued to surface in the tracking polls conducted by the campaign management team.

It no doubt helped that the Bush team grabbed a tired replay of 1988 off the shelf and had no attack that packed the punch of the Willie Horton commercials from the previous election. The Clinton team, for its part, never forgot the motto on the wall of campaign headquarters: "The Economy, Stupid." Perhaps most damaging for the Bush camp was its failure to respond with the necessary flow of psychological reassurances to the voter doubts raised by the Clinton campaign's steady emphasis on the economy. It is an open question as to how much of the damage might have been reversed had the Bush team remembered the first maxim of the new voter psychology: "A reassurance a day keeps doubts away."

The Clinton campaign illustrates this necessary process of short-term image construction, maintenance, and defense with a generally fickle public. Clinton's viability as a candidate hinged on responding to a huge volume of press attacks on his character by going over the heads of the press to convince voters that he was willing to submit his character to direct scrutiny—or, in the electronic age, what passes for direct scrutiny. Welcome to the Clinton campaign of 1992, with its electronic town halls; true confessions on *60 Minutes;* appearances on Arsenio, Phil, and Larry; MTV; madcap bus trips; and more. All of it was aimed at the continuing reinvention of Bill Clinton. He was not called the Comeback Kid for nothing.

Reinventing Bill Clinton on the Campaign Trail

As Clinton learned during the campaign and after the election, the mass psychology of contemporary American politics requires constant attention from pollsters, marketers, and communications advisers. Initially, this fact may have been lost on the candidate. Following the disastrous allegation of a twelve-year extramarital affair with former TV news personality and aspiring singer Gennifer Flowers, Clinton spent a three-hour drive through the snows of New Hampshire brooding and reading Lincoln on leadership.[7] Finally realizing that the Gennifer Flowers incident was not to be solved by Lincoln's advice on leading a nation through civil war, Clinton turned to the campaign team of pollster Stan Greenberg, media consultant Mandy Grunwald, and political strategist James Carville for insight. What emerged was a broad media strategy of continual personal renewal and reinvention that carried the candidate through the primaries and all the way to victory in November.

The first TV appearance in the emerging strategy of "electronic intimacy" was a January 26 interview on *60 Minutes* immediately following the Super Bowl. Although Clinton was outraged with the program's editing, the campaign spin doctors (most notably Carville) went forth on other talk shows to attack both Flowers and the media, while applauding Clinton's willingness to bare his soul before the voters in direct TV appearances. An ABC News poll that week showed that only 11 percent of the voters had been swayed by the Flowers episode. More important for the "reinvention strategy," 79 percent said that the press had no business dramatizing such personal matters, and 82 percent said that they had heard enough about Clinton's personal life.[8] The campaign escaped New Hampshire with a respectable second place finish, to which Grunwald added the right psychological spin by categorizing Clinton as the "Comeback Kid."

Grunwald's symbolic move fits Murray Edelman's (1993) definition of a "category mistake": a label that leads people to ignore important features of a situation as they form their opinions about it. Not only was it unclear what Clinton had come back from (the political undead, one guesses), but the same categorization continued to be offered throughout the primary campaign, the convention, and the general election. (An embattled Comeback Kid was symbolically rescued by the Man from Hope after the convention, setting the stage for the greatest comeback of all—winning the election.) Never mind the contradiction of a candidate recumbent in a perpetual state of comeback; if voters could be induced to think of the endless flow of character problems less as problems and more as occasions for continuing comebacks, negative judgment could be suspended. The psychological margin created by this oxymoronic suggestion of an eternal comeback fit nicely with "reinventing Bill" as the underlying psychological strategy of the entire campaign. Thus, a simple category mistake invited voters to continually suspend negative judgment in the face of information that would have finished off candidates with lesser political strategies.

This strategy also fed nicely into polls showing high levels of public disgust with the personal preoccupations of the press. Similar levels of public discontent over "the character issue" were recorded in 1988, but the Dukakis campaign developed no psychological strategy for playing into that opinion. To the contrary, Dukakis's indignant and offended posturing, along with his awkward denials, may have undermined the kind of intimacy required for the reassurance that a vulnerable and open character is on continual electronic display whenever undecided voters seek relief from their doubts.

The Beat Goes On: Character and Comeback

The continuing media drumbeat on Clinton's character flaws offered the campaign an opportunity to remind voters that they did not like the press preoccupation with candidates' personal lives. Like it or not, of course, that preoccupation created doubts in many voters' minds. Thus, the reminder that such information was distasteful was not in and of itself enough to dispel those doubts. The important next step was the ironic but effective move of countering every new negative input by putting an increasing amount of Clinton's personal life on public display. Thus, the campaign took on a strange dynamic: As more negative personal images emerged in the press and from the Bush camp (and, to a lesser extent, from Perot), the Clinton team found new ways to expose Clinton's private side on morning breakfast programs and through paid "minidocumentary" ads. Even the bus trips displayed a casual, relaxed, "just folks" side of Clinton, who with vice-presidential sidekick Al Gore turned the campaign into a kind of lighthearted buddy movie: *Al and Bill's Excellent Adventure.*

All of these personal campaign episodes were drawn together around a steady schedule of TV town halls in which the serious, issue-oriented Bill Clinton effectively winked to the studio audiences (with a nod to the viewers at home) and communicated the punch line "We know that the press doesn't care about the issues in this election, but we can beat them by having our own face-to-face conversation about the issues right here." When election day rolled around, exit polls indicated that voters found the issue content of the 1992 campaign far superior to that of 1988 and that Clinton owned the issue positions that mattered to the largest number of voters. (See data presented in Bennett, 1994, chap. 10.) It is unlikely that the higher levels of self-reported issue voting were due just to the carefully designed relationship between "personal Bill" and "policy Bill." Much of the elevation in issue voting in 1992 must be attributed simply to the entry of a third candidate in the race, which, as explained by Benjamin Page (1978), disrupts the rational strategy of minimizing issue differences in two-candidate races.

Although the reasons for a resurgence of issue voting may be debated, the personalized campaign strategy (of continual reassurance through staged moments of intimacy) was clearly the context in which the various elements of the Clinton appeal fit together. Thus, the public was continually reminded that the media were the culprits responsible for failing to shift the focus from Clinton's character to more important issues. To make the best of the intrusive press, everyone was invited to hit the electronic road with Bill and Al following the convention (courtesy of the same press pack that kept the character problems flowing). The bus trips, the talk shows, and the town halls all provided the daily intimacy required to answer the character question. At the same time, people looking for an alternative to Bush and Perot were invited into a fantasy of renewal and hope. Indeed, the subliminal message that held this campaign fantasy tour together was *hope*, as in "A Man from Hope" and "A Place Called Hope."

However, the Man from Hope was not an easy invention. He was born of necessity in the midst of a crisis of voter confidence that nearly killed the Comeback Kid. The following analysis tracks the story from the primary trail to the convention and on through the campaign, showing how and why the Comeback Kid was reinvented as the Man from Hope.

Slick Willie Meets the Comeback Kid

In the months after New Hampshire, the Flowers scandal was joined with charges of draft evasion, unpatriotic antiwar activities in England during the Vietnam era, and the marijuana incident that made Clinton the butt of comedians' jokes following his ill-advised "didn't inhale" disclaimer. Opponents soon collected the multiple character blows into the summary slur "Slick Willie," a name that took on a life of its own in the media, making the top ten list of most mentioned terms in newspaper and broadcast coverage of the campaign. These character flaws were never out of public view. During the extended primary period, measured from September 1991 through June 1992, "Gennifer Flowers" and "draft dodging" were among the top ten most men-

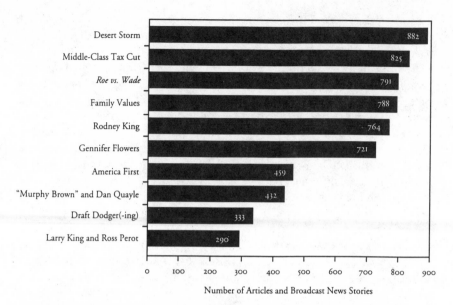

Figure 5.1 Top-Ten Names and Phrases from the Campaign Trail, September 1, 1991–June 30, 1992. Source: Tim Miller and John Pavlik, "Campaign Coverage by the Numbers," in *The Finish Line: Covering the Campaign's Final Days* (New York: Columbia University, The Freedom Forum Media Studies Center, 1993), p. 68. Reprinted with permission. The Freedom Forum Media Studies Center. Copyright 1993.

tioned terms in campaign coverage of all candidates from both parties, as shown in Figure 5.1. And during the final campaign period, from July through election day in November, Clinton had the dubious distinction of scoring four personal character categories ("character issue," "draft dodging," "Gennifer Flowers," and "Slick Willie") among the most mentioned topics in newspaper and TV coverage of all three candidates combined, as shown in Figure 5.2.

Through it all, Clinton was routinely pronounced politically dead by the pundits. In February, for example, Robert Evans and William Novak cited the conventional wisdom among "mainline Democratic politicians" that Clinton was "one of the walking dead who will sooner or later keel over."[9] Not only did Clinton fail to keel over; he also went on to win primaries in the South and collect enough delegates to secure the nomination. The remarkable fact amid all the negative press is that Clinton's poll ratings against Bush held fairly steady in the high 30s and low 40s during a primary season in which Bush maintained a stable 50 percent + rating against the embattled Democrat.

However, a steady 40 percent rating would not be enough to win in November. To make matters worse, the Comeback Kid had begun to wear thin

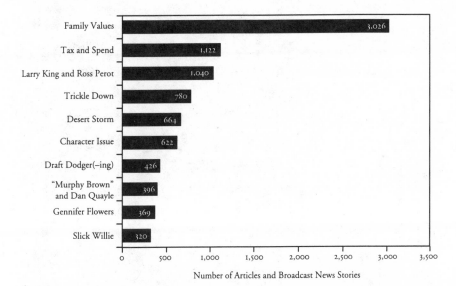

Number of Articles and Broadcast News Stories

Figure 5.2   Top-Ten Campaign Names and Phrases from the Campaign Trail, July 1, 1992– November 3, 1992. Source: Tim Miller and John Pavlik, "Campaign Coverage by the Numbers," in *The Finish Line: Covering the Campaign's Final Days* (New York: Columbia University, The Freedom Forum Media Studies Center, 1993), p. 67. Reprinted with permission. The Freedom Forum Media Studies Center. Copyright 1993.

in the polls toward the end of the primary season. The crucial segments of swing and undecided voters were not sure why Clinton wanted to be president. They did not know why they should care about him. Worst of all, he was rated as just another politician—the kiss of death in an antipolitical age. Thus, with the nomination in the bag, the campaign was in a crisis in June.

The candidate had to be reinvented again. Within the next six weeks, the Comeback Kid was given a new and psychologically more resilient persona as the Man from Hope. From the convention on, Clinton added the famous bus trips to his already steady schedule of talk show appearances. There was a stunning reversal in the poll standings, as Clinton jumped into the 50 percent range as Bush slipped steadily through the 40s and into the 30s (see Figure 5.3). What happened?

Slick Willie Beats the Comeback Kid

The Comeback Kid was Clinton's direct-to-the-public emotional loss leader throughout the campaign, but by June he was clearly losing ground to Slick Willie. As Slick Willie began to take root in the public imagination, the Kid was able to do little more than fight a psychological holding action on the talk

104

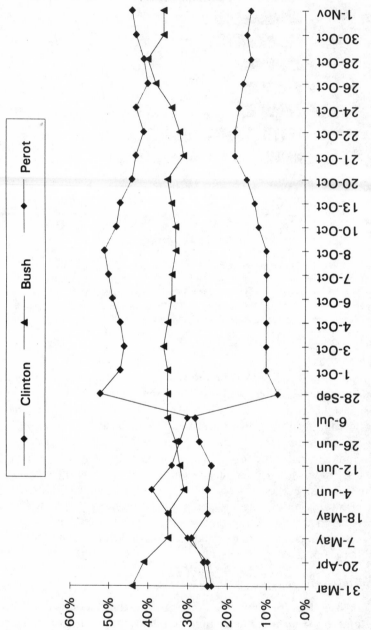

Figure 5.3 Clinton Gallup Poll Ratings in Mock Contests with Bush and Perot. Source: *Gallup Poll Monthly* (January–November 1992).

shows. Each time his poll ratings began to slip, the Clinton campaign launched another barrage of direct talk show appearances, making Clinton the undisputed talk show king of the 1992 election with forty-seven national appearances (and many more local forums) to Perot's thirty-three and Bush's puny sixteen, as shown in Figure 5.4. Clinton's talk show appearances were divided fairly evenly between the primary season (twenty-three) and months leading to the general election (twenty-four). Clinton far outstripped his eventual general election opponents in the crucial character test period of the primaries when Perot scored only fourteen TV talk show appearances and Bush appeared just twice (Smillie, 1992, 21). As Figure 5.5 illustrates, the Clinton TV barrage became heaviest at times when poll ratings began to slip, indicating, at the very least, that displays of electronic intimacy were calculated responses to moments when new character blows began to erode Clinton's position in the polls. (Note that the data in Figure 5.5 do not include all the TV appearances recorded in Figure 5.4; they reflect just the appearances reported in the *New York Times* and the *Washington Post* and detected in a Nexis/Lexis search from January 1 to November 3, 1993.)

The direct media strategy that evolved during the primaries was a crisis management effort to save the ever-embattled campaign. In a postelection interview with *TV Guide* (appropriately enough), Clinton explained how he (and his campaign managers) decided to bypass the news in an effort to regain control of the media content of the campaign:

> TV GUIDE: It's been an incredible year for both TV and politics. When did *you* decide you needed to run a radically different kind of campaign?
> BILL CLINTON: New Hampshire. During the first primary, in February. I started getting bad press [about alleged infidelities and the draft] and nobody wanted to talk about the issues anymore. I wondered if the voters felt the same. So I started having town hall meetings. ... I noticed there were large crowds at our meetings. So I just took that idea to television.
> TVG: [There was] quite a jump—from TV town halls to Arsenio Hall. Was there a particular moment when you and your advisers said "OK, nobody's listening—time for the sax, time for the shades?"
> CLINTON: Yes, during the New York primary. Again ... what I was saying was still not being reported. The media were more interested in the horse race. That's when we decided to go full steam ahead in the new way. When people look back at this year and ask, "What really happened?" I think the two-way communication on TV between the candidate and the people will be the story.[10]

"Two-way communication" in this context is a rarefied term. Loosely translated, it implies the candidate's ability to respond directly to damaging information. As previously noted, that strategy became little more than a public opinion holding action as polling and focus group research revealed new vulnerabilities in the Clinton character. Put simply, the Comeback Kid was

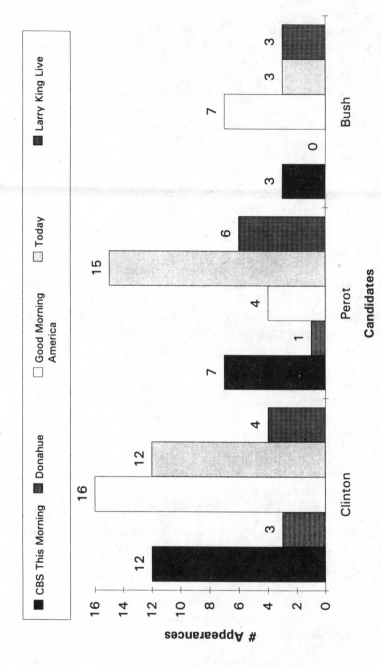

Figure 5.4 Talk Show Tally: Appearances by Clinton, Perot, and Bush from January 1 to November 3, 1992. Source: Adapted from chart by Dirk Smillie, "Breakfast with Bill, George, and Ross," in *The Finish Line: Covering the Campaign's Final Days* (New York: Columbia University, The Freedom Forum Media Studies Center, 1993), p. 125. Reprinted with permission. The Freedom Forum Media Studies Center. Copyright 1993.

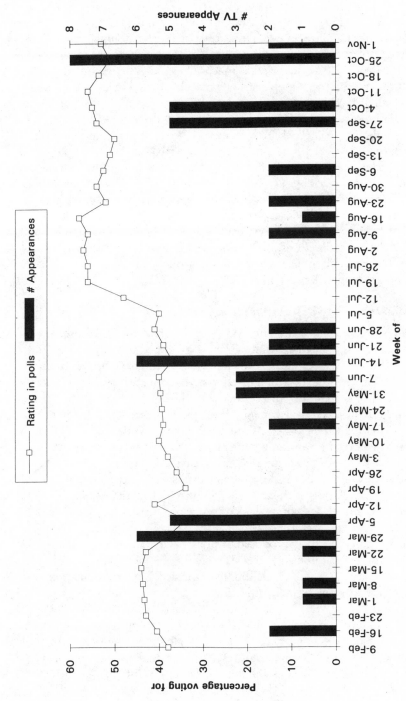

Figure 5.5   Clinton TV Appearances and Gallup Poll Ratings. Source: TV appearances from Nexis/Lexis accounts of *New York Times* and *Washington Post* stories; Gallup Poll data from *Gallup Poll Monthly* (January–November 1992).

not strong enough as a language category to contain the repeated revelations that came after the Flowers episode. As layer on layer of doubt-inducing character attacks surfaced, Slick Willie became all the more damaging, particularly when the image was popularized as much by Democratic opponents such as Jerry Brown as by the Republicans. To make matters worse, as indicated in Figure 5.2, Slick Willie eventually took on a life of its own in the media during the final months of the campaign.

Although the Comeback Kid eventually drove leading challenger Paul Tsongas out of the race, Jerry Brown continued to drill Clinton with the Slick Willie charge. Brown would eventually self-destruct over a poorly developed "flat tax" proposal, losing New York and Pennsylvania, and thereby his presidential hopes, to Clinton. However, Greenberg's polls showed continued vulnerability to the Slick Willie label, particularly when voters were asked to think ahead to an eventual contest between Bush and Clinton. Greenberg's polls showed Clinton trailing Bush by 24 points on honesty and trustworthiness.[11] It was clear that Slick Willie was much too strong a character for the Comeback Kid to combat alone.

The Man from Hope Rescues the Comeback Kid

In June the campaign team launched "a top secret project of research and [character] recasting" that Mandy Grunwald dubbed the "Manhattan Project," both for its secrecy and its reliance on science to develop an unbeatable strategic weapon.[12] Focus group research revealed that the Clinton character had eroded to such an extent on the eve of the convention that the project team reportedly circulated copies of Nixon's Checkers speech for inspiration.[13] As noted earlier, what eventually emerged was the psychological insight that voters did not know why Clinton wanted to be president, a fact compounded by the impression that he was a typical politician, a problem that was magnified further by the devastating trust issue. The campaign was in turmoil following a string of frustrating failures to find anything that moved focus groups of undecided voters to identify personally with the candidate or his proposals.

The solution reportedly proposed by pollster Greenberg was to act quickly to "depoliticize" Clinton and replace his checkered political image with a human persona that was vulnerable, humble, and accessible to ordinary people. The search began for an image that at once alleviated doubts and answered the key questions "Who is Bill Clinton?" and "What makes him run?" The public holding action escalated during this period with the campaign's largest number of talk show appearances to date. While the Comeback Kid gamely made the TV rounds, focus group results began to show that much of the checkered details of Clinton's childhood (alcoholic stepfather, poverty, small town upbringing) actually evoked sympathetic responses. Elements from Clinton's background in Hope, Arkansas, that had been kept hidden from public view seemed to answer those nagging voter questions.

And so "A Man from Hope" was invented, with his allegorical invitation to imagine America as "A Place Called Hope." The new character was launched with a convention video biography and Hillary Rodham Clinton's suggestion of closing the acceptance speech with the Comeback Kid's transition line to the Man from Hope: "I end tonight where it all began: I still believe in a place called Hope."[14] The new character provided an image of Bill Clinton with which millions of undecided voters looking for hope in the election could identify. More important, the Man from Hope appeared to be at least the psychological equal of Slick Willie.

The rest, as they say, is history. Whereas the Clinton campaign found a symbolic defense against its candidate's greatest weakness, the Bush camp never recovered from its disarray. Roger Ailes never joined the team. James Baker was recalled too late from his duties as secretary of state. And there was little time to reconstruct the Bush character in midsummer when public relations expert Sig Rogich was brought in from Iceland, where he was serving as ambassador in reward for his work crafting attack ads in 1988.

Without a market-tested political communications strategy to go on, the Bush campaign became a wooden recast of 1988. Both the speeches and the ads became more negative as election day drew closer.[15] On the campaign trail, Bush's personal attacks turned into ineffectual name-calling. He referred to Clinton and Gore with these taunts, among others:

> "The Waffle Man"
> "Governor Taxes and the Ozone Man"
> "He smokes, but he doesn't inhale. Sure."
> "A couple of yuppies dressed as moderates. Watch your wallet."
> "Those deadly talking heads"
> "Bozos"

As noted earlier, when Bush's daily tracking polls reported that all this unguided negativity appeared to be backfiring, he simply canceled his poll briefings.

By contrast, as Figure 5.3 shows, Clinton never lost his "convention bounce" in the polls, suggesting that the new character unveiled before the nation that week in July did the trick. Greenberg polls not only confirmed a strong Clinton lead but also revealed that he was steadily overtaking Bush on the leadership dimension.[16] That was the final indication that the character problem had been solved—at least long enough to get Bill Clinton elected.

Conclusion

The electronic intimacy at the heart of the Clinton campaign—from the Comeback Kid to the Man from Hope—suffered the defects of all such illusions. In the end, the public is brought no closer to candidates on talk shows or bus trips than on conventional newscasts or meet the press programs; just the opposite may well be true. However, it is the short-term, continually reinforced illusion of intimacy and responsiveness that counts. All of which raises doubts about the kinds of forums that "talk show democracy" and "electronic town halls" actually create. This curious feature of the 1992 election appears to be an unsettling coming of age of Roger Ailes's original use of audience forums to create the "New Nixon" (McGinnis, 1969) in 1968. And in many ways the continuing evolution of this electronic intimacy echoes Daniel Boorstin's (1961) early warning about the threat to social and political credibility posed by media-based pseudoevents.

Perhaps the greatest irony of the 1992 campaign is that at the same time the Man from Hope was being introduced to the voting public with great success, the candidate was found brooding and burdened with doubts about his personal ability to engage effectively with that public. According to one report, Clinton considered his childhood in Hope to be the source of his greatest political weakness because, as one close associate put it, "the trauma of having an alcoholic stepfather who abused his family had made him shy away from face-to-face conflict."[17] It seems that the very image that helped get him elected ended up masking the basis for his own and, more important, the public's sincere doubts.

As Bill Clinton soon discovered, his fragile support (carefully cultivated on a daily basis during the campaign) would soon crumble. Like his predecessor, Bill Clinton felt the sting of public disapproval. Where Bush fell from grace following what appeared to be a career-making victory in the Gulf War, Clinton suffered the shortest presidential honeymoon period to date. Clinton's response appears to involve turning the presidency into a continuing campaign, first by breaking his vow not to bring his image makers into the White House (as James Carville quietly moved into the White House basement) and then by hiring David Gergen, one of the people who learned the secrets of day-to-day communications psychology required to make Ronald Reagan the great communicator.

It may be asking too much to turn Bill Clinton into a great communicator. However, if Bill Clinton thought he overcame voter misgivings by winning the election, he failed to understand the fragile public psychology of the times. Indeed, the turbulent fortunes of the campaign trail must have appeared mild compared to the ups and downs of his first year in office. Even Clinton's budget plan, one of his more successful policy initiatives, was greeted with mixed reactions, as noted in this news account:

The ratings for Mr. Clinton's August 3 budget speech are not in. But a CNN–USA Today opinion poll after the address suggested it was tuned in by about half of adults, but that only about 21 percent persevered to the end. That would seem to place the president perilously close to Bill Cosby's movie "Ghost Dad," which attracted 16 percent of viewers in a network outing some months ago. ...

... The presidency these days is less a bully pulpit than a telephone solicitor, interrupting the dinner hour or "Roseanne" for a pitch that the folks at home either deeply mistrust or simply don't want to hear. Make it quick; we just got home and it's only two hours till bed. And no, you can't have our credit card number.[18]

The ultimate problem with the constant reinforcement psychology required to sell politicians to ever-wary citizens is that it permits little room for public dialogue about the issues and programs that politicians are elected to deal with. As the ties between leaders and citizens become ever-more illusory, the reality of serious issues seems ever-more harsh. It is small wonder that most modern politicians prove better at getting elected than at governing.

Notes

I wish to acknowledge the valuable research assistance of Megan Dahl on this project.

1. Elizabeth Kolbert, "Media Whistle Stops a la 1992: Arsenio, Larry, and Phil," *New York Times,* June 5, 1992, A18.

2. *USA Today,* December 28, 1992, 5B.

3. Maureen Dowd, "How a Battered Clinton Has Stayed Alive," *New York Times,* March 16, 1992, A1.

4. Richard Morin, "Budget Czars for a Day," *Washington Post National Weekly Edition,* November 23–29, 1992, 36.

5. Everett Carl Ladd, "Campaign '88: What Are the 'Issues'?" *Christian Science Monitor,* June 3, 1988, 14.

6. Jack Honomichel, "Richard Wirthlin, Advertising Man of the Year," *Advertising Age,* January 23, 1989, lead article.

7. Reported in *Newsweek* (Special election issue) (November-December 1992):33.

8. Ibid., 34.

9. *Time,* November 2, 1992, 30.

10. *TV Guide,* November 21–27, 1992, 14–15.

11. *Newsweek* (November-December 1992):40.

12. Ibid.

13. Ibid.

14. Ibid., 56.

15. Richard L. Berke, "In Late Onslaught, Nastiest of Politics Rules Radio Waves," *New York Times,* November 2, 1992, A1.

16. *Newsweek* (November-December 1992):78.

17. Ibid., 55.

18. Michael Wines, "Wonked Out: It's August; How Much Policy Can a Nation Take?" *New York Times,* August 15, 1993, D1.

References

Bennett, W. Lance. 1992. *The Governing Crisis: Media, Money, and Marketing in the 1992 Election*. New York: St. Martin's.

_____. 1994. *Inside the System: Culture, Institutions, and Power in American Politics*. Fort Worth, Tex.: Harcourt Brace.

Boorstin, Daniel. 1961. *The Image*. New York: Atheneum.

Campbell, Angus, Phillip E. Converse, Warren E. Miller, and Donald E. Stokes. 1960. *The American Voter*. New York: Wiley.

Edelman, Murray. 1993. "Contestable Categories and Public Opinion." *Political Communication* 10, no. 3:231–242.

Farah, Barbara G., and Ethel Klein. 1989. "Public Opinion Trends." In *The Election of 1988: Reports and Interpretations,* ed. Gerald M. Pomper. Chatham, N.J.: Chatham House.

Hertsgaard, Mark. 1988. *On Bended Knee: The Press and the Reagan Presidency*. New York: Farrar, Straus and Giroux.

Jamieson, Kathleen Hall. 1988. *Eloquence in an Electronic Age: The Transformation of Political Speechmaking*. New York: Oxford University Press.

McGinnis, Joe. 1969. *The Selling of the President, 1968*. New York: Trident.

Page, Benjamin I. 1978. *Choices and Echoes in Presidential Elections*. Chicago: University of Chicago Press.

Smillie, Dirk. 1992. "Talking to America: The Rise of Talk Shows in the '92 Campaign." In *An Uncertain Season: Reporting in the Postprimary Period*. Columbia University: The Freedom Forum Media Studies Center.

Smith, Erik R.A.N. 1989. *The Unchanging American Voter*. Berkeley and Los Angeles: University of California Press.

6

Presidential Psychology and Governing Styles: A Comparative Psychological Analysis of the 1992 Presidential Candidates

DAVID G. WINTER

The Paradox of American Presidential Democracy

Presidential campaigns pose an ironic paradox for many Americans: With nearly universal adult suffrage, we have the power to choose our supreme leader; with the increased importance of polling and primary campaigns, we have a relatively wide field of candidates (at least during the early phases of the campaign); yet we are often unsure how to choose. Here is the problem: We are asked to predict the governing performance of the candidates; yet in terms of demands and opportunities, the presidency is so "unprecedented," so different from any other political position, that we do not have a clear basis for prediction and choice. For example, the behavior and accomplishments of Chester Arthur and Harry Truman once they became president took most observers by surprise. Even an incumbent president can pose a challenge to judgment and prediction. In 1992, for example, who was the "real" George Bush: the decisive leader of the Gulf War coalition or the collapsing banquet guest in Tokyo; the "kinder and gentler" leader of all Americans or the shrill and divisive politician seeking reelection?

Judging Candidates and Predicting Performance

In American presidential campaigns, then, we do not lack information, promises, or claims. But what information is relevant and important? What claims

113

can be believed? First, we can discard candidates' campaign promises as a reliable guide to their future style and substance of governing. For example, in 1932 Franklin D. Roosevelt promised reductions in government expenditure; in 1964 Lyndon Johnson campaigned as the "dove" candidate who would not escalate the war in Vietnam; in 1980 Ronald Reagan promised a balanced budget by the end of his first term; and in 1988 George Bush asked Americans to "read my lips" about new taxes.

Or we might focus on the candidates' previous roles and the kinds of experience embodied in those roles. Since candidates who have been governors have had more administrative experience than candidates who have previously served only as legislators, we might predict that former governors would make better presidents than would former members of Congress. In support of such a prediction we could cite the contrast between both Roosevelts and Woodrow Wilson, on the one hand, and Warren Harding, on the other. But surely the counterexamples of former governors Calvin Coolidge and Jimmy Carter (perhaps also Reagan) versus former legislators Truman and John Kennedy cast doubt on prior role as a reliable basis for prediction.

James Barber (1992) demonstrated that many presidents' performance in office can be understood in terms of the nature of their first independent political success. In retrospect, these interpretations can seem convincing: For example, we can find hints of Truman's surprising presidential success in his early career as a Missouri county administrator. But what shall we count as "political," and how shall we identify, in advance, the "first" success? Thus, was Richard Nixon's first political success the Alger Hiss episode (as Barber believed)? Or was it his essentially passive experience of having been recruited by others to run for Congress in 1946? Was it navy administrative experience and poker playing, his election as student body president in college, or perhaps even his having to mediate between a quick-tempered father and an undemonstrative mother?[1]

In the final round of the 1992 election, voters were asked to evaluate, predict, and choose among three men: the enigmatic incumbent, a Democratic challenger with a contested "character" and contested record as governor of Arkansas, and a super-rich businessman with no prior political experience and ambiguous stands on most issues. In this chapter, I describe a method of assessing and predicting the future governing styles of these three candidates through psychological content analysis of motive imagery in their speeches.

Measuring Personality at a Distance

Because of limited access, conventional techniques for assessing personality cannot be applied to political candidates, but one resource that we do have in abundance is *words:* Candidates talk, and what they say is written down. At the explicit, or manifest, level, such words are of little use in making predictions;

but at the deeper level of imagery and nuance, they may have considerable value because in recent decades psychologists have developed reliable and objective methods of content analysis to measure personality at a distance (see Winter, 1991, on motives; Suedfeld, Tetlock, and Streufert, 1992, on conceptual complexity; Zullow and Seligman, 1990, on explanatory style; and the general reviews in Hermann, 1980a, 1980b; and Winter, 1992).

Motives

Motives are an important but complex element of personality. On the one hand, people's motives are stable and enduring dispositions to seek certain categories of goals. Different people are said to have different characteristics or predominant motives—for example, hunger, achievement, or power. On the other hand, people's motives vary over time and across situations. (Over the course of a life, or even a day, people usually pursue several different goals, and not even the strongest hunger motive leads to eating in every situation.) In other words, motives are said to be differentially "aroused" or "engaged" by different situations. How can we reconcile these two perspectives of stability and variability? John Atkinson's (1982) formulation provides one way: Motives are *stable and enduring dispositions to be aroused by certain classes of stimuli or situations.* On this view, a "high" score on a particular motive can be understood as a disposition to have that motive aroused by a greater number and variety of situations, as a more sharply rising curve of arousal over time, as a higher final asymptote of arousal, or as any combination of these (see also Winter, 1973, chap. 2).

Over the past several years, I have developed content analysis methods of measuring at a distance three important social motives or classes of goals—achievement, affiliation, and power—using adaptations of systematic scoring systems developed by David McClelland and his associates for use with the Thematic Apperception Test (TAT) (McClelland, 1985; Smith, 1992; Winter, 1991). With this technique I have carried out several political psychology studies, including studies of the motives of the major candidates in every U.S. presidential election since 1976 (using announcement of candidacy speeches; see Winter, 1976, 1982, 1988) and every U.S. president from George Washington through George Bush (using first inaugural addresses; see Winter, 1987) as well as a more intensive case study of Richard Nixon (Winter and Carlson, 1988). In the present chapter, I apply the technique to an analysis of the major 1992 presidential candidates.

Characterization of the Three Motives

Table 6.1 presents a brief characterization of the achievement, affiliation, and power motives. The achievement motive involves a concern for excellence. It is associated with preferences for moderate risks, use of feedback to modify

TABLE 6.1 Brief Characterization of Achievement, Affiliation, and Power Motives

| *Characteristic* | *Motive* | | |
	Achievement	*Affiliation*	*Power*
Typical verbal images	Excellence, quality of performance, innovation	Warmth, friendship, unity	Impact on the behavior or emotions of others, prestige
Associated actions	Moderate risks, use of information to modify performance, entrepreneurial success, dishonesty when necessary to reach goal	Cooperativeness and friendliness under safe conditions, defensiveness and even hostility under threat	Leadership and high morale of subordinates if high in sense of responsibility, profligate impulsivity if low in sense of responsibility
Negotiating style	Cooperative and "rational"	Cooperative under safe conditions, defensive and hostile under threat	Exploitative, aggressive
Approach to a negotiating partner	Cooperator	Either fellow worker or opportunist	Yielder, gambler, competitor, resister
Help sought from	Technical experts	Friends and similar others	Political "experts"
Political psychological manifestations	Frustration	Peacemaking and arms limitation, but vulnerability to scandal	Charisma, war and aggression, independent foreign policy, rated greatness

Source: Based on D. C. McClelland, *Human Motivation* (Glenview, Ill.: Scott, Foresman, 1985); D. Winter, "Measuring Personality at a Distance: Development of an Integrated System for Scoring Motives in Running Text," in *Perspectives in Personality: Approaches to Understanding Lives,* ed. A. J. Stewart, J. M. Healy Jr., and D. J. Ozer (London: Jessica Kingsley, 1991), 59–89; D. Winter, "Content Analysis of Archival Data, Personal Documents, and Everyday Verbal Productions," in *Motivation and Personality: Handbook of Thematic Content Analysis,* ed. C. P. Smith (New York: Cambridge University Press, 1992), 110–125; and D. Winter and A. J. Stewart, "Content Analysis as a Technique for Assessing Political Leaders," in *A Psychological Examination of Political Leaders,* ed. M. G. Hermann (New York: Free Press, 1977), 46–47.

performance, and success as an entrepreneur—that is, success in business situations where it is possible to exercise a good deal of personal control over outcomes. People scoring high in achievement motivation are innovators and are willing to try new techniques and sometimes even dishonest or illegal techniques when necessary to reach the goal. However, the achievement motive is not so adaptive in situations where effectiveness depends on motivating and coordinating others. Thus, in politics high achievement motivation by itself seems to enmesh leaders in a cycle of frustration and rigidity, probably because they have only limited control of outcomes and must compromise their aspirations in order to see them carried out. Thus, for example, presidents scoring high in achievement motivation tend to be classified as "active-negative" by Barber (1992).

The affiliation motive involves a concern for warm, friendly relationships. People who score high are often friendly and cooperative, but under conditions of threat they may become "prickly" and defensive. Affiliation-motivated politicians are often peacemakers. They are also vulnerable to scandal.

The power motive involves a concern for impact and prestige. It leads both to inspiring leadership (among those high in responsibility) and a cluster of variables—verbal and physical aggression, risk-taking, alcohol and substance abuse, exploitative sexuality—that reflects a style of "profligate impulsivity." Among politicians, power motivation is associated with war and violence but also with historians' ratings of charisma and greatness. Power-motivated presidents tend to end up as Barber's (1992) "active-positives."

Issues of Method

The motive-scoring technique works only if it furnishes scores that are reliable reflections of the candidates' actual motives. Therefore, before proceeding to the 1992 results, I discuss some methodological issues that often arise in connection with these content analysis studies.

On the one hand, when political speeches are scored for motive imagery, do the resulting scores actually reflect the motives of the candidates or leaders themselves or rather the motives of their speechwriters? And if speechwriters are trying to emphasize salient cultural values in order to create the broadest popular appeal, do the scores really reflect *anybody's* motives? On the other hand, leaders and candidates do select their speechwriters. Speechwriters, in turn, know how to craft words, phrases, and images to fit the style and personalities of their "clients" (see Crown, 1968, 34–38, on John Kennedy and Theodore Sorenson; and Safire, 1975, 316–326, on writing for Richard Nixon versus writing for Spiro Agnew). Finally, for any important speech such as an announcement of candidacy or an inaugural address, the candidate and other close associates review and rework successive drafts until the words feel appropriate and "comfortable." In 1960, for example, Kennedy personally wrote out a late draft of his inaugural address, and he inserted some scorable motive images into Sorenson's penultimate typed draft (see also Scott, 1993, on Clinton and his speechwriters).

To be sure, factors such as audience, campaign issues, popular mood, cultural values, and political stereotypes do affect speech content, but there is evidence that by themselves they do not wholly determine motive imagery scores (see Hermann, 1980a, 344; Winter and Stewart, 1977a, 51). Thus, it is possible for a political leader to talk about different topics, such as the economy, national heritage, and even war and peace, from almost any policy perspective and still either use or not use achievement, affiliation, or power images. In other words, the motive scoring systems seem to pick up the subtle shades of image or emphasis that reflect personal factors rather than the common currency of cultural symbols or ideological stances.

In principle, it would be possible for a speechwriter who knew the motive scoring system to manipulate deliberately the motive imagery of a speech in order to create whatever effect such imagery might have on voters or other leaders (including the political psychologists who make inferences, predictions, and judgments from motive imagery scores of political speeches!). So far, however, there is no evidence that this has happened or is about to happen.

Since the motive imagery content analysis system was derived from TAT scoring systems, which have a reputation for low test-retest reliability (see Entwisle, 1972), many readers may wonder whether this at-a-distance technique is reliable. Actually, several researchers have shown that the common impression of low TAT reliability is not accurate (Atkinson, 1982; Winter and Stewart, 1977b). Moreover, I have shown (Winter, 1991, 70–71) that the at-a-distance adaptation of these scoring systems give over-time reliability coefficients in the range of .62 to .77, which suggests a good deal of temporal stability.

Source Materials for Motive Scores

For the ten major Democratic, Republican, and independent candidates in 1992, I obtained copies of their official announcement speeches from their campaign headquarters. (David Duke's speech was transcribed from a C-Span videotape.) These speeches were scored for motive imagery in the usual way according to the system I developed (Winter, 1991). The results, expressed in terms of both raw scores (number of motive images per 1,000 words) and standardized scores (overall mean = 50 and overall standard deviation = 10), are presented in Table 6.2. Such standardization controls for any effects of announcement speeches as such on motive imagery scores and makes possible comparisons among any candidate's scores on all three motives. Standardization was carried out on the entire group of ten speeches.

To assess how Bush's and Clinton's motives may have changed as they moved from president to candidate and candidate to president, respectively, their 1989 and 1993 inaugural addresses were also scored and standardized on the basis of previous presidents' first inaugural addresses (see Winter, 1987). These scores are also reported in Table 6.2.

Ross Perot presented a problem. At the time of the original scoring (February–March 1992), the precise nature and status of his campaign were not clear since he had not yet made any formal announcement speech. In an effort to get some estimate of his motive profile, however, I scored transcripts of several published interviews with Perot: two lengthy "political" interviews from

TABLE 6.2   Motive Scores of the Major 1992 Candidates

	Raw Motive Scores (images/1,000 words)			Standard Motive Scores (mean=50, SD=10)		
Candidate	Achievement	Affiliation	Power	Achievement	Affiliation	Power
George Bush						
1989 inaugural	7.35	10.81	7.35	57	83	54
1992 announcement	11.99	8.24	17.23	63	69	71
Bill Clinton						
1992 announcement	8.69	4.50	8.04	55	54	45
1993 inaugural	10.23	5.75	9.59	71	60	65
Ross Perot						
1992 interviews	5.75	1.40	4.72	75	41	45
1992 announcement	6.02	2.19	5.47	48	45	38
Other candidates (1992 announcements)						
Jerry Brown	3.83	1.77	9.42	42	44	49
Pat Buchanan	0.69	2.06	12.35	34	45	57
David Duke	2.43	0.00	11.35	38	37	55
Tom Harkin	9.31	1.94	4.65	56	44	36
Bob Kerrey	7.65	2.39	10.74	52	46	53
Paul Tsongas	12.06	7.42	7.42	63	65	44
Douglas Wilder	5.80	2.23	5.80	47	46	38

the spring of 1992 in *Newsweek* and *Time* and two earlier "business" interviews from 1987–1988 in *Barron's* and *Fortune*. Since candidacy announcement speeches and magazine interviews may not be comparable kinds of documents in terms of motive imagery, direct raw-score comparison of Perot and the other candidates may be inappropriate. I therefore standardized Perot's interview-based raw scores on the basis of interviews from a standard sample of world leaders (Winter, 1990). These scores are also shown in Table 6.2.

Having never officially entered the race, Perot withdrew from it on July 16, only to reenter again on October 1. His opening statement at the October news conference announcing his candidacy (the first, 1,827 words, up to the point at which he introduced vice-presidential candidate James Stockdale; see Perot, 1992) is therefore as close to an official announcement speech as we have. Motive imagery scores from this speech, standardized on the basis of the other nine announcement speeches, are also shown in Table 6.2. Inspection of these different scores for Perot shows some major differences, in contrast to the general run of previous experience with multiple scores from the same person over time. (These discrepancies are discussed later in this chapter.)

Motive Profiles of the 1992 Candidates

The most convenient way to present the results is to proceed candidate by candidate: the incumbent Bush, the challenger Clinton, and the outsider

TABLE 6.3   Greatest Similarity Between Each Major 1992 Presidential Candidate and Previous
U.S. Presidents

George Bush (1992)	"And history will tell of a second American Century—when we led the world [*power motive*] to new heights of achievement [*achievement*] and liberty. This is our legacy. This is our challenge. And this is our destiny. And together [*affiliation*], we will win [*achievement*]. I'm certain of that."
Harry Truman (1949)	"Almost a year ago, in company with sixteen free nations of Europe, we launched the greatest cooperative [*affiliation*] economic program in history [*achievement*]. The purpose of that unprecedented effort is to invigorate and strengthen democracy in Europe [*power*]."
Bill Clinton (1992)	"I believe with all my heart that together [*affiliation*], we can make this happen. We can usher in a new era of progress [*achievement*], prosperity and renewal."
Lyndon Johnson (1965)	"For the hour and the day and the time are here to achieve progress [*achievement*] without strife, to achieve change without hatred—not without difference of opinion, but without the deep and abiding divisions which scar the union [*affiliation*] for generations."
Ross Perot (1992)	"I have said over and over again that Solomon, the wisest man in the world [*achievement*], couldn't get this job done alone. The voters are going to have to stay in the room after November. If they do, anything is possible."
Herbert Hoover (1929)	"The questions before our country are problems of progress to higher standards [*achievement*]. ... They ... enlist our sense of responsibility for their settlement. And that responsibility rests upon you, my countrymen, as much as upon those of us who have been selected for office."

Source: Bush and Clinton: announcement speeches; Perot: interview with *Newsweek*, April 27,
1992, 26; Truman, Johnson, and Hoover: *Inaugural Addresses of the Presidents of the United
States* (Washington, D.C.: GPO, 1974), 253, 273, and 233, respectively.

Perot. Motive scores can be interpreted in several ways: as a general thematic
characterization, as independent variables from which specific aspects of governing style and performance as president can be predicted, and finally as a
configuration to compare to previous U.S. presidents. (With the motives of
both candidates and previous presidents standardized on the same scale, and
with the three motives assumed to be independent and orthogonal, the "most
similar" president to any candidate can be defined as that president whose
score has the smallest Pythagorean, or three-dimensional, distance from that
candidate.) Table 6.3 illustrates these similarities with representative quotations. What does it mean to say that a candidate most closely resembles some
particular previous president? Obviously, these similarities do not mean an
identity of personality or behavioral outcomes, but they do suggest possible
similarities of goals and goal-setting style, reactions to the political process,
personal strengths, weaknesses, opportunities, and vulnerabilities.

George Bush

In his reelection announcement speech, Bush scored high in all three motives,
at least 1 standard deviation above the average of the nine major 1992 candi-

TABLE 6.4   Motive Scores of George Bush Over Time

	Standardized Motive Imagery		
Bush Speech	*Achievement*	*Affiliation*	*Power*
1988 announcement of candidacy	61	62	51
1988 nomination acceptance	46	43	62
1989 inaugural address	58	83	53
1992 announcement of candidacy	63	69	71

Source: D. Winter, "Personality and Leadership in the Gulf War," in *The Political Psychology of the Gulf War,* ed. S. A. Renshon (Pittsburgh: University of Pittsburgh Press, 1993), 114.

dates. This was a change from his previous profiles, as shown in Table 6.4, and the differences may help us understand Bush's personality and behavior. In both his 1988 announcement and his 1989 inaugural address, Bush was high in achievement and affiliation but only about average in power. Such a profile seems consistent with his earlier life and much of his presidency. Restless and energetic ("Gotta keep moving. Can't stay in one place all the time"), flexible on beliefs in the pursuit of a goal, and successful as a Texas oil entrepreneur driven by the stimulus of meeting self-imposed "challenges," Bush has been the quintessential achievement-motivated person (see McClelland, 1961, especially chap. 8).

Bush's high affiliation motivation is evident in his striving for comfortable congeniality and consensus with colleagues, most notably in his successful formation of the international coalition against Iraq, but perhaps also in his needless and counterproductive courting of his "base" in the extreme right wing of the Republican party during the 1992 campaign. The less attractive "prickly" and defensive aspect of Bush's high affiliation, which may have roots in his early family life (see Chapter 2), has also surfaced on several occasions. For example, after being called a "wimp" in 1988, he lashed out with a negative campaign that echoed the "dirty tricks" of the Watergate era. Humiliated over his handling of the 1989 Panama coup, Bush went on to unleash a full-scale military invasion to arrest and extradite Manuel Noriega. Forced to retract his "Read my lips: No new taxes" pledge during the 1990 budget negotiations, he was primed to strike out against any threat.

Saddam Hussein—different from Bush in culture, social class, family background, religion, language, goals, interest, and personal style—was the perfect threat stimulus. Even so, the published transcript of the July 1990 Saddam Hussein–April Glaspie interview and other recently disclosed documents suggest that initially Bush actively and energetically courted Saddam Hussein with military, economic, and intelligence assistance, right down to the day Iraqi troops invaded Kuwait. Perhaps Bush had thought that in spite of all their differences, he could still deal with Hussein as a friend. The Iraqi invasion of Kuwait dashed those hopes, and Bush impulsively responded with aggression, suggesting (to modify slightly an old saying) that "hell hath no fury like an affiliation-motivated person who has been double-crossed" (see Winter, 1993).

Sensitive—highly sensitive—to dissimilar people, dislike, and disagreement, Bush responded to such threats not with a constant high level of power motivation but with sharp increases in his power motive score. Thus, in the course of the 1988 campaign his level of power motivation dramatically increased over that of his original announcement speech. And in the elevated power motive score of his February 1992 announcement speech, we can easily discern the aggressive echos of the Gulf War "Big Bang." The fact that when power motivated, Bush can so easily come across to others as petulant suggests that these high power motive scores are not well-integrated and stable features of his personality. In terms of motive profile, the George Bush of the 1988 candidacy announcement and 1989 inaugural was most similar to Richard Nixon among previous twentieth-century presidents; but the 1992 campaigner Bush was most like Harry Truman.

Bill Clinton

In his announcement speech, Clinton scored a little above average in achievement and affiliation and a little below average in power—like Bush in 1988, but lower on all counts. This pattern fits much of Clinton's rhetoric and performance before, during, and after the campaign—goals and aspirations tinged with warmth and compassion and a willingness to modify style, change tactics, and even cut corners that earned the nickname "Slick Willie" from his opponents. But his relatively low power motive score suggests that for all his experience as governor of Arkansas, he might be neither comfortable nor effective in the quicksands of Washington federal politics. His inaugural address, however, showed an elevation of all scores, especially achievement and power, though achievement was still higher than power. Among twentieth-century American presidents, Clinton resembles both Lyndon Johnson and Jimmy Carter, with Clinton the campaigner closer to Johnson and Clinton the president more like Carter. Both of these previous presidents had achievement scores that were high and higher than power motivation; similarly, both entered office with ideals and visions, only to depart several years later mired in frustration and defeat. (What these similarities might mean for Clinton is discussed later in this chapter in connection with predictions about his presidency.)

Ross Perot

As estimated from the interviews, Perot scored very high in achievement, low in affiliation, and a little below average in power. This profile is certainly consistent with his extraordinary success as an entrepreneur and seems to fit the style of the Perot campaign, at least in its first phase. This interview-based profile most closely resembles those of Herbert Hoover (who was also very successful in business before becoming president), Woodrow Wilson (who also went over the heads of "the politicians" to appeal directly to "the people"—but without success), and Jimmy Carter (who also graduated from the U.S. Naval Academy, then quit the navy to become a success in business). In Perot's October 1, 1992, statement officially announcing his candidacy, however, his achievement motivation was much lower—below average and not much higher than affiliation or power. Even so, Hoover remained the most similar president.

Changes in Perot's Motives. Why did a drop occur in Perot's achievement motive score? Actually, an examination of the raw scores for his interviews and announcement speech reveals that the rate of achievement images per 1,000 words is about the same. In other words, the use of different standardization samples for the two kinds of material is the reason for the apparent difference in Perot's achievement motive scores. Is the difference therefore an artifact, or is it real? In comparison to world leaders responding to interview questions, Perot scored high in achievement motivation; in comparison to other candidates making an announcement speech, he did not. What is his "real" level of achievement motivation? This problem can be resolved in several different ways. (1) The apparent drop in Perot's score is simply an artifact of the different comparison samples used; hence Perot's "real" achievement motive score is either high (interviews) or low (announcement statement). (2) The apparent drop occurred because Perot's announcement of candidacy was made as an opening statement in a news conference rather than as a set speech, as were the other candidates' announcements, and was therefore inappropriately standardized. (3) The drop is real, but it occurred because Perot (or his speechwriters) somehow did not adjust his actual level of achievement imagery upward to levels typical of announcement speeches; in other words, his announcement was poorly matched to the demands of the occasion and did not reflect his true high level of achievement motivation.

These are essentially null (or at least methodological) hypotheses, and although they may be correct, they may also obscure an interesting substantive explanation: (4) The drop is real and reflected an actual decline in Perot's achievement motivation, at least as it was engaged during the course of the presidential campaign. (See the previous discussion; and Atkinson, 1982, about the change and stability of motives.) If this is true, then it would suggest other major differences between Perot's "early" and "late" campaigns: in summary terms, that he somehow did not "have his heart in it" after his July withdrawal even though in October he went through the motions of the announcement and the debates. At the time of his July withdrawal, Perot's probability of success, initially high, had been dropping precipitously (Zaller, 1993). Under these circumstances, achievement-motivated candidates tend to get out of the race (Winter, 1982), which is what Perot did. From the perspective of power motivation, however, such a change of direction, calculated as it was, could be politically damaging in the long run because it would alienate supporters. Thus, even though his actual probability of success in the late campaign was much lower than it was at the end of the early campaign (hence not attractive to someone high in achievement motivation), Perot may have gone through the motions of reentry as a strategic maneuver to preserve his base of support for the future. On this hypothesis, Perot in October 1992 was making a pro forma announcement only for long-term strategic purposes. As a result, his announcement statement had lower levels of achievement motivation than it would have had if it had been composed and delivered several months earlier.

(5) Still another explanation of Perot's 1992 behavior that has been suggested by some commentators is that his campaign was never intended as a serious bid for the presidency. Rather, by highlighting fiscal issues and thereby influencing policy, Perot may have hoped to increase the value of his financial holdings and thus his personal wealth ("When in the Course," 1994). Such an interpretation would be consistent with his high achievement motivation and low power motivation scores.

Perot as Hoover? What can we make of Perot's similarity to Herbert Hoover, which was true of both the interview-based and announcement-based profiles? Since Hoover's reputation was so strongly affected by the Depression, it is worthwhile recalling several aspects of his prepresidential career that show striking parallels to Perot—parallels that are also consistent with the high achievement motivation scores of both men (see Lyons, 1964):

1. Each showed entrepreneurial precocity and accumulated great wealth prior to entering politics (Hoover as a mining engineer and executive, Perot in computers).
2. Each organized a freelance international rescue (Hoover at Tianjin during the Boxer Rebellion in China, Perot in Iran after the fall of the shah).
3. Each entered politics late in life, with virtually no prior political experience, running only for the presidency.
4. On entering politics, each had an ambiguous party identification.
5. Each identified himself as "not a politician."
6. Each approached politics primarily as an administrator rather than as a negotiator or broker.
7. Each advocated reorganizing the executive branch of government.

8. Each emphasized diffusion of responsibility away from Washington and toward "the people" (see the Perot and Hoover quotations in Table 6.3).

9. Each was quite uncompromising when he thought he was right.

10. Each focused on national fiscal prudence in a time of social and economic upheaval.

Predicting I: Who Gets Elected?

Could the motive profiles of the 1992 candidates have been used to predict who would get elected? In a study of the 1976 New Hampshire primary, I found (Winter, 1982) a significant correlation between candidates' level of achievement motivation and their percentage of the vote. In a much broader study of American presidential elections from 1796 to 1964, however, I found (Winter, 1987) that the candidates' electoral success was a function not of any one particular motive but rather of the degree to which their motive profiles were congruent with those of the larger American society at the time of the election (as measured through content analysis of popular literature and similar materials). For the 1992 election, we lack any quantitative information about the societal motive profile (but see Chapter 5 for a qualitative description). However, if we assume that Clinton's victory resulted in part from his greater motivational congruence with American society, then we can work backward from the scores in Table 6.2 and conclude that Bush's increased power motivation (1992 announcement speech) hurt him with the voters, who preferred only low-to-moderate power motivation in combination with high achievement and affiliation (see also Chapter 2). More tentatively, we can also conclude that Perot's low levels of affiliation motivation at all times would have reduced his electoral support even if he had continued his campaign at its spring 1992 level of intensity.

Predicting II: How Will Clinton Govern?

Clinton's motive profile is high achievement, perhaps slightly less high affiliation, and moderate power (higher than moderate in his inaugural address, however). We can judge the validity of this profile by comparing the behaviors it suggests (see Table 6.1) with the descriptions of Clinton's behavior and personality in Chapters 4 and 7. Meanwhile, what predictions can we make about his presidency on the basis of this profile? Can we expect to see more of the Slick Willie portrayed by his opponents in the 1992 campaign? Or will we see the Comeback Kid, narrowly escaping from bungled personnel appointments, a seemingly indecisive and ever-changing foreign policy, and military and diplomatic quagmires? What about the Man from Hope, or the pop-culture hero of the inauguration festivities? (See also Chapter 5.) Perhaps each of these campaign images reflects a different aspect of his high achievement, high affiliation profile. Will the final story of the Clinton presidency resemble the triumph of Lyndon Johnson at his best in 1964–1965 or the sad decline of Jimmy Carter at his worst in 1979–1980? From a motivational perspective, what are Clinton's strong and weak points? What are his risks and vulnerabilities?

Predicting from Clinton's Inaugural Motive Profile

High Achievement Motivation. Clinton's high achievement motivation—in standardized terms, much higher in his inaugural than in his announcement speech—is certainly consistent with his many presidential programs and actions directed toward improvement as well as his energetic personal style. The Slick Willie image, which refers to Clinton's tendency to change his views and modify his positions, reflects the tendency of achievement-motivated people to modify their performance on the basis of the results of previous actions. Similarly, the twists and turns of his policy on Bosnia may be taken as awareness of and sensitivity to feedback from other centers of political power as well as an avoidance of high risks—also characteristics of achievement motivation. Taken together, all of these characteristics may be "good business," but in politics they can corrode alliances, alienate supporters, and give the impression of unprincipled opportunism: hence the derogatory nickname so reminiscent of another achievement-motivated president nicknamed "Tricky Dick" (see Winter and Carlson, 1988).

Above-Average Affiliation Motivation. Clinton's affiliation motive is above average and increased slightly from announcement to inaugural, but even so it is not as high as that of Truman, Nixon, or Bush. This suggests that although Clinton will have some motivational capacity or predilection to seek peace and arms limitation, he may not be quite so defensive in his response to criticism as were these predecessors. The fact that Clinton's affiliation score is not as high as his achievement score further suggests that his changes of position and policy are based more on calculations of risk and results than on the influence of close associates. As a consequence, the potential for major scandal may be slightly reduced, although this remains a vulnerability of affiliation-motivated presidents.

Power Motivation Increasing from Moderate to High. In his inaugural, Clinton's power motive score increased over that of his announcement speech to being at least 1 standard deviation above average. This suggests the kind of capacity to get enjoyment from being president that characterized some of the great twentieth-century presidents (Franklin Roosevelt, Truman, Kennedy), who were also high in power motivation. Such a capacity can be seen in small incidents such as the populist "fix" that Clinton seemed to get from the day-after-inaugural White House reception for the public, his ability to laugh at himself under stress (recall his joke about getting a manicure after the "$200 haircut" fiasco), and his projected sense of being at ease in difficult situations such as the budget negotiations.

Balance Between Achievement and Power. From the motivational perspective, the most critical question of Clinton's presidency is whether his enjoyment of power and of office will be sufficient to allow him to navigate through the morass of politics—compromise, frustration, gridlock, independent power centers, difficulties in implementing policy, and so forth. (Recall the previous presidents whom Clinton most closely resembles, who were also much higher in achievement than in power.) In his announcement speech, Clinton resembled Lyndon Johnson—also a visionary reformer, but a president destroyed by a war from which he stubbornly refused to extricate himself until it was too late. In the inaugural, Clinton's profile was closer to that of Jimmy Carter, who also approached Washington as an outsider full of ideas for improvement, but who by the summer of 1979 was retreating to Camp David, his presidency sunk by economic problems and the "malaise" of the political process.

The Problem of Achievement Motivation in Politics. Since achievement-motivated leaders do so well in American business, what exactly is the problem for them in American politics? American corporate culture is a "command-and-compliance" culture, in which a chief executive can insist on the "one best solution" to any problem. Once there is a single best solution, further discussion is often preempted; in the words of Carter's 1976 campaign autobiography, "Why not the best?" (Perhaps this is a latent authoritarian "shadow" of utilitarianism or meritocracy.) In democratic politics, however, different constituencies usually have different ideas about what is best, so that the best usually has to be compromised in order to get the possible. People have to be persuaded, cajoled, and inspired to accept someone else's vision of the best. In the 1861 Senate debates during the secession crisis, William Henry Seward (1861, 344) poignantly expressed the difficulties of reconciling aspirations and realities in politics:

> I learned early from Jefferson, that in political affairs we cannot always do what seems to us absolutely best. Those with whom we must necessarily act, entertaining different views, have the power and the right of carrying them into practice. We must be content to lead when we can, and to follow when we cannot lead; and

if we cannot at any time do for our country all the good that we would wish, we must be satisfied with doing for her all the good that we can.

Then too, the best often costs too much. As historian Frederick Merk (1967, 371) described this problem, "On the floor of Congress a [program and plan], attractively packaged ... is opened. Its items are individually inspected. The price tags on them are read with dismay, especially those still to be paid; mislabelings and confused labelings ... are detected and denounced. Members ... begin throwing epithets and charges at each other. ... The victory celebration ends; the fight over measures begins."

In politics, finally, even after compromise programs are passed, they have to be implemented by less-than-the-best officials, whom the president did not appoint, does not fully trust, and cannot remove. To a power-motivated leader like Franklin Roosevelt or Kennedy, these are not obstacles but rather the very things that make political life interesting. To achievement-motivated chief executives, however, such problems may bring about a small death each day. As a result, achievement-motivated presidents may be tempted to go over the heads of politicians and take the case directly to "the people" (as did achievement-motivated Woodrow Wilson), to take ethical short-cuts (as did achievement-motivated Richard Nixon), or to exhaust themselves in micromanagement (as did achievement-motivated Jimmy Carter).

Clinton's Central Vulnerability

These considerations suggest one central area of vulnerability for President Clinton: that the inherent frustrations of politics may in the end overwhelm his aspirations for change, improvement, and "reinventing government," driving him down the bitter paths trod by Wilson, Johnson, Nixon, and Carter. In other words, over the long run the balance of Clinton's power and achievement motives—in everyday language, his capacity to derive pleasure from the office while at the same time pursuing his aspirations and so avoid frustration, illegalities, or micromanagement—may turn out to be the critical defining feature of the Clinton presidency.

Just how vulnerable is Clinton on this score? From a motivational perspective, the critical question is whether his power motivation is high enough to generate a sense of pleasure in the political process itself. Thus, the relatively higher power motivation score in his inaugural address gives some grounds for optimism, although the relatively higher achievement motive score may indicate that his aspirations still outrun his capacity for political pleasure. However, the discussion in Chapter 7 of how Clinton changed his governing style between his first term as Arkansas governor, in which his immoderate aspirations led to frustration and defeat, and his more "political" and successful subsequent terms, gives additional grounds for hoping that Clinton has learned how to enjoy politics. The most cautious verdict, then, would be that

Clinton's achievement and power motives are both high and that the balance between them could be tipped either way—for example, by fluctuations in motives as a result of external events or even measurement error. At the behavioral level, how has Clinton the president responded to the frustrations of politics? As of January 1994, he had done reasonably well. On the budget, with luck and strong Democratic support, he overcame his tactical mistake of excluding Republicans. On subsequent issues (notably NAFTA), he sought bipartisan support instead of being vindictive.

Signs to Watch

Nonverbal Behavior. What can we predict of the future? What are the signs of frustration or pleasure in office, signs to which we might pay attention? One obvious source of cues would simply be Clinton's appearance and nonverbal behavior: How much does he smile? Does he appear to enjoy the job of being president? Has he maintained his sense of humor? One positive sign might be his ability to recover the appearance of a pleasant disposition after moments of testiness and anger.

Relations with the Press. President Clinton's relations with the press may be a more subtle and complex indicator of his frustration-pleasure balance (or achievement-power motivation balance). All presidents have their difficulties with the press and get angry at reporters. Power-motivated presidents, however, recognize that because politics is largely "mediated" by the media, political goals can be achieved only with and through collaboration with the media. In contrast, achievement-motivated presidents would tend to experience media opposition as attack, not just on themselves as persons but (more important) on their "best" policies. Thus, they view the media as an obstacle to the pursuit of the best, rather than as an indispensable source of help in that pursuit. The contrast between a power-motivated and an achievement-motivated approach to the press, then, can be put in the following terms: Are representatives of the media viewed as challenging but friendly adversaries with whom jousting is fun and friendships rewarding? Or are they portrayed as unfair enemies, from whom only ill will and malice can be expected?[2]

So far, Clinton's relations with the press have been at best mixed, as chronicled in Chapter 9. Clinton's interview with *Rolling Stone* writers ended in off-the-cuff bitter words that recalled Richard Nixon at his most extreme (Wenner and Greider, 1993, 81):[3]

> I have fought more damn battles here for more things than any president has in the last twenty years ... and not gotten one damn bit of credit for it from the knee-jerk liberal press, and I am sick and tired of it and you can put that in the damn article. I have fought and fought and fought and fought. I get up here ev-

ery day, and I work till late at night on everything ... and you guys take it and you say, "Fine, go on to something else, what else can I hit him about?" ...

And you get no credit around here for fighting and bleeding. And that's why the know-nothings and the do-nothings and the negative people and the right-wingers always win. Because of the way people like you put questions to people like me. Now, that's the truth. ...

And I'm sorry if I'm not very good at communicating, but I haven't gotten a hell of a lot of help since I've been here.

Lowered Integrative Complexity and Frustration. Conceivably, another, more technical sign of the president's frustration may be found in his ongoing level of integrative complexity. Although every successful leader has the capacity to simplify messages when conducting a campaign or advocating revolutionary change (Suedfeld and Rank, 1976; Tetlock, 1981), continuing low levels of integrative complexity—that is, overly simplistic thinking—may reflect political frustration and foundering. Even though there are no direct data to support this hypothesis, the findings reported in Chapter 11 do suggest that Clinton's surprisingly low levels of integrative complexity might be understood as a reflection of the frustrations of achievement motivation in politics.

The Political Future of Ross Perot

These same considerations also apply to Ross Perot, in whom all of the tendencies of high achievement motivation are further reinforced by a lifetime of experience within American corporate culture, where consensus can in the end be imposed. On the basis of his motive profile, we could expect from a hypothetical future President Perot an even more intense conflict between achievement motivation and the realities of the political process. For example, consider Perot's own description of his leadership tactics:

> Step one: We have to decide to change it. Step two: Once that starts there will be a raging debate about how to change it, and that will kill all the sunshine soldiers because they can't take the heat. But out of that a handful of leaders will emerge, and from that a consensus will emerge. And that is the way you get things done. (interview with *Barron's,* February 23, 1987, 35)

> [As president] I will be listening, listening, listening to their [leaders'] ideas. They will have ideas better than my ideas. ... We take these ideas to the people, present them to the people. The people say let's do it, and now we have a system out of gridlock and a system that works. That's the process I'll use. (interview with *Time,* May 25, 1992, 37)

Such tactics assume a widely shared rationality on the part of political leaders and the public: a faith that consensus will naturally emerge out of debate and that the one best way will be recognized by most people. But what if there is no consensus? And what if the people do *not* say, "Let's do it"? When this happened in the past (in the navy and at IBM and General Motors), Perot dropped out, as is discussed in Chapter 3. Such episodes of bitterness may represent a wounded sense of entitlement, but they can also be interpreted as a consequence of the imbalance between Perot's achievement and power motives in a quasi-political context.[4]

Motives and the Limits of Prediction

During presidential elections, examining and comparing motive profiles may be an agreeable parlor game, but do motive scores derived from content analysis of politicians' speeches really help us understand and predict a presidential administration? In two articles (Winter, 1991; Winter and Carlson, 1988), I suggested that Richard Nixon's inaugural motive profile provided an astonishingly good guide to his presidency and his life. And at the beginning of Ronald Reagan's second term in January 1985, the substantial increase in his affiliation motivation (Winter, 1990) suggested the possibility of a major U.S.-Soviet arms limitation agreement (when the treaty reducing intermediate range ballistic missiles was not even up for discussion) and a major political scandal (when the Iran-contra affair was just a glint in Oliver North's eye).

Nevertheless, the high affiliation motive score of George Bush's 1989 inaugural address suggested that he would promote peace rather than become involved in a war. Even if it is true that Bush worked for peace and good relations with the Soviet Union, how can such an analysis account for his invasion of Panama and the Gulf War? David Winter, Margaret Hermann, Walter Weintraub, and Stephen Walker (1991, 463–464), drawing on their earlier assessment of Bush's personality, tried to answer such a question:

> Could we have predicted [the Gulf War] in July 1990? Of course not. ... Saddam Hussein's [invasion of Kuwait] was unpredicted, *and from the perspective of our earlier study* [of Bush] *it was unpredictable.* What we can do, however, is interpret Bush's response, *given* that stimulus. Thus most useful and successful predictions from at-a-distance assessments of political leaders' personalities are of the "if/ then" or propositional variety. ... While such an analysis may describe a leader with Bush's personality as inclined toward peace and rational cooperation, it can also spell out the circumstances [e.g., threat from a "dissimilar" opponent] under which such a leader would be likely to go to war.

Like all personality assessments, this analysis of Clinton's motive profile can predict the course of his presidential administration only in broad terms: a series of tendencies, strengths, vulnerabilities, each interacting with the characteristics of his advisers, political counterplayers, rivals, and enemies as well as with the unpredictable course of events. No doubt we could do better by adding in other personality measures (for example, introversion-extroversion, stage of moral reasoning, and self-esteem), as Winter et al. (1991) did.

We must finally recognize, however, the limits of all predictions of political outcomes from the personalities of political actors. Can we confidently predict from the similarity of motive profiles that Clinton will be another Lyndon Johnson or Jimmy Carter? By no means. But we can suggest that the tendency of achievement-motivated leaders to be dragged down by the frustrations of politics should be of particular concern for the Clinton administration.

Notes

1. In one autobiography, Nixon (1978, 5, 6, 8) wrote that "the principle that opposites attract aptly describes my father and my mother." He went on to describe his father as a "strict and stern disciplinarian," given to "tempestuous arguments with my brothers ... that could be heard all through the neighborhood." His mother, in contrast, was "intensely private in her feelings and emotions." In a later autobiography, he (1990, 87) added that "in her whole life, I never heard her say to me or to anyone else, 'I love you.'"

2. The difference between these alternatives can be illustrated by the contrast between John F. Kennedy (whose power motivation was 2.7 standard deviation units higher than his achievement motivation) and Richard Nixon (whose power motivation was 1.3 standard deviation units lower than his achievement motivation; see Winter, 1987, Table 6.1, for presidential motive scores). Kennedy clearly enjoyed his relations with reporters, many of whom he cultivated both as personal friends and as tools for furthering his policy (e.g., Bradlee, 1975; Reston, 1991, 469–470). Nixon, in contrast, maintained a running exchanges of barbs with the media, as in his famous 1962 statement to reporters after losing the California gubernatorial election: "You won't have Nixon to kick around anymore."

3. Appropriately enough, this conversation took place against a backdrop of a portrait of Woodrow Wilson (also much higher in achievement than power motivation) on the wall.

4. Perot's performance in the televised October 1993 NAFTA debate with Vice President Gore may be another example.

References

Atkinson, J. W. (1982). "Motivational Determinants of Thematic Apperception." In *Motivation and Society,* ed. A. J. Stewart, 3–40. San Francisco: Jossey-Bass.

Barber, J. D. (1992). *Presidential Character: Predicting Performance in the White House.* 4th ed. Englewood Cliffs, N.J.: Prentice-Hall.

Bradlee, B. C. (1975). *Conversations with Kennedy.* New York: Norton.

Carter, J. (1975). *Why Not the Best?* Nashville, Tenn.: Broadman Press.

Crown, J. T. (1968). *The Kennedy Literature: A Bibliographic Essay on John F. Kennedy.* New York: New York University Press.

Entwisle, D. R. (1972). "To Dispel Fantasies About Fantasy-Based Measures of Achievement Motivation." *Psychological Bulletin* 77:377–391.

Hermann, M. G. (1980a). "Assessing the Personalities of Soviet Politburo Members." *Personality and Social Psychology Bulletin* 6:332–352. .

_____ (1980b). "Examining Foreign Policy Behavior Using the Personal Character-istics of Political Leaders." *International Studies Quarterly* 24:7–46.

Lyons, E. (1964). *Herbert Hoover: A Biography.* New York: Doubleday.

McClelland, D. C. (1961). *The Achieving Society.* Princeton: D. Van Nostrand.

_____ (1985). *Human Motivation.* Glenview, Ill.: Scott, Foresman.

Merk, F. (1967). *The Oregon Question: Essays in Anglo-American Diplomacy and Poli-tics.* Cambridge: Harvard University Press.

Nixon, R. M. (1978). *RN: The Memoirs of Richard Nixon.* New York: Grosset and Dunlap.

_____ (1990). *In the Arena.* New York: Simon and Schuster.

Perot, R. (1992). "Opening Statement at News Conference." *New York Times,* Octo-ber 2, A12.

Reston, J. (1991). *Deadline: A Memoir.* New York: Random House.

Safire, W. (1975). *Before the Fall: An Inside View of the Pre-Watergate White House.* New York: Belmont Tower Books.

Scott, W. (1993). "Walter Scott's Personality Parade." *Parade,* October 24, 2.

Seward, W. H. (1861). "Speech in the U.S. Senate." *Congressional Globe,* January 12, 36C1:344.

Smith, C. P., ed. (1992). *Motivation and Personality: Handbook of Thematic Content Analysis.* New York: Cambridge University Press.

Suedfeld, P., and A. D. Rank (1976). "Revolutionary Leaders: Long-Term Success as a Function of Changes in Conceptual Complexity." *Journal of Personality and So-cial Psychology* 34:169–184.

Suedfeld, P., P. E. Tetlock, and S. Streufert (1992). "Conceptual/Integrative Com-plexity." In *Motivation and Personality: Handbook of Thematic Content Analysis,* ed. C. P. Smith, 393–400. New York: Cambridge University Press.

Tetlock, P. E. (1981). "Pre- to Postelection Shifts in Presidential Rhetoric: Impression Management or Cognitive Adjustment?" *Journal of Personality and Social Psychol-ogy* 41:207–212.

Wenner, J. S., and W. Greider (1993). "President Clinton: The *Rolling Stone* Inter-view." *Rolling Stone,* December 9, 40–45, 80–81.

"When in the Course of Events It Is Time to Pillory Someone" (1994). *New York Times* (National ed.), March 6, E7.

Winter, D. G. (1973). *The Power Motive.* New York: Free Press.

_____ (1976). "What Makes the Candidates Run." *Psychology Today* (July):45–49, 92.

_____ (1982). "Motivation and Performance in Presidential Candidates." In *Motiva-tion and Society,* ed. A. J. Stewart, 244–273. San Francisco: Jossey-Bass.

_____ (1987). "Leader Appeal, Leader Performance, and the Motive Profiles of Leaders and Followers: A Study of American Presidents and Elections." *Journal of Personality and Social Psychology* 52:196–202.

_____ (1988). "What Makes Jesse Run?" *Psychology Today* (July):20ff.

_____ (1990). "Inventory of Motive Scores of Persons, Groups, and Societies Mea-sured at a Distance." Ann Arbor: University of Michigan. Manuscript.

_____ (1991). "Measuring Personality at a Distance: Development of an Integrated System for Scoring Motives in Running Text." In *Perspectives in Personality:*

Approaches to Understanding Lives, ed. A. J. Stewart, J. M. Healy Jr., and D. J. Ozer, 59–89. London: Jessica Kingsley.

———— (1992). "Content Analysis of Archival Data, Personal Documents, and Everyday Verbal Productions." In *Motivation and Personality: Handbook of Thematic Content Analysis,* ed. C. P. Smith, 110–125. New York: Cambridge University Press.

———— (1993). "Personality and Leadership in the Gulf War." In *The Political Psychology of the Gulf War,* ed. S. A. Renshon, 107–117. Pittsburgh: University of Pittsburgh Press.

Winter, D. G., and L. Carlson (1988). "Using Motive Scores in the Psychobiographical Study of an Individual: The Case of Richard Nixon." *Journal of Personality* 56:75–103.

Winter, D. G., M. G. Hermann, W. Weintraub, and S. G. Walker (1991). "The Personalities of Bush and Gorbachev at a Distance: Follow-up on Predictions." *Political Psychology* 12:457–464.

Winter, D. G., and A. J. Stewart (1977a). "Content Analysis as a Technique for Assessing Political Leaders." In *A Psychological Examination of Political Leaders,* ed. M. G. Hermann, 28–61. New York: Free Press.

———— (1977b). "Power Motive Reliability as a Function of Retest Instructions." *Journal of Consulting and Clinical Psychology* 45:436–440.

Zaller, J. (1993). "The Rise and Fall of Candidate Perot." Paper presented at the Annual Meeting of the American Political Science Association, Washington, D.C., September.

Zullow, H., and M.E.P. Seligman (1990). "Pessimistic Rumination Predicts Defeat of Presidential Candidates, 1900 to 1984." *Psychological Inquiry* 1:52–61.

PART III

The Process of
Presidential Leadership

7

Political Style and Political Leadership: The Case of Bill Clinton

FRED I. GREENSTEIN

My charge is to analyze President Bill Clinton's political style—that is, his outward manner and habitual mode of action. It is the responsibility of Stanley Renshon in Chapter 4 to make inferences about the inner man. Rather as if we were both assessing the performance qualities of an automobile, one of us by observing it in action and the other by looking under its hood, our concerns and approaches converge.

The leadership styles of some political leaders are all of a piece. President Jimmy Carter provides an example. As the declassified record of his presidency begins to emerge, one sees a president who in his private counsels appears very similar to the president evident in such public displays as news conferences and addresses to the nation. In both contexts Carter shows the same preoccupation with the technical details of his policies and the same rather stiff-necked insistence on the correctness of his own positions. Other presidents' leadership styles are layered, as in the case of President Dwight D. Eisenhower, whose homely outward persona concealed a cool, analytically detached political strategist who typically obtained results by indirection (Greenstein, 1982).

The leadership style of William Jefferson Clinton appears to be neither unitary nor layered. Rather, it changes over time in an alternation between two basic modalities—a no-holds-barred style of striving for numerous policy outcomes with little attention to establishing priorities or accommodating political realities and a more measured, pragmatic style of focusing on a limited number of goals and attending closely to the politics of selling his program. I speak of an alternation in Bill Clinton's leadership style rather than an evolution because there is a striking similarity between the course of Clinton's political actions in the state of Arkansas and his actions during his first year in the White House.

After being elected in 1978 as the nation's youngest governor, Clinton moved too fast and too far for the political temper of his state and was defeated two years later but then spent the next two years stumping the state and promising to remedy his ways. He was returned to office, and thereafter his political comportment was by all accounts far more measured and responsive to political realities, enabling him to remain as governor for a further decade (Ifel, 1992; Kolbert, 1992). Similarly, the first 100 days of the Clinton presidency were an exercise in political excess. Having promised to focus "like a laser" on the economy, Clinton confronted the Washington political community with a scattergun of stimuli—gays in the military, a succession of problematic appointments, and a procession of other distractions that negated the positive effects of his occasional tour-de-force performances, such as the much-acclaimed ad lib presentation of his economic program to a joint session of Congress on February 17.

By the 100 days' mark Clinton had a record-low approval rating in the polls. The press commentary on his presidency was suffused with images of failure, and whatever political capital his periodic strong performances had earned him was already squandered. Then, rather as if the punditry occasioned by the arbitrary 100-day mark had provided the same wake-up call furnished by defeat after his first term as governor, Clinton corrected sharply, moved to the center, signaled his willingness to bargain and negotiate, and even conspicuously added to his staff former Republican White House aide David Gergen. Ironically, Gergen had been charged with the public relations aspects of enacting President Ronald Reagan's 1981 tax cut, which produced the mounting deficit that President Clinton's 1993 economic program was designed to combat.

Because my concern is with the outer aspects of the Clinton leadership—with his style rather than his character and personality—I do not attempt to arrive at an answer to the puzzling question of why Clinton appears to require external correction in order to modify his style in ways that are plainly in his interest. Rather, I focus on the particular elements of his leadership that combine in different ways at different periods to account for his two political modes.

Clinton's Leadership Qualities

The account that follows of the components of Bill Clinton's oscillating political style takes the form of a series of observations and clusters of observations, set forth in a somewhat arbitrary sequence. Although this analysis has something of the atomized, static character of trait-psychology inventories of personal attributes, I set it forth in the form of a continuous narrative that is meant to suggest how these components fit together and come into play under varying circumstances.

Policy Concerns

High on any listing of the qualities Bill Clinton brings to his leadership is his passionate interest in public policy, especially domestic policy. Clinton is preoccupied with policy not just in the broad sense of having general policy aims but also in the narrower sense of being fascinated by the specific details of particular policies. Beginning in the Truman years, when the practice of the president presenting an annual legislative program came into being, all presidents have promulgated policies as part of their official responsibilities (Neustadt, 1954). But only a few presidents appear to have had much intrinsic interest in the detailed rationales for alternative policies.

Dwight Eisenhower brought to his presidency a deep concern for the logic of national security, which went back to his early career as a military planner and staff officer. John Kennedy developed a curiosity about the logic of policies while he was in office, largely as a consequence of his interactions with his more specialized advisers. And Jimmy Carter was notable for his preoccupation with the details of his own policies. But Clinton is an aficionado of policy in and of itself, not just the policies of his own administration, so much so that his rhetoric on the stump sometimes has more of the ring of the public policy school than of the political arena.

Interestingly, for a president who is so deeply fascinated with the rationale for and mechanics of his domestic policies, Clinton seemed for much of his first half-year in office to be almost oblivious to foreign policy. Neither his formative experiences as a Vietnam War protester nor his dozen years as governor of a small southern state appear to have led him to address himself in any sustained way to the larger world. Apart from occasional brief periods of intense involvement in foreign affairs on the occasions of his meeting with Soviet president Boris Yeltsin and participating in the Tokyo economic summit, Clinton appears almost to have delegated the larger world to his foreign policy team for much of his first year. He stepped into the commander in chief role only in October, when events in Somalia and Haiti made it evident that, like it or not, as commander in chief and head of state he could not confine himself to leadership in the domestic sphere.

Political Propensity

Clinton also stands out in the extent to which he is a political animal, although in a universe that includes Franklin Roosevelt, Lyndon Johnson, and Richard Nixon, his preoccupation with politics is less distinctive than his passion for policy. He is political both in the public sense of battening on the responses of the mass public and in the private sense of reveling in the arts of persuasion and cajolery. Moreover, he seems to have exhibited these qualities, at least in anticipatory form, from his earliest years. As the editor and compiler (Dumas, 1993, xvi) of a collection of reminiscences of citizens of Arkansas who knew Clinton at various points in his development put it:

> Few Americans ever had the exterior gifts of the politician in such abundance. Bill Clinton was handsome, loquacious, and tireless. He always exhibited a boundless optimism. He met people with grace and facility, and a prodigious memory never let him forget them. He had what seemed to be a compulsive need to meet people, to know them, to like them, to have them like him. These are the instincts of the calculating politician, but they long preceded Clinton's political impulses. Bill Clinton's is the case where a man's deepest human instinct perfectly matched, maybe even gave rise to, his most abiding ambition.

There is no obvious precedent in the modern presidency for a chief executive who combines a concern for and interest in politics and policy to the extent that Clinton does. It is as if the more cerebral side of John F. Kennedy's approach to leadership were writ large and amalgamated with Lyndon Johnson's proclivity to press the flesh, find ways to split the difference with his opponents, and otherwise practice the art of the possible.

Verbal Facility and Proclivity

The link between Clinton's policy and political orientations is his intelligence and formidable verbal facility. The record abounds with evidence of Clinton's seemingly effortless ability to elaborate at length about his policies with modifications of emphasis from audience to audience. The perfectly grammatical 100-odd-word sentences Clinton is able to spin out extemporaneously could not be more unlike the fractured prose of George Bush. Indeed, Clinton sometimes spins out statements of extraordinary complexity with seemingly effortless spontaneity, as in the following vintage utterance to the *Wall Street Journal* staff members to whom he granted his first interview after taking office, which juxtaposes two pairs of if-then propositions:

> The people who say that if I want to go to a four-year phased-in competition model [in connection with health care reform] and that won't save any tax money on the deficit in the first four years, but will save huge tax money on the deficit in the next four years, miss the main point, which is that if we have a system now which begins to move health care costs down toward inflation, and therefore lowers health care as a percentage of the GNP in the years ahead, the main beneficiaries by a factor of almost two to one will be in the private sector. (Clinton, 1992)

As exceptional as Clinton's verbal intelligence is, however, it is not clear whether he can make the kinds of sound, balanced judgments that are commonly summarized in the term *common sense,* and it is not certain whether he has a fundamentally analytic cast of mind that leads him to search for evidence that would lead him to accept or reject the assumptions behind the formulations he can verbalize with such facility. (On multiple intelligences, see Gardner, 1983.) Moreover, precisely because he is so facile, so well informed, and so profoundly political, it is difficult for others (and perhaps Clinton himself) to be sure of when and whether he is advancing a policy on the basis of its intrinsic merit and when he is trimming.

Dynamism and Ebullience

Other elements of the Clinton amalgam are an energy, exuberance, and optimism of truly remarkable proportions. Even when he was deeply beleaguered at the time of the New Hampshire primary, Clinton exhibited an optimism reminiscent of FDR's capacity to radiate confidence under conditions of extreme adversity. But unlike Roosevelt, Clinton has no war or Depression as a foil for these qualities, and he is not a natural dramatist. More fundamentally, he appears to lack a comprehensive strategic sense about how to present himself to the public and advance his policies.

Interestingly, Roosevelt, like Clinton, faced a "character issue" during the period when he was seeking the presidency. Part of the concern was about his very outgoing and cheerful qualities—his critics dismissed him as lacking in presidential stature, in large part because of what Edmund Wilson once described as his "unnatural sunniness." But such skepticism was forgotten in the wake of his magisterial assumption of power in March 1933 (Maney, 1992). Clinton's assumption of power, however, was anything but magisterial. Indeed, during the transition period between his election and his inauguration, Clinton received a quite favorable press for his performance in an economic "summit conference" he convened in Little Rock, Arkansas, and for such initial presentations as his interview with the *Wall Street Journal*. During that period his support, as measured in public opinion polls, was quite high. But by the time the first polls were conducted after he entered the White House, his administration had experienced a series of gaffes that significantly lowered his support levels (Greenstein, 1993-1994).

Lack of Discipline and Failure to Focus

Related to Clinton's energy, enthusiasm, intelligence, and devotion to policy is a cluster of more problematic traits—absence of self-discipline, hubristic confidence in his own views and abilities, and difficulty in narrowing his goals, ordering his efforts, and devising strategies for advancing and communicating the ends he seeks to achieve.

Insensitivity to Organization

Another of Clinton's traits is a predilection to take on large numbers of personal responsibilities and to do little to establish structures of delegation that divide the labor of his presidency and avail him with overall strategic advice.

The paradoxical result is that it is difficult for his administration to move on more than one track at a time, but at the same time he has a Jimmy Carter–like tendency to overload the national political agenda. This is the case in spite of Clinton's many statements during the transition of his intention to avoid Carter's difficulties and emulate Ronald Reagan in the single-minded pursuit of a limited number of major goals.

Because Clinton takes on so many responsibilities, his administration has been slow to make appointments, many of which are held up for clearance in the Oval Office (Pearl, 1993). In general, Clinton's exceptional talents are in great need of management lest he fly off in all directions, but he is not easily managed. Moreover, he appears not to have given much thought to problems of creating an effective staff. In this, he is a striking contrast with Eisenhower, who entered office with a well-developed view of the staff needs of the presidency and for whom effective delegation was an article of faith (Greenstein, 1984).

Given Clinton's energy and intelligence, he probably did not need to be very attentive to staffing in Little Rock, but he plainly does in Washington. He is said to be a student of the presidency and of American history, but he shows little awareness of the uses some presidents have made of well-designed formal organization (Burke, 1992). Indeed, he has acknowledged that he entered the White House with no plan for White House organization, whether at the informal or the formal level, and initially peopled his staff with aides who had little Washington experience and who lacked the stature to help him control his own centrifugal tendencies (Nelson and Donovan, 1933; Watson, 1993). This, of course, was the early story of his White House. Then he turned (with seemingly good results) to such Washington insiders as veteran Republican White House aide David Gergen for staff assistance (Frisby, 1993).

The Not-So-Great Communicator

As articulate as Clinton is, his record of communicating his aims to the public has been poor. Paradoxically, his fluency does not serve him well. He finds it all too easy to deluge the public with details, and it appears to be difficult for him to transcend policy mechanics and convey the broad principles and values behind his programs. Here, of course, he is the antithesis of Ronald Reagan, who was notoriously innocent of policy specifics but gifted at evoking larger themes.

Personal Charm

At the personal level, Clinton appears to be one of the more ingratiating incumbents of the Oval Office. In spite of being rather thin-skinned and having a quick temper, which occasionally is evident in public, he is fundamentally amiable, sometimes to the point where this is counterproductive. Thus, like Franklin Roosevelt, Clinton's congeniality sometimes leaves those who consult him with the false impression that he has accepted their views when he intends only to acknowledge that he has heard them.

Clinton's impulse to be agreeable feeds the familiar charge that he seeks to be all things to all people and reinforces the "Slick Willie" epithet that is turned against him by his enemies. Yet he made surprisingly limited use of his charm and persuasive powers in the early months of his presidency, perhaps because, like many bright, self-confident people, he is impatient with those who do not share his views and is therefore ill-disposed to take them seriously. Thus, he overestimated his ability to win support by appealing directly to the public through cable television, and he failed to cultivate the press. And he did little during the transition to win over such key Washington actors as Senators Sam Nunn (D.–Ga.) and Daniel Patrick Moynihan (D.–N.Y.). And once in office, Clinton was slow to do much to enlist the support of Republican moderates and Democratic conservatives.

Resilience and the Capacity for Taking Correction

I have left for last what seem to me to be Clinton's most redeeming traits— ones that bode favorably for his leadership in the long, if not the short, run: his remarkable capacity to rebound in the face of adversity, his fundamental pragmatism, and his capacity (in spite of his thin-skinned tendencies) to admit his own failings. This cluster of traits helps account for the commonly made observation that he is incapable of sustained error.

The Clinton Syntheses

Most of the components of Clinton's leadership style are not distinctive, but the magnitude of some of them and the way they fit together are. As I have suggested, there appear to be two Clinton syntheses. Under some circumstances his traits combine to form an undisciplined, have-it-all approach, and under others they converge in a more focused, accommodating style. When he is in the first mode, as he was in his initial term as governor of Arkansas as well as in his first months in the White House, Clinton is animated by his policy enthusiasm, his boundless energy, and his impatience with the views of those who do not share his policy vision. Even when he is in the first mode, however, he is no Woodrow Wilson, capable of bringing his own program to defeat by insisting that Congress take its medicine. But when Clinton pulls back after overreaching himself, his compromises are likely to have a disheveled, rear-guard quality, as was the case in his prolonged negotiations over gays in the military.

As I noted earlier, Clinton's second, more pragmatic, and focused mode of operation appears to come into play only after outside forces have constrained him. It is not clear why such an intelligent, politically aware leader, who knows in his heart that he should be laserlike in his focus, began his presidency in a scattered fashion or why he is so dependent on external correction. My task of examining Clinton's style does not require that I reach a settled conclusion about this and other questions that bear on his inner workings, including questions about the continuing uncertainty over who the "real" Bill Clinton is. Some answers are very likely to be found in his upbringing. Clinton and his aides have themselves drawn attention to his alcoholic stepfather, suggesting that Clinton's almost unsettling good cheer reflects the exaggerated need to be agreeable found in children (and stepchildren) of alcoholics (Kaufman and Pattison, 1982; Cruse, 1989). It is also the case that his younger stepbrother had a substance abuse problem.

Clinton's background in a family in which addictions played a significant part has an obvious bearing on his tendency to leave people with the misleading impression that he accepts their views. But his lack of self-discipline would appear to have other roots. At a minimum, Clinton, whose outward characteristics seem almost to have been custom-made to illustrate James David Barber's (1992) active-positive character type, shows the difficulty of categorization in that much of what is puzzling about him stems from inner complexities that do not figure in Barber's (or perhaps any other) classification.

More to the point may be the political psychology of Richard Neustadt, in which the accent is on "political" rather than "psychology." Neustadt's 1960 book nicely anticipated many of Clinton's problems. Neustadt, it will be remembered, stressed the fundamental weakness of the American chief executive in an era in which the nation's problems are huge, especially when there is little readiness on the part of the other members of the Washington community, whose support is needed to bring the president's program into being, to transcend political advantage and rally around him. The president, Neustadt argued, has two basic resources with which to accomplish his purposes above and beyond his executive powers and his ability to use them to bargain: his reputation with other policymakers as a skilled, determined player and their perception that he has the support of the public. (Neustadt's 1960 account remained fundamentally unaltered in its 1990 incarnation. See also the elaboration on Neustadt's formulation by Sperlich, 1975.)

Whither the Clinton Presidency?

In the early months of his presidency, Bill Clinton managed to diminish both of the resources Neustadt saw as the levers of presidential power. His political and policy propensities often converged in a manner that led him to be perceived by other members of the political community as inconstant and disingenuous, not only because he departed from previously held positions but also because his departures often seemed effortless. It would not matter much to members of the Washington community that a president seemed insincere ("What else is new?") if he was seen as having the public behind him. But Clinton was conspicuous for his failure to capture the imagination and enthusiasm of the American people.

Before he modified his style, Clinton was more Carter-like than Jimmy Carter in his seeming assumption that once elected he could put politics behind him. In fact, Clinton made even less effort than Carter to establish a favorable public persona. Once in office, Clinton's tendency was to confine himself to impersonal and distinctly noninspirational messages on such themes as the need to "grow the economy," and he and his associates did little to humanize his presidency. (For discussions of what citizens appear to expect of their presidents and of the president as interpreter of public aspirations, see Greenstein, 1974; Stuckey, 1991.) Then at about the midpoint of his first year in office, he entered into the previously noted transformation.

Once he moved to his second, more strategic mode in the summer of his first year in office, Clinton not only became more focused and accommodating; he also appeared to have realized that he needed to find ways to simplify and dramatize his appeals to the public. Striking deals with dissident Democrats, he brokered through a deficit reduction measure in the summer of 1993 and then departed on a vacation that some felt was as needed by the Washington policy community as by the president and his staff. He returned from vacation with what seemed to be an impossibly demanding political agenda—comprehensive reform of the nation's health system, the controversial North American Free Trade Agreement, and the gimmicky sounding "reinvention of government" proposals. But he used the latter for a remarkably effective set of well-publicized photo opportunities that for once showed his administration in a favorable light. He made a tour-de-force presentation of his health program to a joint session of Congress, shrewdly associating himself more with the program's general aims than with its specific provisions. And he largely delegated the promotion of NAFTA to others until almost the eleventh hour, when he engaged in a whirlwind of promotional and bargaining activity, achieving a victory in the House of Representatives that for the moment put to rest the view that Clinton would never be able to adapt his leadership skills to the complexities of politics in the nation's capital.

The jury was still out on the Clinton presidency at the end of President Clinton's first year in office. Nevertheless, there was little doubt that, whether by dint of his own far-reaching policy aspirations or the very power of the modern president to shape the nation's political agenda, the presidency of William Jefferson Clinton had directed the nation, at least in domestic policies, toward ends that would probably not even have been envisioned if the electorate had returned George Bush for a second term in November 1992.

References

Barber, J. D. (1992). *The Presidential Character: Predicting Performance in the White House*. 4th ed. Englewood Cliffs, N.J.: Prentice-Hall.

Burke, J. P. (1992). *The Institutional Presidency*. Baltimore, Md.: Johns Hopkins University Press.

Clinton, W. J. (1992). "Excerpts from the Interview with President-Elect Clinton." *Wall Street Journal*, December 18.

Cruse, S. W. (1989). *Another Chance: Hope and Health for the Alcoholic Family*. Palo Alto, Calif.: Science and Behavior Books.

Dumas, E., ed. (1993). *The Clintons of Arkansas: An Introduction by Those Who Know Them Best*. Fayetteville: University of Arkansas Press.

Frisby, M. K. (1993). "Communication Guru Gergen Works His Alchemy on Clinton to Improve Chemistry with the Press." *Wall Street Journal*, August 16.

Gardner, H. (1983). *Frames of Mind: The Theory of Multiple Intelligences*. New York: Basic Books.

Greenstein, F. I. (1974). "What the Presidency Means to Americans: Presidential 'Choice' Between Elections." In *Choosing the President*, ed. J. D. Barber, 124–148. Englewood Cliffs, N.J.: Prentice-Hall.

—— (1982). *The Hidden-Hand Presidency: Eisenhower as Leader*. New York: Basic Books.

—— (1984). "Centralization Is the Refuge of Fear: A Policy-maker's Use of a Proverb of Administration." In *The Costs of Federalism: Essays in Honor of James W. Fesler*, ed. R. T. Golembiewski and A. Wildavsky, 117–139. New Brunswick, N.J.: Transaction Books.

—— (1993-1994). "The Presidential Leadership Style of Bill Clinton: An Early Appraisal." *Political Science Quarterly* 108 (Winter):589–601.

Ifel, G. (1992). "Man in the News: William Jefferson Clinton." *New York Times*, July 16.

Kaufman, E., and E. M. Pattison (1982). "The Family and Alcoholism." In *Encyclopedic Handbook of Alcoholism*, ed. E. M. Pattison and E. Kaufman, 663–672. New York: Gardner.

Kolbert, E. (1992). "Early Loss Casts Clinton as a Leader by Consensus." *New York Times*, September 28.

Maney, P. J. (1992). *The Roosevelt Presidency: A Biography of Franklin Delano Roosevelt*. New York: Twain.

Nelson, J., and R. J. Donovan (1993). "The Education of a President: After Six Months of Quiet Success and Loud Failure, Bill Clinton Talks About the Frustrating Process of Figuring Out His Job." *Los Angeles Times Magazine*, August 1.

Neustadt, R. E. (1954). "The Presidency and Legislation: The Growth of Central Clearance." *American Political Science Review* 48:641–647.

—— (1990). *Presidential Power and the Modern Presidents: The Politics of Leadership from Roosevelt to Reagan*. New York: Free Press.

Pearl, D. (1993). "Clinton's Slow Pace in Making Appointments Affects Policy at Some Departments and Agencies." *Wall Street Journal*, August 20.

Sperlich, P. (1975). "Bargaining and Overload: An Essay on Presidential Power." In *Perspectives on the Presidency,* ed. A. Wildavsky, 406–430. Boston: Little, Brown.

Stuckey, M. E. (1991). *The President as Interpreter-in-Chief.* Chatham, N.J.: Chatham House.

Watson, J. (1993). "The Clinton White House," *Presidential Studies Quarterly* 23:429–436.

8

Advice and Advisers in the Clinton Presidency: The Impact of Leadership Style

MARGARET G. HERMANN

As leaders, American presidents face several policy dilemmas forced on them by the division of powers in the Constitution and the large executive bureaucracy that has developed over time: How can they maintain control over policy while still delegating authority (or having it delegated for them) to other actors in the government? How can they shape the policy agenda when situations are being defined and problems as well as opportunities are being perceived and structured by others in the political system? These concerns have precipitated an increase in the size of the White House staff as presidents have worked to improve coordination among the various entities that define and shape policy (cf. Hess, 1988; Light, 1991). As a result, the presidency has become a complex organization or advisory system (cf. Burke and Greenstein, 1991; Feldman, 1990). In effect, as in any organization, the president's staff extends his capabilities by increasing his "available attention, knowledge, and expertise" and by coordinating the behavior of the other units involved in making and implementing policy (Feldman, 1990, 17). Because the president participates in the selection of members of this organization and sets into place the norms and rules that determine its organizational culture, what the president is like (e.g., his personality, background, training) influences what his advisers are like and how his organization tackles policy issues. What the president is like helps shape the relationship among the advisers and his relationship with them. As Fred Greenstein (1988, 352) observed, "Leadership in the modern presidency is not carried out by the president alone, but rather by presidents with their associates. It depends therefore on both the president's strengths and weaknesses and on the quality of the aides' support"—

149

that is, on the nature of the relationship between a president and his associates.

This chapter explores how President Clinton structured his advisory system in the initial months of his presidency. It places Clinton in a framework built from previous studies that suggest how a president's leadership style influences the way he organizes and coordinates his advisory system. (For a review of these studies and a detailed presentation of the framework, see Hermann and Preston, 1994a, 1994b.)

Linking Presidential Leadership Style to Pattern of Authority and Policy Coordination

Pattern of Authority

Presidents appear to differ in the degree of control they need over the policy-making process. Complex organizations include people with different goals and interests. Although such differences generally cannot be resolved through voting, they can be resolved through the establishment of a hierarchy and a pattern of organizational authority (cf. Downs, 1967). How much control a president wants to exert over his advisory system helps shape the nature of the pattern of authority that develops.

Presidential interest in control is evident in the strategies a president prefers for managing information and conflict. If the president wants to make the final decision—that is, have his preferences prevail—he will seek to control what happens in the policymaking process. His is the ultimate authority, and it cannot be reversed. Similarly, such a president is likely to organize authority into a hierarchical system, with himself at the apex of a formal chain of command. Information processing, problem definition, and option generation will occur at lower levels and percolate up to the president. The advisory system will be organized to do things, and authority patterns will be well defined.

If, however, the president is more comfortable when decisions are made through consensus or concurrence, he is less likely to use a formal hierarchical pattern of authority. Who participates in decisionmaking and how structured the process is become determined largely by the situation and problem the president faces. There will be a looseness and informality to the pattern of authority that facilitate the president building consensus. Often leaders in an informal system manage information by putting themselves at the hub of the communications network. In this way they gain control over who gets what information as well as knowledge about what information others know. As a result, they have the basis on which to organize a decisionmaking unit that can reach consensus. In effect, the pattern of authority is more flexible and is structured and restructured in relation to the particular problem at hand. The president is still on top, but he has purposively chosen to involve others directly in decisionmaking and to use more informal channels of authority.

Policy Coordination

Presidents also appear to differ in how they coordinate the policymaking process. Coordination among advisers typically takes one of two forms—either a focus on building concurrence among relevant advisers or a focus on accomplishing a task. Scholarly research on group dynamics suggests that leaders play two major functions in groups—they help the group work through a task, or they facilitate group interaction, participation, and satisfaction (e.g., Bass, 1981; McGrath, 1984; Stogdill, 1974). This theme also appears in the literature on organizations, where researchers talk about the twin goals of leadership as organizational survival and policy achievement (e.g., Hargrove, 1989; Meier, 1989; Miller, 1987).

Building concurrence and a sense of belonging among members of a group and developing a climate of cooperation and support are critical to facilitating group satisfaction and organizational survival. Conflict and disagreement are perceived as dysfunctional in such an environment, as interest is centered around promoting a sense of community. At issue is how members are helped to feel a part of the group or organization and to see their participation as valued and needed. Generally there is little tolerance for conflict, and much attention is paid to providing approval and support. Translated to the presidential advisory system, presidents with a focus on group satisfaction and organizational survival will want advisers who feel empowered, who believe that their opinions and interests count, but who function best in a climate of cooperation and trust. The advisory system becomes a community of interlocking parts with a shared interest in containing conflict and disagreement and in enhancing common values and beliefs.

When coordination focuses on accomplishing the task or policy achievement, attention turns to getting something done. It is not how members feel about the group or organization but how present problems can be solved or defined that becomes the major impetus for action. There is a change from seeing the group as a community to perceiving the group as a producer. The emphasis is on solving problems and taking advantage of opportunities toward some end. There often are a sense of mission and a bottom line. Leadership facilitates movement on the mission and achievement of the goal. Conflict and disagreement are generally valued with such a focus because they introduce different perspectives into the discussion and enhance the chances for innovative solutions as members wrestle with their differences of opinion. Presidential advisory systems with this type of coordination are interested in doing a good job, in addressing issues facing the administration in an effective manner with positive results. Advisers do not have to like each other, but they

TABLE 8.1   Typology of Presidential Patterns of Authority and Policy Coordination

		Authority Pattern	
		Formal	Informal
Policy Coordination	Focus on political process	The chief executive officer (Truman & Nixon)	The team builder and player (Johnson, Ford, & Carter)
	Focus on substance of problem	The director/ideo-logue (Reagan)	The analyst/innova-tor(Franklin Roosevelt)

need to acknowledge and admire each other's problemsolving competencies and skills. This advisory system is like a well-oiled machine, with members both defining and carrying out roles and functions with the quality of the product in mind.

Scholars knowledgeable about the advisory systems of the Eisenhower and Johnson administrations (Burke and Greenstein, 1991, 290) have differentiated between two aspects of political reality testing—"the political component of selling policies and mustering the support necessary to win approval and the substantive component of devising and analyzing policies and the means of implementing them." These two components parallel the two ways of coordinating policy proposed here. The political component is similar to the focus on building concurrence and community; the substantive component is similar to the focus on accomplishing a task or policy achievement. In one, the emphasis is on the process of building support; in the other, the emphasis is on solving the problem and developing good policy.

A Possible Framework

The two types of authority patterns and the two ways of coordinating policy create a fourfold typology of advisory systems based on the president's leadership style. This typology is illustrated in Table 8.1. Each cell in the table indicates a different pattern of authority and policy coordination. The labels in the cells give an overall impression of the way a president's leadership style shapes the advisory system for the corresponding pattern. These labels describe the role that a president with each pattern plays in the policymaking process and, in turn, the kinds of advisers he will choose and how he will organize these advisers. Table 8.1 also suggests examples of presidents who appear to fit each type. The leadership style characteristics associated with each of the types is elaborated in Table 8.2. (These types are described in more detail in Hermann and Preston, 1994b.)

Table 8.3 indicates the kinds of advisers that these four types of presidents are likely to select and the relations they are likely to develop with these advis-

TABLE 8.2   Relationships Between Organizational Functions and Leadership Styles

| | | *Authority Pattern* | |
		Formal	Informal
	Focus on political process	Leader's preferences prevail	Make decisions through consensus or working majority
		Follow formal chain of command	Act as hub of information-gathering process
		Not very willing to tolerate conflict	Not very willing to tolerate conflict
Policy Coordination		Motivated to seek approval and support (power/status)	Motivated to seek approval and support (power/status)
	Focus on substance of problem	Leader's preferences prevail	Decisions made through consensus or working majority
		Follow formal chain of command	Act as hub of information-gathering process
		Willing to tolerate conflict	Willing to tolerate conflict
		Motivated to promote cause (complete task, do what is right)	Motivated to promote cause (complete task, do what is right)

ers. To this point, these four patterns of authority and coordination have been discussed as if they were mutually exclusive and pure types. An argument can be made that some presidents emphasize one or the other of the two dimensions that make up this typology—either authority or coordination—and move across the other dimension depending on the situation in which they find themselves. It can also be argued that presidents change who is involved in the advisory process as the nature of the problem or topic changes. In each case, aspects of the president's leadership style become linked with the characteristics of the context. When a particular contextual variable is present, it elicits certain aspects of the president's style.

James Barber (1977) argued that a president's first political success helps shape the leadership style he will depend on in future political settings. If this style continues to be rewarded with success in the future, it becomes even more a part of a president's repertoire. Presidents begin to rely on this style, and it defines the way they will approach decisionmaking and interpersonal interactions. There may, however, be certain situations in which presidents have

TABLE 8.3   The Influence of Presidential Leadership Style on Advisory Selection and Organization

		Authority Pattern	
		Formal	Informal
	Focus on political process	Loyalty important	Advisers seen as part of the team
		Advisers used as sounding board	Sharing of accountability
		Interested in focusing on important decisions	Group cohesion is valued
		Interested in evaluating, rather than generating, options	Advisers provide psychological support
		Leader-dominated groupthink possible	Options sought that minimize conflict and disagreement
Policy Coordination		Procedures well-defined and highly structured	
	Focus on substance of problem	Advisers selected who share cause/concern/ideology	Experts selected as advisers
		Advisers seen as implementors and advocates	Advisers seen as providing information and guidance
		Advisers tailor information to fit biases	Open to using bureaucracy to get information
		One or two advisers play gatekeeper role for information and access	Time spent on generating options and considering consequences
		Decisions shaped by shared vision	"Doable" solution sought to problem
		Disagreements center on means rather than ends	Disagreement is valued

found their usual leadership style is not useful and have learned to adapt it in order to cope with the demands placed on them. Knowing something about presidents' personalities can help shed some light on when such changes in leadership style are likely.

Elsewhere I (Hermann, 1993; Hermann and Hermann, 1989) demonstrated how leaders' sensitivity to the political context and information about what is happening can influence when contextual factors are likely to shape how they engage in decisionmaking. Leaders who show less sensitivity to contextual cues from their environments tend to be top-down information processors or cognitive misers. In effect, they are more ideological and principled, more reliant on heuristics to guide how they perceive any problem, less willing to deal with discrepant information, and more interested in advocating a specific option than in learning about alternative possibilities. Such leaders are more likely to find a leadership style that is successful in getting them what they want and to rely on it in most situations. These leaders will probably build an advisory system that is fairly stable across time and situation and evidences only *one* of the patterns in the typology.

Leaders who are more sensitive to contextual information appear to be bottom-up information processors or hypothesis testers. They use contextual information to guide what they do, being more pragmatic and opportunistic, interested in learning about discrepant information, and concerned about option generation. Leaders who are sensitive to contextual information are likely to use different types of advisory systems for different types of problems and will probably use information from the environment to guide whom they select to become part of the decision unit on any occasion.

The Bush presidency illustrates this interaction of leadership style and context. For many of the decisions in his administration, Bush used a team approach to decisionmaking, with consensus building and information sharing as the mechanisms for control and with a low tolerance for conflict and a strong need for approval defining what was a comfortable climate in which to operate (see Winter, Hermann, Weintraub, and Walker, 1991). He wanted team players around him who would be loyal and interested in participating in "bull sessions" and building consensus (Dowd and Friedman, 1990, 58). Group cohesion and minimization of conflict were the order of the day. At issue was making decisions that would play well with Congress, the media, and public opinion—"the focus was on managing the reaction" (Woodward, 1991, 81). But what happened to that advisory system when Bush felt himself backed into a corner—before the invasion of Panama, during the rescue of the savings and loan industry, during the Clarence Thomas ratification process? Bush appeared to shift his advisory needs from the type of system characterized by team building to one characterized by formal control and a problem focus. He became a man with a mission, wanting advisers who would act as advocates and implementors of his policy decisions; he became a director and ideologue. Only advisers who shared in Bush's vision became part of the inner circle. In effect, when Bush perceived a threat not only to the policies of his administration but also to policies important to his political well-being, he became more focused and driven to see something happen that would deal with the situation at hand. (For a more detailed look at the Bush administration, see Hermann and Preston, 1994b.)

The Clinton Advisory System

Building on the typology just presented, how would we classify the Clinton advisory system during the initial months of his presidency? In making judgments, I extrapolate from my personality profile of Clinton and his leadership style (Hermann, 1992) as well as from descriptions and observations of Clinton as governor of Arkansas, as a presidential candidate, and as president done by journalists and Clinton associates (e.g., Clift and Cohn, 1993; Dumas, 1993; Friedman, 1993; Goldman and Mathews, 1992; Levin, 1992; Safire, 1993; Turque and Clift, 1993).

Observations of Clinton throughout his political career suggest that he is sensitive to the political context. It has been noted that he is a "networking president," a president who continually runs for election, a president who thrives on friends (see Goldman and Mathews, 1992). A former Clinton chief of staff (Moore, 1993, 93) observed, "He always had boundless confidence in his ability to forge a consensus and work out any problem, if he could just get enough information and talk earnestly to everybody involved." A former legislative assistant (Roberts, 1993, 126) indicated that Clinton's interest in talking with everyone everywhere grows out of his distrust of the sanitized, self-serving sources often found around politicians. "He had learned that the problems, desires, and ideas of average people needed to be thrown into the [political] mix. These random exchanges served as sounding boards for Clinton to test his ideas and to learn what people really thought." His motto in his second gubernatorial campaign highlights the importance of information about the political terrain: "You can't lead without listening" (Levin, 1992, 149). Given this sensitivity to contextual information, we might expect Clinton to organize several types of advisory systems depending on the situation. And, indeed, his leadership style and choice of advisers suggest when he may have a need for different advisory structures.

A personality profile of Clinton (see Hermann, 1992) indicated that he is motivated both by a need to solve problems and a need for approval and support. He has learned to combine these two motives in his networking. By developing an elaborate set of Friends of Bill that cuts across different types of constituencies, groups, and organizations, Clinton maintains an information-gathering system that provides data on a variety of people's needs and opinions as well as on support and interest in him and his ideas. Information is, in effect, power and ensures that what appears to be good public policy can be merged with the political realities of the moment (cf. Roberts, 1993). His interest in solving problems forces him to tackle policy issues head-on, but issues where there is at least a 50-50 chance for success. He is not interested in working for policies that are assured success or for which there is little chance of thoughtful consideration. He wants to take on the causes that challenge his political skills. He appears to be driven by a set of principles that help shape the positions he takes, although "his approach to seeking solutions is now different from that he embraced in his early days in politics. He has learned to listen, and he has come to understand that compromise on details can advance principles more than can uncompromising failure. It might be only half a loaf, but, while it is not cake, it is not an empty plate either" (Smith, 1993, 16).

Clinton does not like confrontation: "Negotiation rather than muscle is an impulse of Clinton's character" (Roberts, 1993, 124). As Jonathan Alter (1993, 32) observed, Clinton is a "gifted carrot man, proffering it with a deftness that even his enemies admire. But the stick has never rested comfortably in his paws." Building a consensus and working out a compromise are natural parts of his personality. Conflict is "learned, labored, and avoided whenever possible" (Alter, 1993, 32). And "his unique ability to bring opposing sides and forces together is legend" in Arkansas (Pryor, 1992, xix). As one administrative assistant (Smith, 1993, 14) noted, "[He sees] the nuances or differences and shades of opinion. Where I assumed that zero-sum choices were the only option, he saw the possibility for greater consensus and sought the advantages for compromise among competing interests." The downside of this ability to see the different hues in the political context is that "it nurtures Clinton's love of detail and obsessive inability to make final decisions" (Turque and Clift, 1993, 21).

Clinton's leadership style predisposes him toward the team-building approach to advisory systems. Like the captain of a football or basketball team, in this advisory system the leader is dependent on others to work with him to make things happen. Such leaders are interested in arriving at decisions through consensus and see themselves at the center of the information-gathering process. Working as a team means that advisers are empowered to participate in all aspects of policymaking and to share in the accountability for what happens. There is a desire to create an environment where all members of the team feel comfortable and have a sense of loyalty to the leader. Moreover, members of the team are sensitive to and supportive of the beliefs and values of the leader. In support of such a description of the Clinton White House, William Safire (1993, 28) commented, "[It is] a loose, free-flowing, grimly anti-hierarchical staff structure, where collegiality is a virtue." As two journalists (Turque and Clift, 1993, 21) observed early on in the Clinton administration: "All roads lead to the president; more than a dozen aides have direct access to the Oval Office. ... The result is an endless seminar on politics and public policy."

An examination of Clinton's terms as governor, his presidential campaign, and his early days in the presidency suggests that he has had to learn each time not to trust his predispositions when it comes to advisory systems. Although aides attest to this type of advisory system for early campaigns and early political offices (see, e.g., Moore, 1993; Roberts, 1993; Smith, 1993), it tends to lead to no one being in charge and a whirlwind of activity that is suggestive of disorganization and can trigger miscommunication and misunderstanding (Goldman and Mathews, 1992). Friends attribute the problems to what they call the Clinton Factor (cf. Clift and Cohn, 1993; Dumas, 1993; Turque and Clift, 1993):

His perpetual lateness

His quick temper

His talking to the very last person at an event

His complaining about lack of free time when all those he has invited actually drop by

His limitless energy

His love of politics and the horsetrading, cajoling, logrolling, and trench fighting that make up consensus building

His desire to be in the center of everything

His thriving on chaos and uncertainty,

His perseverance and determination

Those with him on the team soon lose sight of the big picture and expend their energy in managing his schedule and him. As one aide noted, "He is like Beethoven's Pastoral Symphony—violent storms followed by calm as he takes the longer view" (Mathews, 1993, 40).

In both the presidential campaign and the first months of the presidency, the recognition of these problems led to two types of advisory systems that built to Clinton's strengths. In the presidential campaign, the changes began with the "Manhattan Project" in April 1992; in the presidency they came with what Safire (1993) and others have called the second Clinton administration. Aides realized that when Clinton knows what he wants and has a particular goal in mind, he is interested in taking charge—in playing the chief executive officer (CEO) role as described in Tables 8.1, 8.2, and 8.3. His emphasis shifts to the political process and building the consensus needed to achieve at least some of his policy goals. But when he has little expertise in a problem arena or has not yet settled on an option, Clinton is more interested in gathering information—in playing the role of analyst and innovator. His focus is on problemsolving, and he wants all the perspectives and views he can get—the wider and more diverse, the better.

In each case the advisory system provides the climate in which Clinton can bring his problemsolving and networking skills to bear on the problem. But by separating the formulation from the implementation stages, he can satisfy his need to build a good policy in one setting and his need to gain approval in the other setting. His interest in looking at all sides of a question—in "endlessly circling around a subject" (Clift, 1993, 39)—is engaged in the advisory system that allows him to be the analyst and innovator. His belief that people can reason together is captured in the system that enables him to sell a policy. Both advisory systems play to his skills as a negotiator and consensus builder and to his love of "in-the-trenches" politics. Let us explore each of these advisory systems in more detail.

When he is wrestling with what a particular policy should be, Clinton is the analyst and innovator, wanting to be at the center of what is going on and wanting to have policies argued and debated in front of him. At these times he seeks out expert opinion and encourages presentation of a range of possible options. That positions may be conflicting is not as important as that a variety of perspectives is represented. When Clinton becomes convinced of a particular option, he wants a chain of command that is loyal and skillful in massaging the political process. He becomes the CEO interested in having his advisers facilitate getting others on board. In effect, Clinton prefers an informal setting for shaping policy and a more formal setting for selling it. In his mind there is a difference between how a policy is put together and how it is pushed through politically. A wide-ranging brainstorming session or set of focus groups facilitates the formation of policy, the understanding of the issues, and the shaping of options. A more ordered system, with people knowing their functions and limits, is needed when a policy is being worked through the political process.

Given the Clinton Factor, it has become apparent that if policies are going to be passed and constituencies satisfied, the president cannot be completely in charge of either of these types of advisory systems. In each case the organization needs a manager who can see the big picture and has the authority to define and put into place norms, rules, and procedures. For the CEO-type advisory system and implementation of a plan, James Carville played this role in the presidential campaign with his war room in Little Rock and the sign "The Economy, Stupid." David Gergen assumed this role in the so-called second Clinton administration, adding experience and calming relations with the media. For the analyst-innovator advisory system, Clinton has also selected managers and given them authority to investigate and develop initial options, to find out whom he should hear from, and to keep him abreast of problems. Stan Greenberg took on this role in the presidential campaign in designing the focus of the campaign. For the area Clinton believed most important for his administration—health care—he gave his wife, Hillary Rodham Clinton, this role. He had successfully placed her in charge of formulating a similar critical legislative program on education in Arkansas. As Paul Greenberg (1993, 121) wrote in the *Arkansas Times* at the time, "If anyone deserves more credit than Clinton for awakening Arkansas to the needs of its young people, it may be Mrs. Clinton. As chairman of the statewide committee on standards in education, Hillary Rodham Clinton helped educate a whole state, not excluding her husband." Robert Rubin as head of the new National Economic Council fulfills this same type of role with regard to economic policy.

Clinton's choices of cabinet members also reflect the distinction between process and substance. He has chosen individuals with process skills to lead agencies important to implementing policy in areas where he already has positions and is interested in having things happen. And he has selected people who are known for their innovative ideas for positions where he is uncertain about what needs to be done. Thus, for example, in the economic arena he has put into cabinet positions people who are good at process and can help in working his programs through Congress. In the field of defense he has chosen people who are idea generators and likely to help him explore the new ways of defining national and international security demanded by changes in the international system.

To the extent that Clinton has surveyed the range of opinion on a particular problem before making a decision, this two-tiered advisory organization can work effectively. When, however, key constituents or players are excluded from the problem defining or option selection process, these parties can become difficult during the selling of the policy. The initial exclusion of key congressional and defense personnel from consideration of the policy banning gays and lesbians in the military is a case in point. When these constituencies were told that they were not being consulted on whether to end the ban but only on how best to implement such a change, they raised all kinds of problems with the proposed policy (cf. Mathews, 1993, 35).

This two-tiered advisory organization can also lead to confusion when media, constituents, special interests, and members of Congress do not realize which part of the process they are involved with. When the focus is on shaping policy, Clinton wants to listen to a wide range of opinions and perspectives, to search out those who are affected by what happens, to ask questions and seek feedback on possible options. He is open to people's ideas and continually looks for what will satisfy the problem and the largest number of constituencies. He is interested in figuring out how to bring policy and politics together. People often leave such sessions, however, sure he has accepted their ideas and will do what they want, whereas he sees the sessions as providing him with better information on which to base a choice (see Moore, 1993; Smith, 1993).

When Clinton is selling a policy, he wants to know which constituents see themselves as having interests, pro as well as con, in the particular policy and what building a compromise will take. At this time he sees the political process "like an intellectual game board on which all the players should be willing to sacrifice a few pieces so that they could advance their own positions. His objective [is] not to give up anything that [will] ultimately cause him to lose either his political or policy goals" (Roberts, 1993, 129). He wants a solution that is mutually beneficial to all—or, rather, a compromise in which all gain some of what they want while only having to give up a little of what they want. For those with an adversarial or zero-sum view of politics, where there should always be a clear winner and loser, such tactics make Clinton seem as if he has no principles or, at the least, is wishy-washy and weak.

For Clinton, the bottom line is that politics is the art of the possible. There will always be another chance, another time to try to get more. In effect, there is forever next year. As one Arkansas state senator said, "He's like one of those broad-bottomed toys that when you thump it over, it pops back up. No matter how many times you push it down, it pops right back up again. That's Clinton. We reject one of his plans, and he comes right back at us saying, 'OK, then, why don't we try to do it another way?'" (Ivins, 1993, C7). Quitting is not a word in Clinton's vocabulary—particularly not for those things that he cares about or that he thinks will make a difference. If his advisory systems work well, the result of the formulation stage is a broad-gauged, well-conceived policy that will go a long way toward solving the problem under consideration. The result of the selling stage is that part of the policy that the public and elite will accept at the moment. In Clinton's mind, the policy that is agreed to will probably be more extensive and useful in the long run than if bits and pieces of the policy had been put forward in an incremental fashion. As Ernest Dumas (1993, xvi) observed, however, this style raises the hopes of all constituencies and then disappoints most of them. "Led to expect miracles, they [are] dismayed at simple good works."

Conclusion

This chapter has focused on how the president's leadership style—in particular, that of Bill Clinton—influences the nature of the White House and its organization. As one scholar observed (Hess, 1988), the president's style, his work habits, how he likes to receive information, the people he prefers around him, and the way he makes up his mind are all key to how the White House is organized. In Clinton's case, his style has led to a two-tiered advisory system that changes as the policy process moves from the problem definition and option generation stage to the implementation stage. His is a different kind of presidency because he involves his various constituencies in all parts of the policymaking process. His style is one of "search and check"—search for information that will bring about good policy and check where relevant constituencies stand to see if consensus is possible. Everyone is fair game as a sounding board for ideas and as a person to be persuaded. The structure of the advisory system differs depending on whether Clinton is searching or checking. He prefers getting a variety of perspectives in the search process; but he wants to be in charge and have loyal allies in support during the checking process.

Thomas Friedman (1993, D1) has used a sailing metaphor to describe Clinton and his administration that is appropriate here. According to Friedman, Clinton is arguing that the ship of state can no longer remain in port. "It must head into stormy seas, even if the captain doesn't always know what he is doing or precisely where he is going, because the bay is no longer safe. The unemployed, the underinsured, the undereducated, the crisis of competitiveness, the burden of debt make sitting idle impossible." "Hang onto your deck chairs, folks. This is the Clinton Administration. Its seamanship may leave something to be desired, but you may just get where you are going, and if you like the unexpected, you may even enjoy it."

Notes

This chapter is a revision of an earlier version presented at the 1993 annual meeting of the American Political Science Association, Washington, D.C., September 2–5, 1993. The profiling and theoretical framework on which this chapter is based were completed with support from a grant from the National Science Foundation (DIR-9113599) to the Research Training Group on the Role of Cognition in Collective Political Decision Making at the Mershon Center, Ohio State University.

References

Alter, Jonathan (1993). "Where Are the Bone-Crushers?" *Newsweek,* February 22, 32.

Barber, James David (1977). *The Presidential Character.* Englewood Cliffs, N.J.: Prentice-Hall.

Bass, Bernard M. (1981). *Stogdill's* Handbook of Leadership: *A Survey of Theory and Research.* New York: Free Press.

Burke, John P., and Fred I. Greenstein (1991). *How Presidents Test Reality: Decisions on Vietnam, 1954 and 1965.* New York: Russell Sage Foundation.

Clift, Eleanor (1993). "The Reinvention of Al Gore." *Newsweek,* November 13, 39.

Clift, Eleanor, and Bob Cohn (1993). "Seven Days." *Newsweek,* July 12, 19–29.

Dowd, Maureen, and Thomas L. Friedman (1990). "The Fabulous Bush and Baker Boys." *New York Times Magazine,* May 6.

Downs, Anthony (1967). *Inside Bureaucracy.* Boston: Little, Brown.

Dumas, Ernest, ed. (1993). *The Clintons of Arkansas: An Introduction by Those Who Know Them Best.* Fayetteville: University of Arkansas Press.

Feldman, Martha S. (1990). "Organization Theory and the Study of the Presidency." Paper presented at the Institute for Policy Studies, University of Pittsburgh, Pittsburgh, Pennsylvania.

Friedman, Thomas L. (1993). "Coming About: Clinton's Sailing Isn't Smooth, But It's Sailing." *New York Times,* June 20, D1.

Goldman, Peter, and Tom Mathews (1992). "America Changes the Guard." *Newsweek* (Special election issue) (November-December):20–85.

Greenberg, Paul (1993). "His Finest Hour." In *The Clintons of Arkansas: An Introduction by Those Who Know Them Best,* ed. Ernest Dumas, 116–121. Fayetteville: University of Arkansas Press.

Greenstein, Fred I. (1988). *Leadership in the Modern Presidency.* Cambridge: Harvard University Press.

Hargrove, Erwin C. (1989). "Two Conceptions of Institutional Leadership." In *Leadership and Politics,* ed. Bryan D. Jones, 57–83. Lawrence: University of Kansas Press.

Hermann, Margaret G. (1992). "Profiles of Bush, Perot, and Clinton: How Their Personalities Are Likely to Influence Policy." Address presented at Drew University, Madison, New Jersey, October 30.

_____ (1993). "Leaders and Foreign Policy Decision Making." In *Diplomacy, Force, and Leadership: Essays in Honor of Alexander George,* ed. Dan Caldwell and Timothy McKeown, 77–94. Boulder: Westview.

Hermann, Margaret G., and Charles F. Hermann (1989). "Who Makes Foreign Policy Decisions and How: An Empirical Inquiry." *International Studies Quarterly* 33:361–387.

Hermann, Margaret G., and Thomas Preston (1994a). "Presidents, Advisers, and Foreign Policy: The Effect of Leadership Style on Executive Arrangements." *Political Psychology* 15:75–96.

_____ (1994b). "Presidents and Their Advisers: Leadership Style, Advisory Systems, and Foreign Policy Making." In *Domestic Sources of American Foreign Policy,* ed. Eugene R. Wittkopf, 340–356. New York: St. Martin's.

Hess, Stephen (1988). *Organizing the Presidency.* Washington, D.C.: Brookings Institution.

Ivins, Molly (1993). "Give President Clinton a Little Credit." *Kansas City Star,* August 20, C7.

Klein, Joe (1993). "A High-Risk Presidency." *Newsweek,* May 3, 32–33.

Levin, Robert E. (1992). *Bill Clinton: The Inside Story.* New York: SPI Books.

Light, Paul (1991). *The President's Agenda: Domestic Policy Choice from Kennedy to Carter.* Baltimore, Md.: Johns Hopkins University Press.

Mathews, Tom (1993). "Clinton's Growing Pains." *Newsweek,* May 3, 34–40.

McGrath, Joseph E. (1984). *Groups: Interaction and Performance.* Englewood Cliffs, N.J.: Prentice-Hall.

Meier, Kenneth J. (1989). "Bureaucratic Leadership in Public Organization." In *Leadership and Politics,* ed. Bryan D. Jones. Lawrence: University of Kansas Press.

Miller, Gary J. (1987). "Administrative Dilemmas: The Role of Political Leadership." Political Economy Working Paper. St Louis, Mo.: Washington University, June.

Moore, Rudy Jr. (1993). "They're Killing Me Out There." In *The Clintons of Arkansas: An Introduction by Those Who Know Them Best,* ed. Ernest Dumas, 85–94. Fayetteville: University of Arkansas Press.

Pryor, David (1992). "Introduction" to *Bill Clinton: The Inside Story,* by Robert E. Levin, xvii–xxi. New York: SPI Books.

Roberts, Bobby (1993). "Everyone Will Do the Right Thing." In *The Clintons of Arkansas: An Introduction by Those Who Know Them Best,* ed. Ernest Dumas, 122–130. Fayetteville: University of Arkansas Press.

Safire, William (1993). "Who's Got Clout?" *New York Times Magazine,* June 20, 25–28, 33–34.

Smith, Stephen A. (1993). "Compromise, Consensus, and Consistency." In *The Clintons of Arkansas: An Introduction by Those Who Know Them Best,* ed. Ernest Dumas, 1–16. Fayetteville: University of Arkansas Press.

Stogdill, Ralph D. (1974). *Handbook of Leadership*. New York: Free Press.

Turque, Bill, and Eleanor Clift (1993). "The Staff Shuffle." *Newsweek*, June 7, 20–21.

Winter, David G., Margaret G. Hermann, Walter Weintraub, and Stephen G. Walker (1991). "The Personalities of Bush and Gorbachev Measured at a Distance: Procedures, Portraits, and Policies." *Political Psychology* 12:115–145.

Woodward, Robert (1991). *The Commanders*. New York: Simon and Schuster.

PART IV

*Public Psychology and
President Clinton*

9

President Clinton Meets the Media: Communications Shaped by Predictable Patterns

MARTHA JOYNT KUMAR

It was a warm, sunny, late spring afternoon in the White House Rose Garden. A group of reporters and staff members was assembled for what was to highlight a presidential victory. President Bill Clinton intended to introduce Judge Ruth Bader Ginsburg to the American people as his nominee to fill a vacancy on the Supreme Court. Unwittingly the event turned from being an occasion that framed a successful presidential decision into one that revealed the president's and the White House press corps' mutual disdain. Following Judge Ginsburg's review of her road to the Court, the president opened the news conference to reporters. Brit Hume, the White House correspondent for ABC News, began the questioning with a query relating to the decision-making process used by the White House to select nominees for government positions. He asked, "Mr. President, the result of the Guinier nomination, sir, and your apparent focus on Judge Breyer, and, your turn, late it seems, to Judge Ginsburg may have created an impression, perhaps unfair, of a certain zigzag quality in the decisionmaking process here. I wonder, sir, if you could kind of walk us through it and perhaps disabuse us of any notion we might have along those lines."[1] The president, who considered the news media to be an unfair and unrelenting critic of him and his administration, exploded. "I have long since given up the thought that I could disabuse some of you of turning any substantive decision into anything but a political process," snapped an angry president.[2] He continued, "How you could ask a question like that after the statement she just made is beyond me." His temper dominating, the president bid good-bye to the assembled group of reporters, turned, and left.

President Clinton's first year in office, in fact, was one characterized by occasional public flare-ups with reporters. More important, however, though less obvious, was his recognition of the news media as an essential resource in governing. He may not trust or like reporters or the news organizations they represent, but he now understands that if he is to govern effectively, he must use the press as a channel to his targeted public. Bill Clinton came to office committed to a laundry list of domestic policy issues ranging from the budget deficit and health care to welfare reform, executive reorganization, family leave, and abortion rights. In order to enact legislation in so many contentious policy areas, he must have public support, which is the momentum that drives Congress. With public support, a president can influence reluctant members; without it, neither policy change nor direction is assured. To mobilize public support, a president must clearly define his policies and the legislation he has crafted. News organizations are the interpreters used to translate his initiatives for the public. The president must lay out lucidly his proposed legislation and define how it relates to the problems experienced by the citizenry. The stakes involved in effective use of the news media are high, particularly for a president with a long agenda.

Although Bill Clinton understood how news organizations could spread the word of his candidacy as he ran for the presidency, he did not fully appreciate the role the same organizations would play once he was elected. On his first day in office, reporters were barred from areas within the White House where they had previously been free to roam. The president initially believed that he did not need the traditional press corps, as had other presidents, because he had new outlets to exploit. "You know why I can stiff you on press conferences?" President Clinton badgered his audience as he spoke before a radio and television correspondents association. "Because Larry King liberated me from you by giving me the American people directly."[3] Within his first year in office, the president learned the limitations of his statement. Having appeared only twice on Larry King's television show during 1993, one could say that Larry King was of marginal value in carrying the presidential message. President Clinton might have been able to avoid having press conferences, but he needed the press corps.

Only a day after the Rose Garden rebuke of Brit Hume, President Clinton did an about-face that underscored his recognition of the news media's importance. In a tacit acknowledgment of the institutional roots of the relationship between the presidency and the media, Clinton came to the pressroom. He took questions from reporters, beginning with Brit Hume.[4] In so doing, Clinton confirmed that this tacit understanding requires the president to transcend whatever personal pique he may feel toward individual reporters. Although it is difficult to govern with news organizations breathing down one's neck, it is also impossible to govern without their presence. With this realization, each president learns to direct his responses to news organizations and their representatives in ways that acknowledge this fact. He soon learns the rhythms of the press and shapes his communications strategies accordingly. Presidential displays of anger do erupt from time to time but are soon followed by ameliorative responses, as was the case in the Rose Garden outburst.

Communications strategies are a hallmark of a presidency. Because the president's attitudes and use of news organizations reflect his notions of how a president leads, his relations with news organizations are important to an understanding of his term in office. A president's relations with the press are a product of his personality and his way of doing things, his aims as president, and his party attachment. He is shaped by these factors but also uses them to structure his relations with the public, government institutions, and news organizations. The personal style of a president is important in determining how he will disseminate information to his various publics. All presidents deliver messages through the media. Yet presidents vary in the forums they use, the frequency of their contacts, and the general atmosphere around their dealings with the media. Usually they do what they are comfortable doing. President Clinton (and Ronald Reagan as well) is not comfortable holding frequent press conferences. He prefers to deal with news organizations in other ways, such as through surrogates, daily press briefings by administration spokespeople, and talk shows and studio audience question-and-answer sessions.

A second element important in shaping a president's relationship with news organizations is the party in control of the White House. Party is a barometer of White House organization. Republicans favor a centrally organized staff structure, with communications controlled by the president's most senior advisers. Here long-range planning is an essential element in communications planning. In Democratic administrations, including the Clinton White House, a different pattern emerges. The White House organization is loosely structured, and communications strategies center on daily contacts with news organizations. Planning gives way to keeping up with day-to-day events and monitoring how the president is being portrayed. The differences in how Democratic and Republican White Houses are organized has an impact on the perception of communications' importance in an administration's policy achievements.

A third element in the establishment of communications policies and strategies is found in the goals of an administration. Presidential communications strategies vary depending on what a president seeks to do during his tenure of office. If an administration hopes to bring about reform in the domestic policy arena, as President Clinton surely has sought to do, it adopts a set of communications strategies quite different from those of a president who works to prevent erosion in policies already adopted and in coalitions already formed.

As was true of his predecessors, the mix of these three elements—personal style, party control of the White House, and the goals of the administration— shaped the relationship that President Clinton developed with news organizations in his first year in office. Understanding how he perceives and uses news organizations as a resource in governing is central to an understanding of his presidency. For communications lie at the heart of a presidency. His ability to articulate a program and subsequently rally support for his policies is crucial to the success of his administration. An ability to present himself and his program is essential for any president but is especially important with Bill Clinton's vast agenda. During his first year, Clinton showed a capacity to recognize and correct his deficiencies as a leader. One of the major changes was in the area of communications. Gradually he came to appreciate that a program had to be sold to the public and to Congress through a coordinated effort of administration policy leaders, White House staff, and himself.

The Personal Style of the President

The personal style of a president is critical to the shape of his communications policies and strategies just as it is to the programs he is seeking to enact. His style has both a direct and an indirect impact on his relationship with the news media and his place in print and on the air. Two aspects characterize the direct ways that his personal style influences that relationship with the media: first, his contacts with reporters and news organizations and second, his view of the media as a resource in governing. Indirectly, his style is important in how he organizes his White House and the communications structure within it. For President Clinton initially, the news media represented an impediment to leadership, not a resource. He looked to news organizations as institutions whose impact he wanted to minimize. His interest in his dealings with White House correspondents aimed more at keeping his distance than at winning them over.

President Clinton: The Press as a Nuisance

The news media are an enormous force to be reckoned with on the modern presidential campaign trail. During the months when candidates are winnowed from close to a dozen down to two or three, the judgment of news organizations has been critical to the outcome. If reporters raise questions about the reputation of a candidate during those early months, the candidate is generally the loser. In 1992, however, one candidate survived in spite of the questions that were raised about his marital infidelity and even actions to avoid service in the Vietnam War. That candidate was Bill Clinton. His ability to survive two months of negative coverage during the pivotal New Hampshire and New York primaries might have easily convinced him that he could survive on the national political scene in spite of a negative press.

At a minimum, his early experience shaped his view of the place he would give to the national media in his presidency: as little as possible. News organizations are a permanent nuisance to President Clinton. They write the wrong stories, miss the important topics, and dog him all the while. Early in his term, he told a group representing the Newspaper Association of America how he believed the press worked: "When you're not in a campaign, when you have to stay there and go to work, you are at the mercy of press coverage."[5] To Clinton, news organizations represent an impediment to effective governing, not a resource. He complained that the defeat of his $16 billion economic stimulus package received "50 times the press coverage" that was given the successful budget resolution involving much greater sums. "Why?" he asked. "Because we won. And we won in record time and in short order." The only items that he felt received attention from the press were those policy initiatives that were heading south. "I'm not critical." he said. "That's just the way this whole deal works."[6] To Bill Clinton, a president is at the mercy of the press. He believes there are few resources to influence the manner in which his administration is treated in the articles and pieces that appear about him and his policies.

His opinions, if anything, have hardened. In response to a question posed by William Greider for *Rolling Stone* magazine, President Clinton fingered the press as the institution and its reporters as the individuals who have prevented him from getting his presidency to his supporters in terms that reflected the accomplishments of his administration. "I have fought more damn battles here for more things than any president has in 20 years, with the possible exception of Reagan's first budget, and not gotten one damn bit of credit from the knee-jerk liberal press, and I am sick and tired of it, and you can put that in the damn article," he said to Greider.[7] When asked his reaction to the knowledge that at least one of his early supporters now classified himself as a person disappointed in the president's performance, Clinton responded angrily: "But I do care that that man has a false impression of me because of the way this administration has been covered. It is wrong. That's my answer. It is wrong. I have fought my guts out for that guy, and if he doesn't know it, it's not all my fault. And you get no credit around here for fighting and bleeding. And that's why the know-nothings are the do-nothings and the negative people and the right-wingers always win. Because of the way people like you [William Greider] put questions to people like me."[8]

President Clinton's White House experience with the media has taught different lessons than those he learned on the campaign trail. While never accepting news organizations as a resource, by late spring he understood that they could do him harm. As June began, Clinton found the level of acrimony between himself/his White House staff and the press to be at an unacceptable level. Clearly harm was being done. The public was losing confidence in his leadership. Clinton attributed this to the coverage he was receiving in the press. Realizing that his relationship with news organizations needed reorganizing and that the talent to refashion it did not lie with the coterie of aides in his White House, Clinton reached to the outside for help. He brought in David Gergen, a communications expert from the Nixon, Ford, and Reagan years. Clearly one of President Clinton's personal strengths is an ability to return to a problem and view it from a different angle. He knows when he is in trouble and is willing to go beyond the familiar to get himself out of rocky terrain.

Personal Relations with Reporters

Differences in presidential relations with the media can derive from factors relating to a president's own personality and style. Bill Clinton counts no reporters among his intimates, but others have. John Kennedy, for example, liked reporters and found them engaging as verbal sparring partners. Lyndon Johnson saw reporters frequently because he enjoyed having people around him who listened to him and marked his words. He met formally and informally with reporters, hoping either personally or officially to persuade reporters to be his friends. Gerald Ford also enjoyed the company of reporters and was very responsive to their requests for time with him. He brought reporters into the White House for social occasions, including having the Sperling breakfast group (a group of print media people who informally questioned government officials over an early morning meal) meet with him there. Unlike Clinton, all of these presidents were comfortable with reporters and chose to spend time with them. George Bush also shared this camaraderie. Whether it was calling reporters to come over for lunch on the spur of the moment or to join him for a movie, he sought them out. In addition, he made many spontaneous and unannounced visits to the pressroom just to see if reporters might have questions for him. For each of these presidents, the shape of his media relationship was formed in part through his personal style and interests.

President Clinton, by predilection and in self-defense, has chosen to join a group of presidents who keep their distance from reporters. Jimmy Carter, Ronald Reagan, Richard Nixon, and Dwight Eisenhower all preferred to confine their meetings with the press to formal occasions. Their reasons for doing so may have varied, but the fact of the distance remained. President Reagan, however, was always more willing to meet the media and answer their questions than his campaign and White House staffs wanted him to be. His staffs' efforts were aimed at minimizing his informal press contacts, preferring instead to use him in formal settings, where his talents could be displayed to his advantage. Because of an antipathy for small talk, President Carter only infrequently met with reporters on an informal basis. He did not make light, easy conversation with anyone, not just reporters. That was his personal style. President Nixon was driven by suspicion of the media's true interests in shaping his contacts with reporters. He kept them at a distance, as had President Eisenhower before him.

At Arm's Length: The Washington Press Corps

"Clinton had a great theory that he didn't need us," said James Perry, national political correspondent for the *Wall Street Journal*.[9] "He would do E mail." Even though President Clinton has established a sophisticated computer access operation through the Office of Media Affairs and its director, Jeff Eller, there is no indication that this operation has produced any substantive personal or policy gains for the president. Nor has MTV. A White House communications first, Clinton used MTV to publicize his National Service Corps program. In fact, his first exclusive television interview from the White House was with Tabitha Soren of MTV.[10]

In another first, Clinton held a question-and-answer session in the White House with a group of children even before he held a press conference with the White House press corps. An unusually long two months of his term would elapse before he turned to the more traditional media for an exchange. Town meetings around the country were another forum as he looked to an audience to which he might respond. His enthusiasm for spontaneous give-and-take is understandable considering the nature of the relaxed questions he receives in those venues. They allow greater latitude for personal shaping. A press conference is a different matter. It is not easy being bored in on by reporters who structure questions to get specific answers and who allow as little wiggle room as possible to elicit their desired response. Any president would rather receive and reply as Clinton did at a town hall meeting:

> Q: Hello, Mr. President—President Clinton. My question is, my birthday is tomorrow and I'm twelve years old tomorrow, and my question is, what kind of future am I going to have in store for me and the country?
> The President: That's a neat question, isn't it? (Laughter) I think you've got a very bright future. The world you will live in will be freer of the threat of total destruction than any world we've ever known.[11]

Imitating Cecil Fielder, Clinton stepped up to the question and hit it approximately 450 feet into the upper deck. Generally press conferences with the White House press corps do not allow a president such leeway. Not surprisingly, the president showed little relish for the press conference as an open question-and-answer session with reporters. Even though he held thirty-eight press conferences during 1993, twenty-five of them were ones held jointly with visiting heads of state. In such circumstances, reporters' questions reflect the meetings held between the leaders. Scheduled press conferences, where reporters have a couple of days' notice and where no other people are appearing with the president, are situations he continues to avoid. They are not events where a president can easily bob and weave around questions he does not want to answer.

Nonetheless, the president must come back to the traditional press corps. Whether the newspaper is the *Wilmington New Journal* or the *Providence Journal,* White House coverage comes from the wire services—Associated Press and United Press International—and the wires of the *New York Times* and the *Washington Post.* The presidential news on a citizen's doorstep in the morning in New Castle, Delaware, is delivered by Ann Devroy, Terence Hunt, and Thomas Friedman, all White House correspondents whose articles are circulated on the wires and printed in the *Wilmington News Journal.*

Despite similar presidential reservations, the press operation in the Carter White House never lost sight of the importance of White House press report-ers. Carter's press operation also reached out to out-of-town news organiza-tions but at the same time maintained a satisfied at-home press corps. Throughout most of the Carter presidency, press conferences were alternated with meetings with out-of-town newspaper editors. Regular mailings were sent to out-of-town news outlets, and a radio actuality operation was estab-lished for out-of-town radio stations. The Carter brand of reaching out to news organizations around the country did not detract in any substantive way from the quality of information the White House press corps received. Al-though Jody Powell did not have experience in Washington, nor did his depu-ties, his access to the president and understanding of his mind and views were unaccustomed assets in a novice press secretary. There was no attempt to reach the country through local outlets as a substitute for dealing with the press corps in Washington. As a result, the Carter press operation did not raise the ire of White House reporters and was able to expand its base without rais-ing any hackles.

Press Concerns as a Low Priority in the Clinton White House

President Clinton's minimal esteem for White House correspondents and their news organizations has been evident in the low priority given to keeping the press corps informed through the formal resources of the Press Office and its press secretary. President Clinton was the first president to appoint a woman as press secretary, but he chose a person to fill that spot who had not served in his close circle of advisers. In an article in the *New York Times Maga-zine,* William Safire identified the thirty most influential people in the Clinton administration in terms of their access to the president's ear.[12] Press Secretary Dee Dee Myers did not figure among them. Few would argue with Safire's as-sessment. Many correspondents have complained about her lack of knowl-edge of presidential decisions and decisionmaking. "She is often left out of what is going on," said one reporter.[13] "She came out and said she didn't know anything about a staff shake-up, and five minutes later the president in the Oval Office said they had been discussing it for five weeks."

In the staff shake-up following the Travel Office firings, the press corps that relied on formal briefings as a source of news were the weaker for the changes. George Stephanopoulos relinquished his role as communications director to Mark Gearan, a person who came from Vice President Al Gore's staff. Stephanopoulos then moved out of the public eye to serve as a senior-level political factotum for the president. A veteran Washington journalist who has followed several administrations pointed to the quality of information lost when Stephanopoulos moved off the pressroom podium: "Stephanopoulos was then and is now still a member of the inner circle of which there are only several: Hillary Clinton, McLarty, Gergen, Gore. We had access to one of them on a regular basis and now we only have access to the deputy of one. We are the losers."[14]

Nevertheless, reporters who work for national news outlets retain their access to senior-level White House aides. Ann Devroy, senior White House correspondent for the *Washington Post,* is not at a loss for information coming out of the building. In fact, it almost cascades in her direction. The same could be said for the *New York Times.* Such national news outlets continue to have access to those serving close to the president and, on occasion, to the president himself. The same opportunities do not exist for news outlets whose national impact is only marginal. Those organizations must still rely on the White House Press Office for their information.

Unintended Consequences: The Impact of Hiring People with No White House Experience

With no experience in either Washington or the White House and a victory under his belt, President Clinton did not feel the need to surround himself with people who had served in earlier Democratic White Houses. The gap of twelve years between Democratic presidents made it difficult, if not impossible, to recruit from those who had served inside the building. President Carter also experienced an eight-year gap and had a similar situation. As a result, he and Clinton both suffered from staffs deficient in White House experience. This hiatus proved costly for both teams. A modest example demonstrates the pothole that one can fall into. For both the Carter and Clinton White Houses, skirmishes with the chair of the Senate Finance Committee highlight the perils of employing an uninitiated staff. In the early days of the Carter administration, a large number of members of Congress were invited to a meeting with White House officials to air a fast-building list of grievances. Russell Long (D.–La.), chair of the Senate Finance Committee, declared to the assembled White House staff group who he was and what congressional position he held. Although the Carter aides no doubt were aware who Russell Long was, he believed they were not acting as if they did and took umbrage. Like most administrations limited in their respect for the lessons of the past, the Clinton White House made the very same mistake. Speaking of Senator Daniel Patrick Moynihan, chair of the Senate Finance Committee, an anonymous White House aide said, "He's not one of us, and he can't control Finance like Bentsen did."[15] "He's cantankerous, but he couldn't obstruct us even if he wanted to," the aide observed, adding fuel to the fire. And then he added, "We'll roll right over him if we have to." In addition to being grossly incorrect, such bravado made life more difficult for the new administration. At the end of Bill Clinton's first year, Senator Moynihan criticized the administration for its priorities and political conduct and publicly questioned the priority the president gave to health care legislation, calling instead for welfare reform to head the 1994 legislative agenda. At the same time, Senator Moynihan was the most prominent of the Democratic lawmakers to publicly call on the administration to appoint a special counsel to investigate the Clintons' Arkansas business dealings in the Whitewater land development project.

When a president enters with a staff lacking prior White House experience, there is no cognitive map of Washington's power centers or knowledge of how they relate to your man. Such ignorance can prove especially costly in the early stages of an administration, traditionally a time when both Congress and the public are focused on the new president's agenda. Both the Carter and Clinton White Houses tried to graft experience onto the staff structure they employed. In some cases, such as with Anne Wexler, director of the Office of Public Liaison in the Carter years, the graft takes, but it requires time to knit, if it ever does. Hedrick Hertzberg, chief speechwriter in the final years of the Carter administration, discussed the problem that Carter had in bringing new people into his administration in a substantive way:

> There was a pretty sharp line between the people that were with him when there was nothing apparently to be gained by being with him, and people who joined as a way of their getting big government jobs. He was unlike Reagan, who was able to take somebody like Jim Baker for example, and make Jim Baker part of him. Because Reagan has incorporated Jim Baker, Reagan is bigger. Carter really only thought of that small group that he brought with him as being part of himself, and he had a very hard time making new people part of himself.[16]

In the Clinton White House, the decision not to employ people with past experience was a deliberate effort to avoid being linked with the previous Carter administration. "It was a calculated decision to employ as few people [from the Carter White House] as they could," noted James Perry.[17] "They knew the Carter record was so unpopular that they didn't want to have people from it." When cracks appeared early on, President Clinton reached to the Republican administrations' David Gergen for help. He has grafted well with the president, but how well he fits in with those who have been with Clinton from the early campaign days is not clear. High-profile staff aides who receive praise in print for the victories of an administration earn the contempt of those on the staff whose names are aired publicly in association with presidential failures. With the constant praise Gergen has earned from news organizations for Clinton successes, he is in danger of receiving too much ink.

Inexperience in the communications area resulted in two similar errors in the early days of both the Carter and Clinton administrations. The first was choosing one communications staff member responsible for both long-range planning and daily press operations. This decision resulted specifically from the lack of White House experience in the communications area. Jody Powell in the Carter administration and George Stephanopoulos in the Clinton White House both initially had responsibility for both long-range planning operations and daily press routines. In each case this proved to be an impossible mixture. Initially, Press Secretary Jody Powell was responsible for the direction of the Press Office and at the same time handled speechwriters, the Photographers Office, News Summary, Media Liaison, and the public information officers in the executive departments. All of which was a totally unwieldy combination. The public information officers, for example, were left to their own devices. In the Clinton White House, Communications Director George Stephanopoulos also tried to serve both as a daily briefer and as the person responsible for long-range planning. For both Powell and Stephanopoulos, the demands of the daily press briefing dominated their day. A conundrum is why the Washington experience of Stephanopoulos and Jeff Eller, who heads the Office of Media Affairs, was not put to productive use early in Clinton's term. Both had worked on Capitol Hill—Stephanopoulos for Representatives Edward Feighan (D.–Ohio) and Richard Gephardt (D.–Mo.) and Eller for Representative William Bonner (D.–Tenn.). Experience in Congress was not enough; how it was used was the overriding point.

The White House as a Reflection of the President

The personal style of a president permeates every corner and every crevice in the building and influences the actions of every individual. Staff members take their cues from him both in the priorities they establish and the messages they send out. It is only through an understanding of the individual holding the office that one understands what is moving individuals and institutions. The same is true with Bill Clinton as it has been with every other president. "You can't understand this place if you don't understand Bill Clinton," observed senior economic adviser Gene Sperling.[18] "The principal economic and domestic policy adviser in this administration is Bill Clinton," noted another.[19] For Clinton, organizing a system that works involves setting up one where he deals personally with many staff members, often at the same time. In mid-

February as he prepared for an Oval Office address, for example, a photographer captured the group as he shot the president with thirteen aides, reworking his speech.[20] Bruce Lindsey, one of the senior aides closest to President Clinton, discussed the process through which the president traveled to reach a decision. It "is not a real structured sort of deal," Lindsey said.[21] That observation could serve as a wrap-up for how the communications operations have functioned under President Clinton. A president's decisionmaking style will be mirrored in those who serve him. Their weaknesses in the end are really his.

Party Control of the White House and Communications Strategies

The priority Democrats give to setting up a White House staff is directly opposite that of Republicans. For Democrats, the White House staff is something a presidential candidate runs against and uses as an example of government waste rather than as a resource in governing. The presidential campaigns waged by John Kennedy, Jimmy Carter, and Bill Clinton all reflected this bias. Having run against the staff, therefore, their priority once elected was to make good on their promise to reduce its numbers. Both Carter and Clinton pledged to cut the White House staff by 25 percent.[22]

If Republican presidents establish White Houses that are process oriented, Democratic presidents establish ones that are president centered. The position of chief of staff demonstrates the difference in structure signaled by a change in party control. "Jack Kennedy was his own Chief of Staff," commented Theodore Sorensen about the president he worked for as a close assistant.[23] The same could be said of all of the other post–World War II Democratic presidents as they came into office. Only Bill Clinton began his presidency with a person designated as a chief of staff, Mack McLarty. There were clear limits, however, on the actual role played by that man. "The president really likes to see a wide range of people," observed McLarty. "He likes to meet face to face, so I see my role much more as a support role, a facilitator, a coordinator, than a gatekeeper."[24] McLarty's observation about his role in the Clinton White House follows the pattern of Democratic presidents who set up staff systems that fit their particular personal needs. A Democratic White House remains president centered, with the chief of staff, if there is one, functioning simply as one of several staff members taking direction from the president.

The presidential staff structure is highly significant in terms of the White House's relationship to news organizations and the execution of the president's own communications policies. Coordination of delivery of messages, long-range planning, and the amount of time devoted to daily press operations are all outgrowths of the staff structure and the type of presidential thinking it represents. Communications within Democratic and Republican administrations have vastly different meanings.

Integrated Policy and Planning: Scheduling Events and Conducting Damage Control

The organization of the White House is a true demonstration of the adage that procedure is substance. A White House structure that functions through integration in its units and commits a considerable share of its resources toward planning results in an institution that normally can get ahead of events and shape how they are portrayed.

Getting Ahead on the Release of Information: The Republicans. One of the reasons that a Republican White House devotes attention to organization is to create a structure strong enough to allow for and encourage integrated planning. How things are done, what units are set up, and how they behave toward one another are paramount. The Reagan White House, where integration was both a reason to establish certain units and an approach within the remaining ones, is a good example. Behind it was the view that people, events, and institutions had specific places. Each had to be coordinated with the other so as to highlight the value of each. Their operation for the coordination of information among government units provides another good example. "This office's most basic role is to coordinate our spokesmen all over the government and to provide them with information on our policies and achievements," said Marion Blakey, who headed the Office of Public Affairs, a unit responsible to the communications director.[25] "From the ambassador in Mozambique to the under secretary of commerce, we make sure they have the same information and are all singing from the same choir book."

The programs the president wants and his timing for them are more important than the wishes or interests of any one of his department secretaries. Both the organization and the product of an administration are designed to reflect that fact. "One of the things you learn in an agency is you avoid running into White House stories. White House stories are on page 1," said a White House staff member with department experience.[26] "You only want the A section." In the Nixon administration department planning meant releasing news on Wednesday, something of a down day. Such a schedule meant that the departments and White House did not step on each other's stories. Clearing speeches and press releases also ensured that these messages would be consistent with the president's program and statements.

The Reagan White House had procedures in place to minimize the impact of actions and events that likely would generate criticism of the president. "You have to be strongly proactive and not let it wash over you in a big wave," said a White House staff member in the Reagan years about the staff's response to bad news.[27] The Press Office dealt with immediate news, and the long-range planning operations kept up with stories that had the potential for generating criticism of the president. Actions such as a possible veto of an ethics in government bill were items that had to be considered. "We met with Legislative Affairs on the question of legislation coming in, and a veto was a dynamic issue while the presidential campaign was on," the aide said. On the issue of Reagan's veto of legislation that would have required plants to give a three-month advance notice to employees before closing down operations, there was a communications plan to implement.[28] "That was a case of minimizing press coverage," the aide said. "A straight case."

This same staff member indicated that a White House response had three basic parts to it: timing, argumentation, and spokespeople. In the plant closing case timing meant, "Release it after everyone's deadline so you force it to a second day story";[29] also make sure it is a day "when the readership is not strong," such as a Saturday. Then "[consider] what else you are offering at the same time. If you know, you can pair it with something to offset it," the staff person suggested. Then work on putting forward spokespeople to argue the issue. "Develop your strongest argument with your strongest people," the aide recommended. But sometimes it is best to say little. "Some part of it is not to say anything. It is harder to keep it going if no one speaks, if no one is available for talk shows."

Holding Up the Walls and Ceilings: The Democrats. If a White House fails through its planning mechanisms to get ahead of situations, as has been the case in the Clinton White House, then it is forced backward by the motion of events. The previous description of the atmosphere in the Carter White House could also apply to the Clinton White House as it manages a myriad of foreign crises involving American troops and interests as well as a full domestic agenda. A senior staff member who served in the Carter administration described the impact of being unable to keep ahead of events:

> There is such a tendency to become a reactive force in the White House. There are so many issues bubbling up and coming in through the windows from all directions that need to be dealt with urgently that there is little time and no resources to look ahead and try to anticipate and do the necessary planning. ... I guess you'd have to be in the White House to feel the dynamic of it. You just feel the walls and ceilings caving in on you daily. It's something that's always got to be done today or tomorrow or next week. I mean next week is long range planning in the White House.[30]

When people join an administration, they cannot imagine such a scenario. They arrive believing they have a clean slate to govern as they promised they would, on a timetable of their choosing, and with an agenda that they draft. Not even a month passes before they find their calendar full of events, particularly congressional dates, requiring their response. They are in a reactive mode before they know it.

Being in a reactive mode can involve not understanding the forces at play on an issue and mishandling it, as was the case in the public firings for "gross mismanagement" of seven Travel Office staff members in the Clinton White House. The firings, which were announced publicly to reporters in a briefing by Dee Dee Myers, did not initially include a discussion of the charges with the employees involved. The history of the Travel Office operation was not properly assessed, and the actions of the president's close friend Harry Thomason and Clinton's distant cousin Catherine Cornelius were not ade- quately monitored. The result was a series of events that resulted in two weeks of bad publicity cascading out of the Clinton White House.[31] Staff efforts to legitimate the firings included having the Federal Bureau of Investigation (FBI) make a statement that the bureau had evidence sufficient to warrant an investigation of the Travel Office for criminal activity. The facts did not bear out the charges. In addition, once they were made Attorney General Janet Reno became publicly upset over the White House contacting the FBI with- out going through normal bureaucratic channels. What had begun as a bad story for the White House soon became a disaster as cover-up efforts became apparent.

A lack of preparation for events can lead the president into territory he should scrupulously avoid. A good example of this occurred during a period when President Clinton was under heavy fire for having lost his focus. The staff arranged for a town hall meeting to be held in the White House Rose Garden. The hosts of the *This Morning* show on CBS, Harry Smith and Paula Zahn, appeared with two hundred tourists rounded up outside of the White House, who served as the audience. It was an operation that had the earmarks of a serious lack of advance work. Early in the program, with President Clin- ton standing in tow, Harry Smith discussed the results of recent public opin- ion polls and then, taking liberties, asked the audience to respond to a ques- tion:

> I know you don't pay attention to this sort of stuff—polls. You never pay atten- tion probably, right? The negatives are now higher than the positives in the polls. And I want to tap into something here, because there's a feeling in the country and I think the people here reflect it. I think people in America want to see you succeed, but I just want to see a raise of hands this morning—and don't be intimi- dated just because you're in the Rose Garden—(laughter)—do you feel like he could be doing a better job? Raise your hand if you think so. Don't be intimi- dated. Don't be intimidated. There's a lot of folks who feel that way. Do you feel like there's a gap between the promises of the campaign and the performance thus far? If you think so, raise your hands. A lot of folks feel that way. What went wrong?[32]

The president was asked to stand in his garden while a television host encouraged invited guests to raise their hands as an expression of criticism of the president. Clinton must have wondered how he had got himself into such a situation and who had done the advance work for the event.

Synchronizing Public and Private Messages

There is a major difference in the ability of Democratic and Republican administrations to synchronize public and private messages. Frankly put, the Republicans are very successful at it, and the Democrats almost universally fail at doing so. The Carter administration, and now the Clinton one, had problems with the way private, pessimistic messages pushed the upbeat public message out of the headlines. "The Democrats are more disposed to send out two different messages. The Republicans are more disciplined with a message-of-the-day, the official viewpoint," noted Dennis Farney, White House correspondent for the *Wall Street Journal* during the Carter and early Reagan years.[33] "It is harder to get them to admit differences." Clinton White House staff members have proved remarkably accommodating to reporters wanting stories about the troubles within their administration. Consider the following information that White House staff members provided a reporter for his story: "'I don't know what mistakes are out there that we *haven't* made,' a presidential aide says. A second one breaks into uncontrollable laughter during conversations. A third doesn't read the newspapers. Still another is described by friends as 'homicidal.' And another describes himself as 'seething' one day and saying 'What can I say?' the next. 'It's true, we have no political strategy,' someone with direct, regular access to the president said."[34]

The Carter people often hurt themselves by promoting both a public and a private message within the same story. On legislation being proffered by the administration to Congress, for example, White House officials would often openly discuss the difficult prospects for passage of the very legislation that they had just put forward. Such was the case with their energy program. "The public message was overtaken by the private one sometimes in the same day," commented Farney. "They would shoot down their own message in private."

The Clinton administration has demonstrated the same tendencies. Three months into President Clinton's term, the headline on the front page of the *Washington Post* declared, "Panetta: President in Trouble on the Hill." The subheading declared, "Agenda at Risk, Trade Pact 'Dead.'"[35] This was a disappointing start for a week during which the White House had hoped to highlight the accomplishments of its first 100 days and reinforce the possibilities that lay ahead. Budget Director Leon Panetta, speaking on the record to a group of reporters, expressed his doubts about the directions the administration was taking not only on the economy but also on health care, aid to Russia, and the North American Free Trade Agreement.

Meanwhile over at the Office of Media Affairs, Jeff Eller and his crew were preparing for distribution thousands of copies of a publication lauding the president's feats.[36] "What will come from what we accomplished here—more economic growth, comprehensive health and welfare reform, a new system of national service, and the like—is new opportunities for achievement, empowerment and progress for middle-class Americans, and a new direction for us all. It is indeed America's season of renewal," declared the White House analysis of the administration's first 100 days.[37] For all its zeal, the Office of Media Affairs assessment went unnoticed in the press, except as an effort to put fresh shingles on a leaky roof. Instead, the Panetta interview was fodder for two days of front-page stories that served as lead-ins for traditional 100-day pieces.

The Clinton White House has also suffered from a continuing inability to focus on a single message. On August 11, the day after President Clinton signed his major legislative initiative, the budget and tax package, the front pages of the major national newspapers were taken up by a report released the day before on the suicide of White House counsel Vincent Foster and by the swearing-in ceremony for Supreme Court Justice Ruth Bader Ginsburg. The bill signing was on page 4 of the *Washington Post* and page 11 of the *New York Times*. The ceremony could have provided an occasion to educate the public about the contents of the legislation. Instead, the president took the ceremony off the front page with two events that he knew would be front-page material.

Democrats are not able to enforce a one-message-a-day policy because they fail to set up the institutional structure to create the message and choose no one to enforce it. Robert Beckel, who worked in the Carter administration on the passage of the Panama Canal Treaty, discussed the problem and its source. "One day we could have Jody [Powell] saying something in the White House, and Hodding [Carter—the press spokesperson at the State Department] would be over in the State Department saying something else," he said.[38] "There was a lack of communication. I think it was a real lack of discipline and that the fault may well have been with the president." The same could be said for the Clinton administration.

Interest Groups in the Democratic Coalition. President Clinton is constantly under attack from groups within the Democratic coalition. He is experiencing what previous Democratic presidents have found in their relationship with groups within their electoral coalition: They attack their own. David Rubenstein, deputy director of the domestic policy staff in the Carter White House, once observed that the groups within the Democratic coalition "want 100% of what they want."[39] In the first month of the administration when the president was considering whom he was going to nominate for attorney general after the first two nominees were withdrawn, the leaders of the National

Organization for Women and the National Women's Political Caucus warned the president not to waiver in his resolve to appoint a woman to the post.[40] They had no praise or encouragement for the president, who only the day before had signed into law the advocated family leave bill. Environmental groups were next, and then gay rights organizations followed with their publicly expressed reservations about the timing and substance of the administration's policy proposals. News organizations prominently chronicled these and other criticisms of the president's programs and actions.

The Focus of an Administration

The focus a president chooses for his term in office determines his conceptualization of the media as he seeks to govern. Presidents who choose to crystallize movement for and implementation of change have one view of the media's role in their administration. Presidents who are interested in previously initiated reform work see the media in a wholly different light. A reformer gears his strategies toward developing broad policy support from the public. As a president committed to political change, Bill Clinton's need for the press is significant. Media are the basic channel, both directly and indirectly, through which the information he wants the public to have will travel. A president such as George Bush, however, whose agenda is designed to reshape, or prune, reforms established by earlier incumbents, need not go to the public well for support.

Three types of focus characterize a president's term in office. He may mobilize for change, consolidate programs and coalitions, or fall into an atomized state with no real focus. Depending on term length, a president may use one or more of these tactics. A mobilization for change focus emphasizes major shifts in policy. A consolidation of programs and coalitions focus is designed to tinker with, rather than draft, grand designs. It is essentially a reaction to complaints emanating from an earlier set of reforms. It is directed to holding the presidential ground without benefiting the opposition. This focus is related to control and definition of the agenda. An atomized focus occurs when a president spends his energies buffeted by events and initiatives of others within the political system. In this situation, control is beyond a president's reach and definition of the issues beyond his grasp. Here the president's focus shifts frequently without a clear sense of direction.

Mobilization for Change

Mobilization for change is one focus of an administration. A presidency of change, such as those of Bill Clinton and Ronald Reagan, requires all the instruments of governing. The president must employ his full arsenal of weapons if he is to move the political system in his chosen direction. Because change is never easy to bring about, any resource the president can muster toward that end is valid. News organizations especially are a critical resource for this president in mustering the coalition of public support essential for change to occur. Tom Griscom, White House communications director in the latter Reagan years, stressed the importance of effective presidential use of the media in the success of the Reagan agenda: "What became apparent was that this President had an extraordinary ability to communicate his message in precise language: a positive tool for any President, but particularly for one who came into office with an established agenda. To reach his goals, domination of the message was essential."[41]

For Bill Clinton, too, domination of the message is important. Two issues that other recent presidents considered only rhetorically he has tackled substantively: health care and the budget deficit. These lightning rod issues draw the intense energy of hundreds of groups and individuals focused almost exclusively on their own interest. In his first year, however, with the exception of a carefully crafted health care effort, President Clinton did not equal Reagan's precise delineation of his programs and priorities. Instead, Clinton seemed to revel in simultaneously juggling several policies.

Steps Toward Change

Mobilization for change is a three-step process: establishment of themes, legitimization of the notion of change, and realization of change. The president must develop support for the concept of change and then present an agenda the public can agree on and support. A publicly approved agenda is the product of interaction between the president and the citizenry. The media are the agent of this interaction, integrating information within the political system and between the system and its publics. Bill Clinton and Ronald Reagan began emphasizing the need for reform during their campaigns.

Establishing Themes. A change agenda requires a president to define parameters for reform under a manageable umbrella. Presidents have traditionally done this by establishing a theme, which calls attention to a need. Themes run from sobriquets, such as the New Deal or New Frontier, to firmly established policy priorities, such as budget and tax cuts. News organizations are often loath to repeat a president's policy pronouncements, but they are more than willing to repeat often the slogan or announced theme of an administration. A theme is also a useful reminder to the public of the president's priorities. President Clinton has had difficulty establishing themes. Early on the newly elected president veered from a budget reduction message to announce his support for a deregulation of gays and lesbians in the military. Good news was replaced by controversy on the front page.

Legitimizing Change. Public awareness of the need for change and substantial support for it are key to effecting change. The president is best situated to weave the threads of support into a coalition that can actively pressure other institutions in government for reform. His ideas give the shape of change its necessity. Legitimization of change was very much what President Clinton had in mind when he assembled economists in Little Rock, Arkansas, a month after his victory. His two-day conference was closely followed by the national media, with long segments aired live on television. The American people saw that reform was on his mind and that he would move strongly to this broad legislative area once in office.

Effecting Change. With the development of reform proposals, the media become a conduit to inform the public of the nature and status of change. This conduit is somewhat different from the channel the media provide during the early period in which the need for change is under development. As a channel, the media are simply a venue, a place rather than a voice. They are the place through which the president and his staff work to send out the signals and messages that they have created. Strategies for using the media as a channel emphasize decisions on how frequently the president himself should appear and in what setting. The president is the key person both in developing the contours of change and in creating the required support for it. Success in using the media as a channel means acquiring airtime from television networks and getting the attention of news organizations and their front-line reporters.

Media Strategies for Change Mobilization

When creating change, the White House has intense interest in the media. An effective president carefully chooses people for senior staff positions who have communications experience. Ronald Reagan chose seasoned people to work with the national media in presenting the changes he sought in the economy, relations with the Soviet Union, and the organization of government. Even though the details of change were not explained, the general contours were in place. Staff was needed to translate support for the president as measured by his popular vote into an actual program for change. The president hired James Baker as chief of staff specifically because of his accumulated Washington experience. Baker, in turn, hired David Gergen because of his previous success in formulating communications strategies for President Ford. President Clinton, to his initial disadvantage, came to Washington with no mature staff with White House experience. This missing element cost him, and he brought in people from Vice President Gore's staff, including Roy Neel and Mark Gearan.

In a major communications reorganization ploy, President Clinton hired David Gergen on the strength of his work for President Reagan. With reform momentum seriously eroding, Clinton reached back for a person with a successful communications track record. The president's frustration over his inability to define the issues and direct attention to programs was clearly expressed: "The economic program was announced one month into my presidency and then I went to work on it in Congress. And what really is news is sort of around the edges; is he losing this or winning that or whatever. It becomes a process debate and the American people tend to lose sight of what is the major focus of my every day, which is how to pass that jobs program and the economic program. That is simply a function of how the news works."[42] Only because the stakes were so high did the president select someone from the opposition party to serve on his personal staff.

News Coverage and the Critics of a Reform Agenda

Presidents who present a reform agenda are met with resistance from a variety of quarters. When opposition appears, news organizations are quick to report it. In most administrations, congressional opposition expresses an early willingness to work with the new government and begins criticism only when specific legislation is proposed and executive orders are presented. House Speaker Tip O'Neill (D.–Mass.) voiced support for Ronald Reagan when he came to Washington two weeks after the 1980 election. As early as election night November 1992, however, Senator Robert Dole (R.–Kan.), the Senate minority leader, was announcing that he would be keeping a weather eye on the new administration and provide storm warnings when the clouds leaned left. He has been true to his word.

Senator Dole has been an effective critic not only because of his willingness to attack Clinton and the administration but also because of his ability to insinuate himself into a presidential story. In the Travel Office abuse stories, for example, he took to the Senate floor with his criticisms in early afternoon. By moving then, he was able to get on the evening news programs as well as the afternoon CNN news hour. Since Senate proceedings have been televised only since 1982, this communications ploy is new. Clinton's predecessors, except for George Bush, did not have to deal with senators taking to the air from the Senate floor to oppose their actions and initiatives from the moment they begin their terms in office.

Congressional critics are also found in President Clinton's own party, not just in the opposition as represented by the Republicans and by Ross Perot. Representative Charles Stenholm (D.–Tex.) organized members against the president's budget proposal, as did the Republicans. In the final tally in the House, Clinton did not get a single Republican vote and lost the support of thirty-three Democrats. In contrast, Ronald Reagan had two Republican defectors and won over the support of fifty-five Democrats when his budget was considered in the House. Such a significant difference in results is bound to produce news stories with different tones and content. Two members of the House leadership—House Majority Leader Richard Gephardt and Democratic Whip David Bonoir (D.–Mich.)—organized congressional opponents of NAFTA, a centerpiece of the president's hemisphere and trade policies. Their opposition was a natural focus of congressional and presidential media coverage. A contemporary "man bites dog," such conflict is the stuff of which news is made.

Consolidation of Gains

A second presidential focus is one that consolidates gains. Reforms do not always work and often fail to work as intended. A shakedown period following consolidation of gains seems to be inevitable. The consolidation of both programs and coalitions is important. Each is crucial to a president trying to weave reform into the fabric of the system. Communications strategies in this case emphasize specific electoral and program audiences. There is little need for an evening address from the Oval Office or East Room unless a crisis or foreign policy event occurs. President Clinton, with a 43 percent electoral margin and with proposals rather than enacted reforms, does not need to emphasize the strategies associated with consolidation. Instead, his first-term task is to build a firm coalition of supporters and a legislative record of achievement. Should he have a second term, however, consolidation will most likely be his focus during those years.

Program Consolidation

The development and passage of reform proposals are followed by a period during which programs are consolidated. Both reform programs and those that are generating problems as candidates for review are retained. Neither may work out as originally anticipated, and support may unexpectedly erode. Taken together as a group, the reforms may also be perceived as too harsh. This was the case in such Reagan policy changes as reduction of social welfare benefits. In Lyndon Johnson's terms, his reforms were regarded as too costly and were trimmed as soon as he left office.

Coalition Consolidation

A second strengthening technique consolidates the policy and electoral coalitions. The electoral coalition is key to governing. As president, the electee must be able to keep the support of those who were behind him in his election. He needs to keep those who were with him as he entered office and who continue to provide a strong support base for policy action. Different policy issues bring out different groups of interested individuals and groups. The harsher the weather gets in Washington, the more he must have reliable supporters. A president looks first to those who have been with him over a period of time and draws from that well when he needs support.

Media Strategies in Consolidation

White House communications strategies during the period of consolidation are a critical element in a president's bid to stabilize electoral supporters. Bill Clinton's slim popular vote demands that he forge a support base for himself and for his programs. When it comes to governing, however, his strategy is to dismantle earlier Republican programs, not consolidate them. George Bush was the typical president of consolidation.

Atomization

When an administration lacks a clear focus, it inevitably gets caught up in others' agendas. President Carter showed us that. He had no single policy focus; instead he had several. In his first three months, major initiatives included executive reorganization, energy, education, congressional water projects, welfare reform, human rights, and the Middle East. Such a policy explosion results in an atomized focus, which causes energies to dissipate fairly quickly and not revitalize. President Clinton showed signs of falling into the same trap with the full policy plate he presented in a short space of time. His initial policy efforts included gays and lesbians in the military, budget reductions, tax increases, NAFTA, a national service program, health care, grazing fee increases on federal lands, and timber clearance reduction in national forests.

The Place of Events

Once an administration loses its own energies, other people and events move in to take center stage. For Jimmy Carter, public attention was rapidly drawn to the Arab oil embargo and the bruising blows delivered by the decade's most severe winter. Foreign policy events involving Bosnia, Somalia, and Haiti presented similar challenges to Clinton's domestic policy focus. President Ford also had difficulty developing a focus. He came to office with no coalition behind him and escalating events that eclipsed his presence. His pardon of Richard Nixon, an action conceived to lay the Nixon presidency to rest, instead disinterred the corpse. Ford linked himself to an ongoing story that dominated his early administration well beyond the former president's tenure. In short, Ford, who had been viewed as above the fray, became part of the tangled Nixon web. He was never able to cut clear. He was, however, able to establish a focus: the legitimacy of the presidency as an institution.

The Lack of a Coalition

A weak coalition of presidential supporters is one hallmark of an administration whose focus is atomized. A strong coalition, by contrast, pressures the president to direct his energies toward its agenda. President Carter, for example, had few people who were primarily Carter supporters. His closest support was from the traditional Democratic coalition, his electoral coalition. He was forced to rely on diverse Democratic party groups for support in Congress. Unfortunately, they proved to be weak partners. When he needed them, they voted for him, but did so while complaining about him and his brand of leadership. A group that loyally supported Carter and defended him never materialized. Only those on his White House staff were true defenders. President Clinton has been successful in getting priority issues through the Congress, but members of his party have also sharply complained along the way.

Media Strategies in Atomization

Media strategies associated with atomization are much like the presidency responsible for them: not in control of the agenda. Either through force of events, institutions beyond its control, or lack of a clear agenda, the administration is not able to get ahead and stay ahead of events. Atomization media patterns reflect the inability to take the initiative. Always behind the action, the administration expends its energy catching up.

Concentration on Daily Routines

Once behind, future planning is a luxury an administration cannot afford. The present situation becomes the focus of everyone's attention. The press secretary directs his or her energies to conducting the daily briefing and putting the best face possible on what is happening elsewhere. The publicity staff also directs its attention to providing the daily releases the press requires. The Carter White House, for example, was barely able to keep up with unfolding events as it took office in 1977. Even though the communications staff was ultimately able to get ahead, it was never actually on the offensive. Jody Powell kept both the long-range and short-term press responsibilities in his office and was reluctant to give them up. Under Clinton, George Stephanopoulos followed the same route until the communications operation was redesigned to get ahead of events.

Lack of Coordination Between Policy and Publicity

Coordination among units within the White House and its many departments and agencies is even more of an unaffordable luxury for those buried under current events. Diverse policy focuses are difficult to coordinate and are especially impossible with press operations geared to respond to momentary events and actions. The Ford administration's early energies were squandered in dealing with the Richard Nixon story. Not until late 1975 was the Ford White House able to put in place an operation involving coordination between policy actions, such as budget initiatives, and publicity.

Bill Clinton's First Year in Office:
The President as a Lightning Rod

The first six months of the Clinton administration were ones during which the president and his staff were constantly dealing with negative stories coming from seemingly every corner of the White House. In the final six months, however, the president's reviews improved. The favorable stories reflected the way in which the president and his staff were effectively coordinating his programs and communications initiatives. In fact, during this period he became a formidable political force. His public support rose from his 43 percent electoral margin to a 60 percent approval rating at the end of his first year.[43] His ratings gains came in part from a public recognition that he is a man who enjoys the exercise of power, even if the public is not always confident that his solutions fit the problems.

A willingness to take on difficult problems characterized President Clinton's first year. He had no fear of taking on issues that had no clear solution or of raising false hopes. For he believes that there is an inevitable gap between aspirations and reality. It is the president's job to provide hope at the same time he fashions policies. When confronted with a protester shouting him down during a speech dealing with AIDS, Clinton told his audience not to be so upset with the demonstrator. "Part of my job is to be a lightning rod," he said in response to the protestor's actions.[44] "Part of my job is to lift the hopes and aspirations of the American people, knowing that as long as you try to lift hopes and lift aspirations, you can never fully close the gap between what you're reaching for and what you're actually doing."

Indefatigable, President Clinton demonstrated an ability to organize legislative victories even in the face of what his critics characterized as almost certain defeat. NAFTA represented a strong victory in the face of a well-organized opposition that included groups from the Left and the Right. News organizations, strong supporters of NAFTA, rallied to his side against the likes of Ross Perot. Their partnership at year's close was quite different from the beating President Clinton had received in print and on the air in the early months of his term. That change was brought about through changes in the president's own effectiveness and in his ability to rally public support. News organizations are among the first to recognize a winning hand.

Notes

This chapter is a slice of a forthcoming book, *Wired for Sound and Pictures: The President and White House Communications Policies* (Baltimore, Md.: Johns Hopkins University Press, forthcoming). Reprinted by permission of Johns Hopkins University Press. Segments appeared in an earlier paper presented to the American Political Science Association, "Freelancers and Fogmeisters: Party Control and White House Communications Activities," September 1993.

1. "The One-Question News Conference," *Washington Post,* June 15, 1993, A13.

2. Ibid.

3. As quoted in Dan Balz, "Changing the Capital, But More So the Man," *Washington Post,* January 17, 1994, A6.

4. "Excerpts from Clinton's News Conference at the White House," *New York Times,* June 16, 1993, A20.

5. "Remarks by the President in Question and Answer Session During 1993 Newspaper Association of America Annual Convention," Marriott Copley Place Hotel, Boston, Massachusetts, April 26, 1993 [boston.txt].

6. Ibid.

7. Jann Wenner and William Greider, "President Clinton: The *Rolling Stone* Interview," *Rolling Stone,* December 9, 1992, 81.

8. Ibid.

9. Interview with James Perry, Washington, D.C., July 24, 1993.

10. She interviewed him March 1, 1993, the day before he introduced the national service bill and then again on September 21, 1993, as the bill was passed.

11. "Remarks by the President in 'A Town Hall Meeting with Bill Clinton," KGTV Studio, San Diego, California, May 17, 1993 [townhl.txt].

12. William Safire, "Who's Got Clout," *New York Times Magazine,* June 20, 1993, 25.

13. Interview, 1993.

14. Interview, 1993.

15. Sydney Blumenthal, "A Beautiful Friendship," *The New Yorker,* July 5, 1993, 35.

16. Hedrick Hertzberg, Project on the Carter Presidency, interview with speechwriters, White Burkett Miller Center for Public Affairs, University of Virginia, December 3–4, 1982.

17. Perry interview.

18. Burt Solomon, "A One-Man Band," *National Journal,* April 24, 1993, 970.

19. Ibid.

20. Ibid.

21. Ibid.

22. For a discussion of President Clinton's prospective cuts in staff in the Executive Office of the President, see Ann Devroy, "Cutting Noses at the White House," *Washington Post Weekly Edition,* April 26–May 2, 1993, 34.

23. Samuel Kernell and Samuel Popkin, eds., *Chief of Staff: Twenty-Five Years of Managing the Presidency* (Berkeley and Los Angeles: University of California Press, 1986), 27.

24. Thomas Mack McLarty, White House chief of staff, March 7, 1993, C-Span, text, 14.

25. Interview with Marion Blakey, director, Office of Public Affairs, Washington, D.C., January 17, 1989.

26. Interview with a White House staff member, 1989.

27. Interview with a White House staff member, 1989.

28. The legislation became law without President Reagan's signature in the fall of 1988. In May he vetoed a similar provision included in the omnibus trade bill. The discussion here refers to the May 1988 veto action.

29. Interview with a White House staff member, 1989.

30. Interview not yet released for attribution, Carter Presidency Project, White Burkett Miller Center of Public Affairs, University of Virginia, January 1982.

31. The fullest running account of the episode can be found in articles written by Ann Devroy, senior White House correspondent of the *Washington Post*. The firings took place May 19, 1993, with the articles chronicling the events beginning the following day.

32. "Remarks by the President During CBS This Morning Town Hall Meeting," May 27, 1993 [cbs.txt].

33. Interview with Dennis Farney, Washington, D.C., April 16, 1981.

34. Sidney Blumenthal, "Dave," *The New Yorker,* June 28, 1993, 36.

35. David Broder, "Panetta: President in Trouble on Hill, Agenda at Risk, Trade Pact 'Dead,'" *Washington Post,* April 27, 1993, A1.

36. "Clinton Administration Accomplishments and Actions: First 100 Days" (April 1993). Distributed by the Office of Media Liaison through its White House computer network [100days.txt].

37. "The First 100 Days, Administration of President Bill Clinton, January 20–April 30, 1993" [dys100.txt].

38. Robert Beckel, Carter Presidency Project, White Burkett Miller Center of Public Affairs, University of Virginia, November 13, 1981.

39. Interview with David Rubenstein, Michael Grossman, and Martha Kumar, Washington, D.C., January 6, 1981.

40. Ruth Marcus and Mary Jordan, "Attorney General Search Resumes; Feminists Express Rising Anger," *Washington Post,* February 7, 1993, A16.

41. Tom Griscom, "Presidential Communication: An Essential Leadership Tool," in *The Presidency in Transition,* ed. James Pfiffner and R. Gordon Hoxie (New York: Center for the Study of the Presidency), 339.

42. "Remarks by the President in Question and Answer Session with National Association of Broadcasters, The Naval Academy, Annapolis, Md.," April 1, 1993. Text released by the Office of the Press Secretary, the White House.

43. As quoted in David Broder, "Economy, Foreign Policy Give Clinton Boost in Poll," *Washington Post,* January 25, 1994, A5.

44. Ann Devroy, "AIDS Patient, Protester Ask Clinton to Do More," *Washington Post,* December 2, 1993, A31.

10

Public Opinion in President Clinton's First Year: Leadership and Responsiveness

LAWRENCE R. JACOBS AND ROBERT Y. SHAPIRO

Few days go by without some report in the media about the latest public opinion poll revealing the president's public approval rating or current support for his policies. Research has shown that the president's public standing can be a resource in subsequent political actions (cf. Neustadt, 1980; Lowi, 1985; Page and Shapiro, 1985, 1992, chap. 8; Edwards, 1983, 1989; Peterson, 1990; Kernell, 1986; Cornwell, 1965). But this standing is influenced by the president's own leadership efforts and recent performance in office. For better or for worse—and we think the jury is still out on this—presidential leadership in the twentieth century has increasingly involved presidents weighing and mobilizing public opinion. Modern presidents have devoted more attention than their predecessors to *responding* to or *directing* public opinion. In doing this, they have made use of public opinion research and political communications and public relations activities that have in fact been institutionalized in the White House (see Chapter 9).

Some critics have argued that reliance on presidential rhetoric and direct communications to the public (see Kernell, 1986, on "going public") has occurred at the expense of traditional and more effective instruments of governing—most notably, institutional deliberations involving the president, Congress, and the executive bureaucracy (see Tulis, 1987). Thus, efforts to take the measure of and respond to public opinion, or to influence public opinion through political communication, take time away from ostensibly more effective (from both a technical and consensus-building standpoint) institutional

195

processes. The public is best left to ratify or reject during the next elections the policies of the officeholders (intertwined with how this reflects on the officeholders' character) that result from these superior political processes (cf. Schumpeter, 1950).

Other criticisms have focused on presidents' responsiveness and direction separately. For one, even though presidents who simply respond to what the public wants might be governing "democratically"—in effect letting the people rule—whether the resulting policies are effective and wise will depend on the quality of the information that led the public to its decisions. Even recent authors, including ourselves, who have been most optimistic about the public's capabilities and ultimate "rationality" do not believe that the mass public can or should autonomously inform itself and make policy decisions (e.g., Page and Shapiro, 1992, chaps. 8–10; Popkin, 1991).

We agree with V. O. Key, Jr. (1961) that political leaders and other elites must play a very important role in educating and leading the public. However, this direction alone can be undemocratic when it produces a "circular" process by which political leaders influence public opinion and then "respond" to the public's preferences, which these leaders have substantially, if not fully, determined (Lindblom, 1977). This circularity would completely undermine liberal democracy if the public was regularly manipulated or deceived through false or misleading information (Page and Shapiro, 1992, chap. 9). This process could also involve political elites acting independently of the public in the guise of following opinion polls, elections, and other democratic institutions and procedures. The effect would be to lull the public into legitimating a system that is not responsive to its citizens' genuine wants and needs (see the "captive public" thesis in Ginsberg, 1986).

We are, however, more optimistic than these critiques. We fully appreciate the need for institutional bargaining and deliberating, but we do not think that in modern-day democracies the public should be excluded from ongoing policy debates and be heard from only at election time (see Page and Shapiro, 1983, 1992; Hartley and Russett, 1992; Jacobs, 1993). Nor should political leaders be kept from educating and directing the public; they *must* do so. Responsiveness and direction of public opinion should not be thought of as mutually exclusive processes. In fact, they can coexist in a reinforcing fashion through a process that can be described as *responsive leadership.*

We argue that presidents can lead by adopting strategies that involve both direction and responsiveness to public opinion. Presidents can use their resources, including formal authority, to formulate workable government policies that respond in part to the public's wishes; they can then use the visibility of their office to mobilize public support for particular courses of action (see Wilson, 1908, 1925, 1952; Jacobs and Shapiro, 1992; Tulis, 1987). This is an attractive strategy because some responsiveness can enable presidents to exercise strong direction. But presidents must not be equivocating Hamlets: In their initial response to the public's general attitudes or policy preferences, they have to offer a clear and essentially unwavering course of action.

Based on the limited evidence available so far, in this chapter we examine the extent to which President Bill Clinton responded to and attempted to direct the American public during his first year in office. Overall we find that Clinton emphasized responsiveness to the public's wishes—as he had during the campaign—over efforts to direct the public. The outcome, however, was decidedly mixed during most of the year, though with surprising success in the last two months. The sheer scope of his policy agenda contributed to this uneven record (see Light, 1982). It was quicker and easier, at least initially, to offer and focus on policies that already had public support than to propose a number of specific policies that lacked public interest or support.

Persuading the public to accept specific policies that evoke skepticism or serious doubts requires a strategy for persuasion and some time (cf. Neustadt, 1980, on the president's "power to persuade"). Clinton clearly tried to do this in the case of national health care reform, to a much lesser extent in his economic and budget reduction program, and belatedly but successfully in the case of NAFTA and other issues by the end of the year. In foreign affairs he began surely enough by responding to the public's general preference concerning the post–Cold War world, but he then failed when it came to formulating specific U.S. and multilateral actions for which he could mobilize and sustain public support. He still has the opportunity and time to remedy this before the 1996 election—and experts and the public have both recognized that he learns from his mistakes.

Our Research

The evidence that we assembled for our analysis is, to be sure, preliminary since we completed our analysis and writing at the end of Clinton's first year in office. We are accustomed to doing more systematic research, making use of archival materials and interviews in addition to the public record, as we have done in studies of Presidents John Kennedy and Lyndon Johnson (Jacobs and Shapiro, 1992, 1993, forthcoming). We have now leaped ahead by shifting our attention from Johnson in the 1960s to Clinton in 1993 (in the future we will examine the presidents from Richard Nixon to George Bush).

In addition to obtaining information about enacted and proposed policies that was readily available through the mass media and published sources, we normally would want to know how a political leader learns about public opinion, what he learns, and what he does with this information. This kind of direct evidence is not yet available. In our previous research on Kennedy and

Johnson, we examined confidential White House analyses of its private polls as well as published poll results.

Recent presidents have had private pollsters; this began in full swing, in an institutionalized fashion, with the Johnson White House (see Jacobs, 1993; Jacobs and Shapiro, 1993). Clinton is no exception; his private pollster, Stanley Greenberg, provides public opinion polling, focus groups, and other public opinion analysis and is not paid by the government but by the national party. Greenberg and others also have access to publicly available polling data and public opinion analyses (in fact, at his request we have sent him our own data and writings on public opinion about health care policy: Jacobs and Shapiro, 1994; Jacobs, Shapiro, and Schulman, 1993). We would expect that analyses of public opinion data by Greenberg and others in the White House can be approximated by our own analysis of some of the data and reports about public opinion that are publicly available. And the fact that we can identify responsiveness confirms this. Greenberg himself offered a more direct confirmation of the use and impact of poll results at a panel of presidential pollsters sponsored by the American Enterprise Institute in Washington, D.C., in December 1993 (Berke, 1993, A20).

Evidence of Responsiveness and Direction

Our research on Kennedy and Johnson revealed that when they were running for election in 1960 and 1964, respectively, they both tended to be responsive to the public. They were highly attentive to public opinion and took responsive positions on issues that their private polls showed were important. Aided by information from Louis Harris's polls conducted in several states for his campaign, Kennedy emphasized particular issues, such as medical care, Social Security, education, unemployment, inflation, national defense, and prestige in foreign affairs, in order to shape his image as a leader for electoral purposes (Jacobs and Shapiro, forthcoming). Although Johnson did not need to do this to get votes (as it was clear early on that he would defeat Republican challenger Barry Goldwater), his responsiveness to the opinions revealed in the state surveys done by his pollster, Oliver Quayle, was geared toward strengthening his position to direct the public on domestic social goals after the election (Jacobs and Shapiro, 1993). Although we have not systematically studied Clinton's two predecessors, George Bush succeeded in directing public opinion in foreign affairs, and on taking office Ronald Reagan directed the nation in a conservative direction on economic and social issues against a substantially more liberal public opinion (Page and Shapiro, 1992, chaps. 3–4).

Making use of Greenberg's and others' polls and focus groups, we determined that Clinton's 1992 campaign strategy of responsiveness seemed to be somewhat similar to Kennedy's. Clinton focused on the economy as the most important issue. He also emphasized the need for health care reform and staked out positions on other salient domestic issues for which there was already substantial public support. Unlike Kennedy—and perhaps justifiably by the end of the Cold War—Clinton was less concerned with foreign affairs. Domestic issues, individually and collectively, helped shape his image as a "move ahead," change-oriented national leader.

Clinton followed up on these campaign issues once in office. His sensitivity to public opinion has been striking, and there may be several reasons for this. First, his campaign style and strategy may have simply been instinctively transferred to his presidency—along with his public opinion and public relations apparatus. This is not unusual, as other presidents have done this. Greenberg, James Carville, Mandy Grunwald, and George Stephanopoulos and others from Clinton's campaign, for example, remained or were brought back as his advisers. W. Lance Bennett's analysis in Chapter 5 attributes this running of the presidency like a campaign to the changes that have occurred in the psychological relations between voters and candidates and presidents; Martha Joynt Kumar shows in Chapter 9 the extent to which the Clinton administration did not like dealing with the press, apparently preferring to communicate with the public directly, at least until David Gergen was brought on board to handle White House communications.

Second, Clinton's personal style and some deeper psychological influences may have produced this responsiveness. These may have developed from his rocky experiences during the presidential campaign, from his shaky first term and subsequent electoral defeat as governor of Arkansas, or from his earlier experiences. As Fred Greenstein (1993) suggested—and we can point to much supporting evidence—Clinton consistently tried to show people and the public as a whole that he had responded to their wishes; this activity reached a point where it appeared that he had a psychological need to appear responsive (or he was a consummate actor). This responsiveness was most apparent when he participated in a several-hours-long town meeting on ABC TV after he had announced his health care reform plan in a national speech. Clinton was quite effective at showing people at the meeting that his plan was responsive to their needs. During the broadcast, moderator Ted Koppel presented to Clinton and the audience the results of the latest ABC/*Washington Post* poll revealing the difficulty that the public had with parts of Clinton's proposal. Clinton's response was very revealing. For one, he took the survey responses seriously, which indicates that he routinely takes polls seriously. For another, he attributed the public's distress to its lack of detailed knowledge about how the current health care system worked and how his specific proposals in fact dealt with the problems cited in the polls.

Third, Clinton's responsiveness on many fronts may have been the product of the sheer scope of his policy agenda. It was quicker and easier to offer in general terms what already appeared to be acceptable than to propose a number of specific policies likely to divide the public. (Pressure caused by the actions of Ross Perot and by Clinton's receipt of only 43 percent of the popular vote may have contributed as well; having far less than majority electoral support for his presidency, Clinton had an incentive to boost this standing by taking popular stances [see Lammers, 1993, 15–17].) This focus on responsiveness appears to have detracted from efforts to direct already existing public preferences into support for the details of proposed policies. Building on general support and persuading the public to support *specific* policies that evoke skepticism or serious doubts require time; they also require that many details of the policies be worked out. This approach has been taken in the case of health care reform and, though perhaps to a lesser extent, in the economic and budget reduction program.

Responsiveness to general opinion has to be followed, as needed, by direction on the more detailed components of the policies—such as how to fund them, implement them, and related matters—and by the offering of new initiatives that can build on previous successes. This responsiveness requires that presidents alter their leadership strategies after the election campaign has ended and they have to govern. We found that Johnson initially did this quite effectively in 1964 and 1965. Johnson's election campaign was responsive to public opinion, but he clearly shifted gears during his new full term in 1965. He and leaders in Congress converted public support for medical care reform and civil rights, for example, into the enactment of Medicare and another major civil rights act (the Voting Rights Act of 1965, which followed the Civil Rights Act of 1964). He also offered more direction in other ways in 1965 than in 1964, most notably in the cases of his war on poverty and his mobilization of support for escalating the war in Vietnam. Support for these initiatives did not emerge autonomously from the public but were the result of presidential leadership—or manipulation (Jacobs and Shapiro, 1993). That the Vietnam War doomed Johnson's administration and that the war on poverty underachieved had little to do with the president's responding to and then trying to direct public opinion in 1965. Rather, they had to do with what transpired in Vietnam, how Johnson misled the public on this issue virtually from the beginning (see Page and Shapiro, 1992, chaps. 6, 9), and how the war made it more difficult financially and otherwise for his administration to address domestic matters such as social welfare policy.

In Clinton's case, a number of his first-year policies continued the pattern of responsiveness that he had established during his campaign. But with the election over, he had difficulty seizing the opportunity to direct public opinion on the specifics of several of his proposed policies, and in some cases he failed to offer clear and unequivocal proposals. Of course, his lack of an electoral mandate, the ideological makeup of Congress (despite the Democratic majority in each house), uncertainty after the Cold War, and pressures from organized groups contributed to this difficulty. We also think, however, that the enormous number of policies that Clinton attempted to deal with produced this uneven record. These policies included cases in which responsiveness produced easily enacted policies; cases in which it produced problems; foreign policy cases in which Clinton's initial reactions responded to the public's general preference but in which he fell short when it came to specific U.S. and multilateral actions; and cases in which he exercised effective responsive leadership. We describe these further in the sections that follow.

Responsiveness

Quickly on taking office, Clinton had some clear successes on policies that he had long supported and that were consistent with overall public opinion. Among the new president's first actions was his executive order to end the "gag order" on doctors at public clinics providing advice and information about obtaining abortions. This shifted national policy toward the status quo existing before the Bush administration had imposed the restriction. The best interpretation of the available public opinion data (involving patterns and trends in responses to different survey questions) is that a public majority has long and quite steadily supported the *Roe* v. *Wade* decision and opposed heavy-handed federal restrictions (see Page and Shapiro, 1992, chap. 3). A June 1993 NBC News/*Wall Street Journal* poll reported that 63 percent of the public "agree strongly" that "the government should not interfere with a woman's right to have an abortion."

Congress repassed and Clinton signed the family leave bill, which had had substantial public support but which outgoing President Bush had vetoed. In an October 1992 *New York Times*/CBS News poll, 55 percent said that Bush should have signed the bill. A January 1993 *NYT*/CBS survey later reported that 65 percent favored (only 28 percent opposed) "requiring employers to guarantee 12 weeks of unpaid leave for parents of new children or an employee caring for a sick family member." In a June 1993 NBC/*WSJ* poll, 67 percent responded that "requiring that employers allow parents to take leave from work to care for a new baby or sick child would be an effective government action" (an additional 24 percent said "somewhat effective").

The bill containing the "motor voter" and related voter registration reforms to make registration not only an easier task but also a formal government responsibility played out similarly to the family leave bill: Bush had opposed it, and it was enacted shortly after Clinton took office. This issue was apparently less salient than others in terms of the president's (and Hillary Rodham Clinton's) time and effort (William Lammers [1993] reported that Clinton devoted *no* attention to it in his public speeches and remarks).

In response to the Midwest floods, Clinton did much better (having the good sense to cut short his rest stop in Hawaii on returning from an important trip to Japan) in anticipating public reactions to federal relief efforts than Bush did in reacting to the massive hurricane in Florida. Only 14 percent of the public thought he had done a bad job in responding to the floods, according to a July 1993 NBC/*WSJ* poll.

These efforts to be responsive to public opinion did not always produce success. This can happen particularly if public opinion is misread or if opinion survey results are ignored. Such misreading can also result in failed opportunities to be responsive. Two of Clinton's early failures fit this description.

Clinton moved quickly on proposing to end the ban on gays and lesbians in the military. He and his advisers did not think that the opposition would be as strong as it was and apparently thought that the issue could be dealt with not much differently from the executive order on abortion regulations. Clinton was clearly responding to the wishes of some of his core supporters during his election campaign, for whom this was an important issue. Public opinion data, however, have long shown that 80 percent of the public think homosexuality is "always" or "almost always morally wrong" (though this did drop to a still-high 71 percent in the February–April 1993 National Opinion Research Center [NORC] General Social Survey). Public opinion has been much more evenly divided on permitting homosexuals in various occupations, including the military (Page and Shapiro, 1992, chap. 3). Gallup Poll data since 1977 and *NYT*/CBS surveys have shown that, although the public has become a bit more accepting toward homosexuality, it is still evenly split on whether "homosexual relations between consenting adults should or should not be legal." Unlike the abortion case, Clinton was offering a new policy proposal, not restoring a previously existing one, so that deeply rooted attitudes toward homosexuality warranted a different strategy than the one followed. *NYT*/CBS polls in January and February 1993 found the public just slightly opposed to or evenly split on "permitting homosexuals to serve in the military." Subsequently, NBC/*WSJ* polls consistently found that just over a majority of those with opinions opposed "allowing openly gay men and lesbian women to serve in the military." A majority (56 percent in a July NBC/*WSJ* poll), however, came to agree that the "don't ask, don't tell" proposal was a good compromise, but 56 percent (July, NBC/*WSJ*) also rated Clinton badly in his leadership on the issue. As early as the second week of February, 56 percent (*NYT*/CBS) thought Clinton was paying too much "attention to the needs and problems of homosexuals"; 66 percent thought government should not "give a lot of attention to" the issue.

Clinton's failures in attempting to appoint Zoe Baird and then Kimba Wood to head the Justice Department also illustrate his misreading of public opinion. The controversy in these appointments had to do with the appointees' employing and paying Social Security taxes on household workers, who, in addition, may have been (as it was publicly perceived) in the country illegally. The issue substantially turned on whether the nominee for this chief post in federal law enforcement broke the law. Baird had broken the law, and she paid back taxes and penalties, whereas Wood had not broken the law. Seeing that Wood's case might be perceived and interpreted by the public as virtually identical to Baird's (Baird's problem had caught Clinton by surprise), Clinton withdrew Wood from consideration. Although the public may have seen similarities in the two cases, Clinton did not attempt to show how the cases were in fact different. (There is substantial research demonstrating that the public is quite capable of making distinctions concerning issues and proposals [see Page and Shapiro, 1992].) The Wood nomination would have been an opportunity for directing the public on an issue that would continue to come up rather than admitting yet another mistake in making executive appointments.

In picking problems and policies to pursue, Clinton, like other presidents, avoided issues on which the public supported actions he was unwilling to take. Immigration was one on which Clinton was essentially silent during his first year, whereas the public viewed the increasing immigrant population as a growing problem.

Clinton also clearly staked out positions on trade—particularly the North American Free Trade Agreement—for which he did not initially have public support. The public initially remained split on NAFTA, with, according to one poll, a slowly dropping plurality of about 35–40 percent saying that they had not heard enough or were not sure about the agreement; about a third opposing it; and only 25–30 percent favoring it (data from NBC/*WSJ* polls, January–October 1993). Had the agreement not already been made by President Bush and left for the new president, it is likely that Clinton would have handled the North American trade issue differently. Clinton was forced on this issue to drop it in order to focus more strongly on other matters or to become more directive on it. He opted for the latter, hoping that he could build on Republican support for Bush's agreement and his own party's votes and in doing so persuade the large undecided percentage of the public. (For example, a November 11–14, 1993, *NYT*/CBS poll showed that the public was evenly split on NAFTA, with 22 percent "don't know's"; the poll strongly, though circumstantially, suggested that support for NAFTA tended to increase as people heard more about the agreement.) Clinton obtained congressional support decisively—and surprisingly. He then attempted immediately to use this victory as a resource in trade talks with Asian leaders (Sanger, 1993).

Falling Short in Foreign Policy

In his handling of foreign affairs generally, Clinton clearly responded to public support for generally maintaining U.S. activism in world affairs (see Hinckley, 1992; Wittkopf, 1990; Page and Shapiro, 1992, chaps. 5–6) and for making sure that the Cold War had indeed ended. Specifically, the public supported *multilateral* activism that was coordinated with allies or international organizations. *NYT*/CBS surveys in late 1992 to June 1993 found that 62 percent or more of the public thought that "the United States has a responsibility to give military assistance in trouble spots around the world when it is asked by (its allies/other Western countries)." Such activism as well as foreign policy more generally was made more complex by the ending of the Cold War. This was especially the case for the public now that the Cold War's struggle with Soviet and other brands of communism was no longer there to simplify foreign policy issues by structuring and framing them in a way that, after more than forty years, was quite familiar.

The public agreed that it was important to pay attention to what was occurring in Russia to prevent the reemergence of any communist threat. Both Bush and Clinton maintained close relations with Russia and monitored the situation there after the fall of Soviet communism. In an April 1993 NBC/*WSJ* poll, 63 percent of respondents said that Clinton was paying the "right amount of attention" to Russia. After the departure of the Bush administration, the public—and Clinton—continued to support Boris Yeltsin. Providing aid to Russia, however, was a more specific and consequently more complex issue. Opinion polls revealed more of a split opinion on this issue than on support for Yeltsin, depending on what was emphasized in the survey questions. An April 1993 NBC/*WSJ* survey found that 73 percent agreed that it was in the national interest of the United States that Russia become democratic and have a free market economy; just a plurality (though a clear one, 48 percent) agreed that it was "important that the United States do whatever it can to see that Boris Yeltsin remains president of Russia." A June 1993 *NYT*/CBS poll revealed an increase from 41 percent to a plurality of 49 percent in public support for "the United States giving economic aid to Russia in order to help Russia reform its economy."

In the case of the Middle East, the public supported peace between Israel and the Palestinians and Arab nations, and it backed the U.S. diplomatic efforts toward facilitating negotiations. For Clinton, this meant doing nothing to rock an ongoing process involving, as it turned out, some important behind-the-scenes foreign mediation from Norway. Critical questions, however, might arise if the president requested that Congress appropriate funds for the Middle East and Russia. Even with the euphoria about the unexpected Israeli-Palestinian agreement, 59 percent of the public (NBC/*WSJ*, September 1993) believed that both sides "will not be able to form a lasting peace agreement." Furthermore, 70 percent responded that the United States "should not make contributions to help pay for the costs of the peace agreement." In Clinton's policies toward the Middle East as well as Russia, it is too early, at this writing, to call these cases of responsive leadership. The same applies to policies toward Iraq, about which much is still unresolved.

The crises in Bosnia and Somalia were major and visible failures for the Clinton administration during its first year, and they illustrate problems that arise in attempting to be responsive without offering clear direction. U.S. policy in these cases was consistent with the public's support for multilateral activism. With the end of the Cold War, pre–World War II isolationist sentiment had clearly not returned. But even with the success of the United States and its allies in the Gulf War with Iraq, there was no longer support for the unilateral U.S. activism that had occurred during the Cold War era.

In the case of Bosnia, the public clearly saw that the United States alone had no responsibility there. In a January 1993 *NYT*/CBS survey, 67 percent of respondents said that the United States had no "responsibility to do something about the fighting between the Serbs and the Bosnians." Specifically, there had been clear and persistent majority opposition to the use of ground troops to fight the Serbs. Even though there was at one point, according to a January 1993 *NYT*/CBS survey, support for sending troops to help get food and medicine through to civilians, 82 percent also responded that before taking any military action, the United States should insist that other European countries help. A September 1993 NBC/*WSJ* survey and an August NBC poll found majority support, 58 percent and 53 percent, respectively, for "having the United States and its European allies conduct air strikes against the Serbian military forces" if they "continue to attack Bosnian cities or the United Nations peacekeeping troops in Bosnia."

Clinton has not drifted far from public opinion on Bosnia, which may turn out to be wise given the complexity of the problems and the difficulty in acting militarily and unilaterally there. But multilateral action of the sort that the public might support and that might lead to the end of the civil war in Bosnia has proved difficult to formulate and orchestrate. And this has been perceived as indicating the Clinton administration's weakness and lack of expertise in foreign policy—its apparent incapacity to help its European allies and the United Nations work out specific multilateral strategies in the post–Cold War world (cf. Ruggie, 1993). In this first year in office, the Clinton administration treated public opinion as a constraint rather than trying to build on the public's support for multilateral activism.

Somalia turned into a visible failure of U.S. foreign policymaking. Again, building on the public's support for multilateral actions, President Bush was able to get public support for sending troops to Somalia for the humanitarian purpose of making sure that food was delivered to prevent further starvation there. Clinton continued this policy. Three December 1992 and January 1993 *NYT*/CBS polls found that 66 to 69 percent of the public supported "sending U.S. troops to make sure food gets through to the people of Somalia." Even as the U.S. mission there became drawn out, support continued to remain high: A June 1993 *NYT*/CBS poll reported that 52 percent approved (only 21 percent disapproved) of Clinton's handling of the situation in Somalia; 66 percent thought it was a "good idea" for U.N. troops to try capturing enemy clan leader Mohammed Farah Aidid. But by September 1993, Americans' backing had begun to sour because no end to the mission seemed in sight. This erosion in public support occurred *before* American troops were killed and wounded (and one soldier was captured and publicly humiliated) in early October as the result of what was initially reported as ineffective coordination of U.N. forces and underarmed and undersupported American troops. By September 1993, a NBC/*WSJ* survey was reporting that only 42 percent of respondents supported the use of U.S. military forces for humanitarian purposes versus 52 percent who responded that the military should "be used only when our national interests are at stake." In the same poll, 52 percent said that the United States was too deeply involved (or its efforts were not under control) in Somalia.

In the case of Somalia, the Clinton administration's loss of control and lack of a clear policy or position, whether unilateral or multilateral, became quite apparent. Something of the same sort occurred when Clinton encountered problems in making his Justice Department and Supreme Court appointments. But in the cases of foreign policy in Somalia and Bosnia (and, again, in the case of further U.S. intervention in Haiti), the stakes were more immediate and larger for American forces and for the people of the foreign areas involved.

Responsive Leadership

It is clearly not easy for presidents to turn the public's general attitudes and support into directives or proposals for specific policies. Clinton was just barely able to do this in the case of his economic and budget deficit reduction program. After being unable to push through his expected economic stimulus and jobs program, he nearly lost the slim majority support for his broader economic program (NBC/*WSJ* polls from April to September 1993). He had some success, however, in using this support to keep or reformulate some of the important components of his program.

On several issues related to the budget, Clinton's compromises echoed public preferences. In a July 1993 NBC/*WSJ* poll, 61 percent of the respondents said that Clinton should compromise by reducing the deficit by $100 billion less than he had proposed in his original plan. Moreover, although the public did not like the idea of more taxes, it was willing to pay a small amount of additional taxes toward deficit reduction: In four *NYT*/CBS surveys from February to June 1993, majorities consistently said they were "willing to pay $100 a year more in taxes in order to reduce the federal budget deficit."

However, in what form the taxes would come mattered to the public, and Clinton pursued different, though not always the most satisfactory, options on taxes. His BTU tax turned into a 4.3 cent increase in federal taxes on gasoline. In three *NYT*/CBS polls from February to June, support declined from 41 to 28 percent for "a tax on all forms of energy such as gasoline, electricity, and heating oil" to reduce the budget deficit. In a July NBC/*WSJ* poll, the public was more evenly divided on the 4.3 cent tax on gasoline, and in a NYT/CBS poll a month earlier, 56 percent of respondents stated that a tax on gasoline would be fairer to them than a tax on all forms of energy.

The public came to support most of the other proposals in Clinton's economic program. A July NBC/*WSJ* poll showed opinion split on slowing the growth of Medicare and Medicaid spending, but there was majority support for "taxing most Social Security benefits from couples earning over forty thousand dollars per year." Fully 72 percent supported "increasing the tax rate from 31 percent to 36 percent for people in upper-income categories," according to a July NBC/*WSJ* poll. NBC/*WSJ* also found that 72 percent preferred to see taxes raised on upper-income individuals rather than on business and that 52 percent disapproved of Republicans in Congress opposing the deficit reduction plan because of the tax increases in the program.

As part of deficit reduction—and as a result of changes in U.S. defense needs deriving from changes in world affairs—Clinton continued Bush's policy of reducing defense spending; this policy reflected a long-term trend in public support for spending less on national defense (e.g., Hartley and Russett, 1992; Page and Shapiro, 1992, chap. 6). The February–April 1993 NORC General Survey found the proportion of respondents saying that "we" are spending "too little" on defense near an all-time low, 11 percent, with 43 percent saying "too much" and the rest saying "about right." This meager support for defense spending was unaffected by the recent cuts in spending and the announced closings of military bases.

Clinton engaged in a full-scale effort at responsive leadership in the case of health care, and it is the issue for which we know most about public opinion. Medical care was an issue high on Clinton's agenda, and as an indication of its importance, he entrusted the coordination of research and development of this health care reform plan to Hillary Rodham Clinton.

Clearly, according to the substantial public opinion data that are available, large majorities of the public wanted reform in the nation's health care system (for the data summarized here we draw heavily on Jacobs and Shapiro, 1994; and Jacobs, Shapiro, and Schulman, 1993). Americans have been quite satisfied with their own medical insurance and care—though they have voiced some insecurity about cost and the ability to keep insurance coverage. Nevertheless, Americans have increasingly perceived that others have not been served adequately by the present system.

The public had two general reactions to the Clinton plan after it was announced. First, citizens were concerned with how they might be hurt by some of the details of the plan. Second, they thought it was fair to others, and they supported the plan overall (though there is some evidence, at this writing, that this support has waned a bit).

Several of the components of the plan and its funding were quite acceptable to the public from the start. In all the polls we have seen, public support for taxes of the sort Clinton proposed on cigarettes ran about 70 percent or more. The public would have supported increased taxes on alcohol, too, but such taxes were not included in the proposal. There was also slightly less but still large majority support for mandating that employers provide insurance. According to Greenberg, opinion poll results contributed to Clinton's decision to require employers to buy insurance for their employees instead of opting for a new value-added tax to finance the health care plan (Berke, 1993, A20). Clinton also proposed malpractice reform, which was supported by the public, though most experts agreed that this was a trivial source of rising costs in health care. Clinton's nationally televised speech introducing his health care plan to the nation appeared to us to be the defining moment of his early presidency, and health care reform offered an opportunity for responsive leadership on an enormous scale given the scope of the proposed reforms.

Clinton also had some other opportunities and successes, some very late-breaking ones, at responsive leadership. One small one was his national service program, which also provided an additional kind of assistance to individuals for education. The public supported the idea of a national service act, and though it was scaled back, the basic elements that the public supported were passed.

There were other problem areas that had always been ripe for responsive leadership because of the public's support for government activism in them. Clinton did not miss out on raising these issues and supporting and overseeing progress. These policy areas included environmental protection, crime (including gun control), drugs, education, congressional campaign finance reform, and welfare reform (for a summary of public opinion trends on many of these issues, see Page and Shapiro, 1992). The last area, welfare, was one in which Clinton had promised bold reform of the sort that the public in principle supports—favoring employment, education, and the family over dependence and the breakdown of the family—and it evidently has high priority after health care on his reform agenda during his second year (though there is some doubt, at this writing, as to how aggressively the administration will be able to push a welfare reform bill [see Claiborne, 1994]).

Clinton's much-hailed speech to black ministers in Memphis on November 13, 1993, claimed in a loud voice and in a highly moral tone his concern for crime, violence, drugs, guns, and the plight of poor families in cities. After the passage of NAFTA, crime and gun control in particular took center stage at the very end of the year. The public had long supported more stringent national gun control laws (though it has not generally favored banning the possession of most guns, including handguns [see Page and Shapiro, 1992, chap. 3]), and the administration latched on to the increase in public salience of crime as an urgent national issue and the lobbying for the Brady bill (on the agenda for several years and requiring a five-day waiting period, allowing for a background check, before a buyer can take possession of a purchased gun). Without much administration lobbying, the Senate on November 19 passed the administration's crime bill, which had striking bipartisan support once compromises were reached on the $23 billion bill (the bill went to a House-Senate conference committee in early 1994 to deal with it and anticrime provisions passed by the House; a revised bill was close to passage at this writing). Within two weeks, after some intense debate and last-minute politicking and theatrics, the Brady bill itself was finally passed and signed into law with much fanfare on November 30. Within another two weeks, after the occurrence of nationally publicized shooting incidents (especially the random killings by a gunman on the Long Island Railroad), Clinton was urging the development of still more national legislation on gun licensing (see Dowd, 1993).

There was progress on campaign finance reform and environmental protection: The House and Senate passed bills (to be resolved in a conference committee) that included voluntary limits on congressional campaign spending; they also passed bills (again to be resolved in conference) adding controls on mining. One last issue that the Clinton administration drew attention to in somewhat striking fashion concerned government organization and efficiency. The American public has been always supportive of cutting waste and inefficiency, and Clinton initiated a major debate on reform—ostensibly grander than the work of the Grace Commission under Reagan and of Dan Quayle under Bush—under the direction of Vice President Al Gore. This debate aroused public interest and support: In a September 1993 NBC/*WSJ* poll, 73 percent of the respondents thought significant savings were possible through such reforms, and more important, 55 percent thought "that the commission on reinventing government, which is headed by Vice President Gore, ... is a genuine effort to reform government."

Conclusion

We have offered a preliminary summary and assessment of Clinton's efforts to respond to and direct public opinion. This review also provides a scorecard for the performance of his administration. The ultimate effectiveness of his leadership and presidency is likely to hinge on how well he balances his responsiveness to general public attitudes with direction in formulating the details of his policies and any new policy initiatives. This is no easy task given the breadth of his activism—the number of problems and policies he tried to take action on in less than a year. His failures made his subsequent actions and proposals all the harder. As George Bush found out, the public remembers recent failures better than past successes. Clinton will have to learn from his mistakes, which his election campaign and his track record on the domestic policy front, including trade issues, have shown he is quite capable of doing. Foreign policy may turn out to be a different story since it has not been his strongest suit. Clinton has banked his best leadership efforts on health care reform and his economic program, which will probably determine whether he will be a one-term or a two-term president.

Notes

We thank John Young and Bill Schneider for their comments, and Marianne Ide, Wynne Pomeroy, Michael Kagay, Arthur Chien, and Sunita Parikh for help in assembling public opinion data. Some of the data were obtained from the POLL data base of the Roper Center for Public Opinion Research, Storr, Connecticut.

References

Berke, Richard L. (1993). "Clinton Aide Says Polls Had Role in Health Plan." *New York Times,* December 9, A20.

Claiborne, William (1994). "Bank on Clinton Submitting a Welfare-Reform Bill, But Don't Bet on His Pushing Too Hard for Its Passage." *Washington Post National Weekly Edition,* January 3–9, 29.

Cornwell, Elmer E. Jr. (1965). *Presidential Leadership of Public Opinion.* Bloomington: Indiana University Press.

Dowd, Maureen (1993). "Moved by Killings, Clinton Urges Action on Gun Legislation: The Public Mood on Crime and Weapons Is Heard." *New York Times,* December 9, B10.

Edwards, George C. III (1983). *The Public Presidency.* New York: St. Martin's.

———— (1989). *At the Margins: Presidential Leadership of Congress.* New Haven: Yale University Press.

Ginsberg, Benjamin (1986). *The Captive Public: How Mass Opinion Promotes State Power.* New York: Basic Books.

Greenstein, Fred I. (1993). "The Presidential Leadership Style of Bill Clinton: A Provisional Analysis." Paper presented at the Annual Meeting of the American Political Science Association, Washington, D.C., September 2–5.

Hartley, Thomas, and Bruce Russett (1992). "Public Opinion and the Common Defense: Who Governs Military Spending in the United States?" *American Political Science Review* 86 (December):905–915.

Hinckley, Ronald H. (1992). *People, Polls, and Policymakers: American Public Opinion and National Security.* New York: Lexington Books.

Jacobs, Lawrence R. (1992). "The Recoil Effect: Public Opinion and Policy Making in the U.S. and Britain." *Comparative Politics* 24 (January):199–217.

———— (1993). *The Health of Nations: Public Opinion and the Making of American and British Health Policy.* Ithaca: Cornell University Press.

Jacobs, Lawrence R., and Robert Y. Shapiro (1992). "Public Decisions, Private Polls: John F. Kennedy's Presidency." Paper presented at the Annual Meeting of the Midwest Political Science Association, Chicago, Illinois, April 9–11.

———— (1993). "The Public Presidency, Private Polls, and Policymaking: Lyndon Johnson." Paper presented at the Annual Meeting of the American Political Science Association, Washington, D.C., September 2–5.

_____ (1994). "The New Public Philosophy: Public Opinion's Tilt Against Private Enterprise." *Health Affairs* 13 (Spring): 285–298.

_____ (forthcoming). "Issues, Candidate Image, and Priming: The Use of Private Polls in Kennedy's 1960 Presidential Campaign." *American Political Science Review.*

Jacobs, Lawrence R., Robert Y. Shapiro, and Eli C. Schulman (1993). "Poll Trends: Medical Care in the United States—An Update." *Public Opinion Quarterly* 57 (Fall):394–427.

Kernell, Samuel (1986). *Going Public: New Strategies of Presidential Leadership.* Washington, D.C.: CQ Press.

Key, V. O. Jr. (1961). *Public Opinion and American Democracy.* New York: Knopf.

Lammers, William W. (1993). "Presidential Leadership Styles in the First Year: Going Public from Roosevelt to Clinton." Paper presented at the Annual Meeting of the American Political Science Association, Washington, D.C., September 2–5.

Light, Paul C. (1982). *The President's Agenda.* Baltimore, Md.: Johns Hopkins University Press.

Lindblom, Charles E. (1977). *Politics and Markets.* New York: Basic Books.

Lowi, Theodore J. (1985). *The Personal President: Power Invested, Promise Unfulfilled.* Ithaca: Cornell University Press.

Neustadt, Richard (1980). *Presidential Power: The Politics of Leadership from FDR to Carter.* New York: Wiley.

Page, Benjamin I., and Robert Y. Shapiro (1983). "Effects of Public Opinion on Policy." *American Political Science Review* 77:175–190.

_____ (1985). "Presidential Leadership Through Public Opinion." In *The Presidency and Public Policy Making,* ed. George C. Edwards III, Steven A. Shull, and Norman C. Thomas. Pittsburgh: University of Pittsburgh Press.

_____ (1992). *The Rational Public: Fifty Years of Trends in Americans' Policy Preferences.* Chicago: University of Chicago Press.

Peterson, Mark (1990). *Legislating Together: The White House and Capitol Hill from Eisenhower to Reagan.* Cambridge: Harvard University Press.

Popkin, Samuel L. (1991). *The Reasoning Voter.* Chicago: University of Chicago Press.

Ruggie, John Gerard (1993). "The U.N.: Wandering in the Void." *Foreign Affairs* (November-December): 26–31.

Sanger, David E. (1993). "Clinton Now Turns to Widening Trade Across the Pacific. Resistance Among Asians. President, Fresh from Success in North America, Pledges to Open More Markets." *New York Times,* November 19, A1, A6.

Schumpeter, Joseph A. (1950). *Capitalism, Socialism, and Democracy.* New York: Harper.

Tulis, Jeffery (1987). *The Rhetorical Presidency.* Princeton: Princeton University Press.

Wilson, Woodrow (1908). *Constitutional Government in the United States.* New York: Columbia University Press.

_____ (1925). *Congressional Government: A Study in American Politics.* Boston: Houghton Mifflin.

_____ (1952). *Leaders of Men.* Ed. T. Motter. Princeton: Princeton University Press.

Wittkopf, Eugene R. (1990). *Faces of Internationalism: Public Opinion and American Foreign Policy.* Durham, N.C.: Duke University Press.

PART V

The Clinton Presidency and the Psychology of Public Policy: Dilemmas and Opportunities

11

President Clinton as a Cognitive Manager

PETER SUEDFELD AND
MICHAEL D. WALLACE

The first year of the Clinton presidency was characterized by administration attempts to follow up on campaign promises and to develop detailed plans and implementation that would turn possibilities into reality. Such implementation depended on three general components: putting into crucial positions people who would be both dedicated to the goal and competent to reach it, establishing a detailed and realistic series of concrete actions based on factual data, and persuading Congress, the media, and the public (not necessarily in that order) to accept at least the major aspects of each proposal.

The administration's success in reaching these goals was mixed, with a surprising degree of controversy and failure. During the first half-year, a number of high-profile appointments were blocked or withdrawn under pressure, and several strongly advocated policy changes and initiatives were abandoned, defeated, or modified beyond recognition. Although the record improved later in the year, the administration's political maneuverings seemed well summed up by Clinton's own comment at a July 1993 press conference in regard to his final decision on logging in the Pacific Northwest: "We know that our solutions may not make everybody happy. Indeed, they may not make *anybody* happy" (italics added). Even more positive outcomes seemed to be due more to the absence of controversial initiatives than to the winning of important controversies. The passage (after considerable doubt and with a very narrow margin) of NAFTA was one of the very few hard-fought battles that ended in a victory for the administration. This record is even more surprising given the solid majority of the president's own party in both houses of Congress, usually *the* most powerful predictor of presidential success (Simonton, 1993).

It seems reasonable to hypothesize that the president's approach to decisionmaking and decision implementation has an important influence on the date of his proposals. Other chapters in this book examining his leadership style imply that his success rate should have been much higher and more consistent than it has in fact been. Contributors to this book have described him as "sensitive to the political context," highly oriented to information seeking, willing to compromise and work as a team player rather than as an autocrat, analytical and innovative, reveling in "the arts of persuasion and cajolery," highly intelligent and verbal, and pragmatically flexible. Nevertheless, it is true that personality traits alone do not provide a good basis for predictions of leadership quality because particular motivational profiles are associated with good and bad outcomes, intelligence and presidential success have an ambivalent relationship (Simonton, 1993), and simple approaches to even complex problems may sometimes be more successful—and morally more defensible—than complex ones (Suedfeld, 1988; Tetlock, Armor, and Peterson, 1993).

Our own analysis of President Clinton's leadership is based on a relatively parsimonious and, to some extent, even simplistic model. This is the assessment of the president as a cognitive manager.

The Cognitive Manager Model

One commonly recognized aspect of decisionmaking is resource allocation. In any problem situation, resources are limited: There are only so much time, so much energy, so much information, so many people to assign to tasks, so much money to spend, and so many possible solutions. Every resource used in attempting to solve one problem is, at least temporarily and sometimes permanently, unavailable to deal with other problems.

The cognitive manager model (Suedfeld, 1992) proposes that the psychological resources that a good decisionmaker will devote to solving a particular problem are commensurate with the importance of the problem. Vigilance, information search and processing, reexamination of alternatives, and the other components of ideal decisionmaking exact a cost; when the potential benefit is worth the cost, these processes will be utilized. It is also important to bear in mind that problems do not come singly, nor are they solved by perfect machines: It is the importance of a problem in relation to others and the resource repertoire of the problemsolver at that time that determine resource allocation. The resource repertoire, in turn, varies with time, personality, health, the situation, and so on. Thus, for example, leaders under severe prolonged stress will have fewer cognitive resources to allocate to the solution of even important problems. Our research focuses on how, within that limited pool, the available resources are allocated.

One implication of the cognitive manager model is that the good cognitive manager will use shortcuts to solve less important problems and will reserve high levels of cognitive effort for more important ones. Furthermore, once all of the criteria of cognitive preparation have been met, the decision itself may be made in a simple or a complex fashion—for example, either as a final and unchangeable answer to the problem or as a proposition open to further compromise—depending on the situation. In other words, we can expect flexibility in response to resource availability, on the one hand, and to the challenges being confronted, on the other.

A variety of analytic methods is available for studying resource allocation and flexibility in decisionmaking. Some of these are intrusive, setting up artificial experimental or simulation situations in which the participants know that they are subjects in a study. Others involve the insertion of an observer while actual problems are being confronted. Least intrusive are archival methods, which analyze documents produced by decisionmakers before, during, and after specific problematic episodes. We have chosen to use the last of these approaches and to score Mr. Clinton's policy statements and other utterances for integrative complexity.

Integrative Complexity

There have been a number of operational definitions of cognitive complexity, but the construct basically refers to the extent to which decisionmakers search for and monitor information, try to predict outcomes and reactions, flexibly weigh their own and other parties' options, and consider potential strategies. Integrative complexity has two measured components: *differentiation,* the recognition of more than one dimension of, or legitimate perspective on, an issue; and *integration,* the recognition of interconnectedness among these dimensions or perspectives through, for example, syntheses, trade-offs, compromises, or higher-level conceptual schemata (Schroder, Driver, and Streufert, 1967; Suedfeld, Tetlock, and Streufert, 1992). It is important to remember that integrative complexity scoring assesses the structure, not the content, of thought. Any specific policy or view of the source can be chosen, explained, defended, or criticized at any level of complexity. So, for example, there is no reason to expect general complexity differences between pro- and antiabortion policies, pro- and anti-immigration policies, liberal and conservative policies, and so on.

Figure 11.1 illustrates the four nodal levels of integrative complexity: the most simple, in which the issue is considered unidimensionally, with no gradations, shadings, or alternatives; differentiation in which different aspects or qualities of the issue are recognized but no relation among them is perceived; differentiation with some understanding of linkage across dimensions; and,

One Bipolar Perspective

No differentiation,
no integration

Unrelated Dimensions

Unrelated Perspectives
Differentiation, no integration

Differentiated Dimensions

One Combinatorial Perspective
Moderate differentiation,
low integration

Differentiated Dimensions

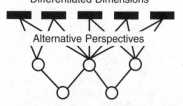

Alternative Perspectives

Superordinate Schemata
High differentiation, high integration

FIGURE 11.1   The Structure of Integrative Complexity

TABLE 11.1   Integrative Complexity Scoring

Score	Characteristics
1	No differentiation, no integration
2	Transition
3	Differentiation, no integration
4	Transition
5	Differentiation, low integration
6	Transition
7	Differentiation, high integration

the most complex, differentiation with a multilevel set of cognitive schemata integrating the differentiated dimensions.

Complexity is typically scored along a 7-point scale, where 1 represents the absence of both differentiation and integration, 3 indicates differentiation only, 5 connotes both differentiation and integration, and 7 shows maximal levels of both, as, for example, in an articulated systems perspective (see Table 11.1). Scores of 2, 4, and 6 are assigned when there is some indication that the passage being scored exceeds one of the nodal levels of differentiation and integration but there is no clear evidence that it has reached the next higher level. To become a qualified scorer, one must reach a reliability of at least 0.85 with established scores on standardized test materials, usually after an intensive training workshop and with the use of a detailed manual (Baker-Brown, Ballard, Bluck, de Vries, Suedfeld, and Tetlock, 1992).

Table 11.2 shows examples of passages and their scores, all taken from a speech on the international economy made by President Clinton on February 26, 1993. There was no passage scored 7 in that speech, but the characteristics of such a score can be inferred from the explanation of the score of 6.

Integrative complexity scores have been derived in studies using a wide variety of methods, which include traditional social psychological laboratory procedures, the scoring of interview transcripts, complex simulation games, and archival analyses of documents generated in the course of domestic and international politics. Situational variables that have been shown to affect complexity include accountability for one's decision, a conflict between or a danger to important values, time pressure, information overload, social role, and the occurrence of societal upheaval such as war. Internal states or events also influence complexity. Among these are high stress, aspects of memory, political ideology, emotional engagement, pre- or postdecision status, and individual differences in "trait" or conceptual complexity as well as in cognitive flexibility (see, e.g., Schroder et al., 1967; Suedfeld et al., 1992; Tetlock, 1983).

Three points should be noted in relation to the scoring of integrative complexity from archival material. First, there is the issue of what happens when the purported source of the material being scored may not be the actual author of the material. We have found that when important writings, speeches,

TABLE 11.2   Sample Passages and Complexity Scores

(a) "We are in a constant race toward innovation that will not end in the lifetime of anyone in this room. What all this means is that the best investment we can make today is in the one resource firmly rooted in our own borders. That is, the education, the skills, the reasoning capacity, and the creativity of our people."

(Score = 1. *Explanation:* one perspective—the best investment for assisting the country toward innovation—is presented, followed by a list defining that investment.)

(b) "Look now at our immigrant Nation and think of the world toward which we are tending. Look at how diverse and multiethnic and multilingual we are, in a world in which the ability to communicate with all kinds of people from all over the world and to understand them will be critical. Look at our civic habits of tolerance and respect. They are not perfect in our own eyes. It grieved us all when there was so much trouble a year ago in Los Angeles. But Los Angeles is a county with 150 different ethnic groups of widely differing levels of education and access to capital and income. It is a miracle that we get along as well as we do. And all you have to do is look at Bosnia, where the differences were not so great, to see how well we have done in spite of all of our difficulties."

(Score = 2. *Explanation:* One basic perspective, the positive aspects of the diversity of the U.S. population, is presented, with the qualification that imperfections are recognized.)

(c) "We also know that regional and bilateral agreements provide oportunities to explore new kinds of trade concerns, such as how trade relates to policies affecting the environment and labor standards and the antitrust laws. And these agreements, once concluded, can act as a magnet inducing other countries to drop barriers and to open their trading systems."

(Score = 3. *Explanation:* Different dimensions of agreements affecting differentiated concerns are identified, as is the eventual additional dimension of expanding free trade with other countries.)

(d) "Our leadership is especially important for the world's new and emerging democracies. To grow and deepen their legitimacy, to foster a middle class and a civic culture, they need the ability to tap into a growing global economy. And our security and our prosperity will be greatly affected in the years ahead by how many of these nations can become and stay democracies."

(Score = 4. *Explanation:* Various dimensions of the needs of new democracies are noted, and an interaction—as opposed to a unidirectional effect—with the global and U.S. economies is implied but not explicitly stated.)

(e) "By now we are woven inextricably into the fabric of a global economy. Imports and exports, which accounted for about $1 in $10 when I was growing up, now represent $1 in every $5. Nearly three-quarters of the things we make in America are subject to competition at home or abroad from foreign producers and foreign providers of services. Whether we see it or not, our daily lives are touched everywhere by the flows of commerce that cross national borders as inexorably as the weather."

(Score = 5. *Explanation:* Magnitude of change in value of imports and exports and competition are recognized as differentiated dimensions of the impact of the global economy on the United States; integration with the U.S. economy and daily life is further made explicit in the first and last sentences.)

(f) "We have got to focus on how to help our people adapt to these changes, how to maintain a high-wage economy in the United States without ourselves adding to the protectionist direction that so many of the developed nations have taken in the last few years. These barriers in the end will cost the developing world more in lost exports and incomes than all the foreign assistance that developed countries provide, but after that they will begin to undermine our economic prosperity as well."

(Score = 6. *Explanation:* This passage shows a differentiated perspective; interaction between high wages and protectionism and between policies of developed nations and effects on developing ones. Comparison of short- and long-term effects of trade barriers on developing nations, and the comparison of these effects with those of foreign aid imply, but do not explicitly delineate, a superordinate system.)

Source: Remarks made at American University, February 26, 1993, as reported in *Weekly Compilation of Presidential Documents.*

interviews, or press conferences are analyzed, it does not matter much whether the material was actually prepared by the presenter or by an aide (e.g., Suedfeld and Tetlock, 1977). Presumably, the identified source will select writers who reflect his or her own level of complexity and will reject or modify specific parts of the material whose complexity level is incongruent. Furthermore, there appears to be very little, if any, complexity difference in prepared and spontaneous speeches by the same individual (Ballard, 1983).

Second, the question is sometimes raised as to whether we are measuring how the individual thinks or only how the individual expresses his or her thoughts. Obviously, thoughts cannot be measured directly; therefore, our data are indirect reflections of the cognitive process. They do have a high level of construct and predictive validity as well as reliability, and the correlation between complexity and various measures of verbal fluency is quite low.

Third, there is controversy about the extent to which complexity can be consciously manipulated by speakers or writers whose goal is to project a particular image (Suedfeld et al., 1992; Tetlock, 1981). Although this issue is not yet settled—in fact, no good way to settle it has been found—complexity scoring has been shown to predict decisions accurately when an analysis of content would lead to deceptive conclusions. In other instances, complexity has changed in directions opposite to that which would be compatible with good public relations. Therefore, the complexity of the utterance appears to be a relatively (although not absolutely) faithful index of the complexity of thought.

Complexity Implications of Qualitative Analyses

Media commentary about the Clinton administration, quotations from people on its staff, and social science analyses all show consensus on some of the salient cognitive characteristics of the president's leadership. The most common remarks concerning the policy process and its outcomes have focused on Clinton's flexibility and readiness to compromise, his hands-on involvement in many policy details, and his desire for ever-more information.

These characteristics—exhaustive information search and processing, wide consultation, willingness to take the perspective of others, refusal to eliminate any alternative prematurely—imply a high level of integrative complexity and what Irving L. Janis (e.g., 1989) would call vigilant problemsolving. In fact, Janis's "symptoms of defective decision-making" (Herek et al., 1987) are best avoided by flexibility, extensive information search, attention to detail: in short, President Clinton's famous strong points. David Winter's analysis in Chapter 6 agrees with this view: "[Clinton's] changes of position and policy are based more on calculations of risk and results than on the influence of close associates." In other words, the president is seen as a fact-oriented, flexible information processor.

But a closer look at some of the analyses shows a somewhat different picture. For example, Stanley Renshon's characterization of Clinton's leadership style in Chapter 4 would lead to the following extrapolations as to complexity scores:

1. Confusing his own understanding of issues with how the public understands those issues would be scored as a lack of differentiation (score of 1).

2. Pursuing too many discrete initiatives simultaneously would be scored as high differentiation, no integration (score of 3).

3. Quibbling about errors would be scored as qualification or implicit differentiation within a unidimensional perspective (score of 2).

4. Wanting to "have it all" would be scored as an undifferentiated, unidimensional perspective (score of 1).

5. Having a narrow group of advisers whom he dominates to achieve consensus would be scored as showing limited search for alternatives and avoidance of differentiation (score of 1).

6. Failing to discuss his policies in trade-off terms and, as has been described in the case of NAFTA, moving from such terms to considering only the benefits of his own proposals and only the drawbacks of alternatives would be scored as perception of only one legitimate perspective on the issue (score of 1 or 2).

7. Self-imposing time pressures (any time pressure generally results in reduced complexity).

Some of the president's other behaviors, as described, for example, by Renshon, lead to similar conclusions. For example, consensus building may involve the recognition and inclusion of each participant's point of view (differentiation and integration), or it may rest on the leader's forcing through a conclusion that he prefers and his advisers' accepting it (no differentiation). Clinton's seeking out of loyalists (e.g., the Friends of Bill) as advisers reflects the latter tendency. Flexibility may reflect the successive recognition of new ideas and facts and their incorporation in a modified and integrated (complex) strategy, or it may reflect the abandonment of one position and the adoption of a new one without consideration of trade-offs or syntheses. Many of Clinton's policy speeches include a presentation of a list of possible policies, each of which is considered and found to be inadequate and dismissed, except the last: the president's own. This, too, is a low-complexity strategy.

The need to build a new coalition for each issue implies the need for high complexity: coalition building requires that one recognize and accommodate the goals and views of various groups (even if only on the specific issue at hand). Someone operating at a level below integration would not be likely to have a high success rate with this strategy—as Clinton so far has not. With these points in mind, let us look at the actual complexity data.

Findings of the Current Study

An analysis performed in September 1993 (Suedfeld, 1994) was based on the scoring of a large number of verbatim quotes made between the spring of 1992 and mid-August 1993. We had started with the hypothesis, based on the consensus of the media, that Clinton's problems arose out of an excessively high level of complexity and an inability or unwillingness to take a simple, firm, and uncompromising stand when such a stand was needed. Much to our surprise, we found President Clinton's mean complexity score to be quite low. It reached only the level of moderate differentiation, with scores of around 2.0–2.5. Another striking and unexpected finding was Clinton's decrease in complexity from the time of the presidential campaign to the period after his inauguration. This was true in general—that is, on all topics considered together—as well as on individual major policy issues.

The statements analyzed for this chapter greatly expanded the database to reduce the likelihood of sampling errors and to make more refined analyses possible. We also obtained independent scores from additional trained scorers to minimize the possibility of scorer bias. These scorers generally did not know from what specific time period a particular quote had come, they varied quite widely in their own political orientation and their opinion of President Clinton, and, most of them being Canadians, they had relatively little personal involvement in the topic.

The findings, set out in Table 11.3, were compatible with those of the September data set. Clinton's overall complexity level still hovered in the low differentiation range and still showed a consistent drop from before the election to his months in office. Other issues on which there are inadequate data for a full comparison bear out the conclusion that Clinton's policy-related speeches are generally low. For example, the mean score across a large number of comments regarding the issue of homosexuals serving openly in the armed forces was 1.84; for several speeches concerning Haiti, in October and November 1993, 1.68; for speeches about Bosnia, in August–November, 1.38; for a speech on black violence, in November, 1.80; for a speech on AIDS, in December, 2.29.

In addition, just as in the earlier analysis, the data contradicted some of our most confident predictions. For example, we expected to find a consistent trend of complexity changes as the president gained more experience in office, presumably upward as he became increasingly complex in the course of learning the complications of developing and then selling his policies. Surprisingly, a quarter-by-quarter analysis showed the opposite: a small but consistently

TABLE 11.3   Clinton's Mean Complexity Scores, by Month and Topic

				Topic			
Period	General Economy	Education (National Service)	Health Care	Environ-ment	NAFTA	Middle-Class Tax Cut	Economic Stimulation
1992	2.3	2.2	2.2	2.3			
1993							
Jan.			2.1				
Feb.	2.4	1.3		1.7	2.2		1.3
Mar.		1.1	2.4	2.1	2.3		1.8
Apr.	1.5	1.6	1.9	2.6	2.7		1.4
May	2.2	1.4	2.6	2.8	1.8	1.5	1.8
June	1.8	1.2			1.8	1.3	1.0
July		1.3	1.7	2.9	1.5	1.5	1.6
Aug.			2.0		1.6		
Sept.		1.4	1.9		1.3		
Oct.			1.4	2.0	1.6		1.5
Nov.			1.6		1.8		
Dec.	1.8		1.4				

Note: Data points based on fewer than five paragraphs are omitted.

TABLE 11.4   Clinton's Mean Overall Complexity Scores, by Quarter

Period	Mean Complexity	Number of Passages Scored
Campaign '92	2.31	432
Jan.–Mar. '93	2.10	329
Apr.–June '93	1.90	409
July–Sept. '93	1.86	669
Oct.–Dec. '93	1.68	199

downward trend over the first year of the administration (Table 11.4). For comparison, the table includes the mean integrative complexity figures for speeches during the 1992 election campaign. These were the highest Clinton had reached by the end of 1993; the last quarter of his first year was the lowest to that point. The overall mean does not exceed 2.0 for any quarter of 1993 after the first. The large size of each sample indicates that the scores were not significantly influenced by a few outliers.

We also expected that we might find an audience effect. Complexity might differ depending on whether the passages came from a presidential news conference, an address to Congress, a town meeting or other direct presentation to the public, or remarks to a friendly group convened because it was interested in the topic and could be expected to support the president. Previous research (Tetlock, 1983, 1985a, 1985b) had established that speakers tended to be more complex when addressing possibly hostile audiences and audiences that it was important to persuade; a similar sensitivity to listeners could be expected to characterize Clinton's materials. Again, we were proven wrong: Even speeches to Congress, an audience crucial to the implementation of policy proposals whose views were known to be mixed, ranged only around 2.2. When addressing an "issue public" (Elkins, 1993)—people sharing a salient policy interest—Clinton showed no consistent trend. For example, a speech on NAFTA to an Export/Import Bank conference rose to 2.67, very high for him; but on the same topic to a business roundtable his speech rated 1.67.

Still another possibility was that the president's complexity would increase as a particular policy approached the moment of truth: a vote in Congress or other decisive event. It could be expected that in the course of negotiating a last-minute acceptance of one of his controversial proposals, Clinton would exhibit increasing complexity concerning its features. However, on those policies voted on so far, no such pattern was evident. There was no consistent trend in Clinton's public statements either on the economic stimulus package, which was defeated, or NAFTA, which was passed.

Last, we thought that we might find consistent differences across topic areas. Some policy proposals, after all, were more controversial than others; some were more important in the president's overall political values than others; some were still in the stage of development before being put to Congress; still others had already been dealt with in whole or in part or were closer to a vote. Here, in fact, we did find one situational effect: The environment was treated with a higher level of complexity than any other topic.

Implications of the Findings

To examine the importance and implications of our results, we put Clinton's complexity scores into a broader context. This context includes comparisons with the complexity data of other twentieth-century U.S. presidents and also looks at complexity patterns among other national and international leaders. We consider what different patterns of complexity imply for the success and failure of such individuals. Last, we consider the paradoxical relationship between President Clinton's cognitive strategies and how these are perceived and evaluated by observers in the media and in academe.

Comparison with Predecessors

How does Clinton's information processing compare with that of other major leaders? One interesting exercise is to compare him with other American presidents? Philip E. Tetlock (1981) scored the complexity of twentieth-century presidential speeches during election campaigns and in the first month, second year, and third year of each president's first term of office. He studied only those presidents who were elected to that office, omitting those who first acceded to the presidency by finishing an incumbent's term. The absolute level of complexity of President Clinton's statements is in the lower range of

TABLE 11.5   Mean Change in Integrative Complexity

President	Preelection	1st Month	% Change
Eisenhower	1.9	3.4	+79
Kennedy	2.1	3.6	+71
F. D. Roosevelt	2.2	3.5	+59
McKinley	2.1	3.1	+48
Taft	2.4	3.5	+46
Wilson	3.2	3.9	+29
Nixon	2.5	2.9	+16
Carter	2.7	3.1	+15
Harding	2.2	2.5	+14
Clinton	2.3	2.2	−4
Hoover	3.8	2.8	−26

Source: Comparison data are from P. E. Tetlock, "An Integratively Complex Look at Integrative Complexity" (Paper presented at the Annual Meeting of the American Psychological Association, San Francisco, California, August 1991).

other presidents in this century (Tetlock, 1981). In fact, Clinton's complexity score in the first month after he took office was lower than *any* of the ten other presidents in Tetlock's study, most of whom reached a level of about 3.5, showing not only clear differentiation but also some integration (Table 11.5).

Almost all of the presidents showed an increase in complexity from before the election to their first month in office. There was no consistent change thereafter, indicating that complexity during the first month was a fairly good predictor of future complexity. To see how President Clinton fits into this pattern so far, Table 11.5 incorporates his statements during the first month of his term into Tetlock's table. Our version of the table is rearranged: Tetlock's original listed the presidents in chronological order, whereas ours has them ranked from those who showed the greatest complexity increases to those who showed the smallest increases and then those who actually decreased in complexity from before to after taking office. Clinton ranks toward the bottom of this list in a category that comprises some of the least esteemed presidents of recent history: Richard Nixon, Jimmy Carter, Warren Harding, and Herbert Hoover.

Implications of Leader Complexity in Historical Context

It appears that, contrary to the implication of some other analyses, President Clinton deals with policy issues at a consistently low level of integrative complexity. We may ask, so what? After all, the cognitive manager model argues that simple decision strategies are not necessarily worse than more complex ones (e.g., Suedfeld, 1992; Tetlock, 1992). Should we be concerned about Clinton's complexity pattern?

TABLE 11.6   Positive and Negative Aspects of Simple and Complex Decisionmaking

Type of Decisionmaking	*Costs*	*Benefits*
Simple	Overlooks trade-offs	Achieves quick resolution
	Is susceptible to biases such as belief perseverance, overattribution, and overconfidence	Minimizes dissonance and cognitive strain Is unlikely to be exploited for long
	Risks being insufficiently empathic toward opponent	Has decreased susceptibility to biases such as dilution and worst-case thinking
	Suffers impression-management liabilities: rigidity, self-righteousness, dogmatism	Possesses impression-management pluses: decisiveness, principles
Complex	Takes time	Is aware of trade-offs
	Produces emotional and cognitive strain (e.g., cognitive dissonance)	Has reduced susceptibility to biases such as belief perseverance, overattribution, and overconfidence
	Risks appeasing aggressors	Is likely to identify mutually beneficial solutions to conflicts of interest
	Is susceptibile to biases such as dilution and worst-case thinking	Possesses impression-management pluses: flexibility, thoughtfulness, cool-headedness
	Suffers impression-management liabilities: weakness, confusion, indecisiveness	

Source: P. E. Tetlock, "An Integratively Complex Look at Integrative Complexity" (Paper presented at the Annual Meeting of the American Psychological Association, San Francisco, California, August 1991).

One answer comes from looking at the strengths and weaknesses of simple and complex information processing. Table 11.6, based on an analysis by Tetlock (1991), shows such a comparison. Note the Clintonian characteristics that fit the descriptors of simple decisionmaking: overconfidence, self-righteousness, insufficient real (as opposed to strategic) empathy, rapid responses in the face of time pressure, and minimization of dissonance.

The presence of these features does not necessarily predict a negative outcome. As we have said, different kinds of problems are particularly amenable to complex or simple decisionmaking. There is general agreement that simple strategies are optimal when, for example, a decision must be made quickly, one is confronting an implacably hostile opponent, crucial values are at significant risk; and it is important to project an image of decisiveness and strength (Suedfeld, 1988). With the possible exception of the last of these points, Clinton's first-year policy controversies do not seem to fit these criteria, and on the last criterion his performance has paradoxically combined low complexity with a public image of insufficient firmness. His low level of complexity might have been just right for a different set of circumstances and problems, but it appears to be too low for the optimal resolution of the policy dilemmas that he has confronted.

Absolute level of complexity is not the only relevant variable. Another, and perhaps even more important, one is the ability to adjust that level as circumstances change and particular levels of complexity become more or less adaptive. The theoretical origin of integrative complexity is in conceptual complexity theory (Schroder et al., 1967), which treated complexity as a personality characteristic, a stable trait that underlies information processing across situations. Conceptual complexity theorists would propose that Clinton may be operating at a low level of trait, not merely of state, complexity. This would explain his strikingly consistent scores across time periods and issue domains. Subjects low in (trait) conceptual complexity have been found to function inadequately in many situations requiring the processing of high levels of changing information, a condition that must be the prototype of most presidential decisionmaking.

The cognitive manager model suggests that people differ in their ability to recognize the need to change their level of complexity in response to environmental demands and/or in their ability to effect the change once the need to do so is recognized. President Clinton's very restricted range of complexity scores, regardless of audience, topic, proximity to a decision, and so on, indicates that his cognitive strategies are unresponsive to the environment. Clinton may not recognize when circumstances indicate the desirability of moving to higher levels of complexity—perhaps his famous optimism hampers his ability to foresee the possibility of failure—or even if he realizes the need, he may be unable to formulate a more complex approach.[1]

Previous studies have found that particularly successful leaders are more likely to show significant complexity increases under conditions of national difficulty. As in the case of American presidents, successful leaders of revolutionary movements showed a consistent increase in complexity from the period of revolutionary struggle to the consolidation of the new post-revolutionary government. Leaders who during the latter period continued to operate at low levels of complexity were likely to lose their position and sometimes their life. Incidentally, leaders who were highly complex during the period of revolutionary combat also tended to fall by the wayside afterward, confirming the importance of a flexible match between environmental demands and the complexity of the response (Suedfeld and Rank, 1976).

At the individual level, we may look at Andrey Gromyko, whose career as a diplomat was unparalleled in the almost continuous occupation of high-level posts in administrations from Joseph Stalin's through Mikhail Gorbachev's. Gromyko was characterized by a unique rise in complexity during crises that resulted in complexity decreases among both his Soviet colleagues and his American adversaries. Similar patterns were found for such consistently successful figures as the duke of Wellington and Lester Pearson (Wallace and Suedfeld, 1988).

As we have seen, Clinton not only fails to show an increase in complexity; he also shows very little situation-specific change of *any* sort. This unresponsiveness to environmental conditions is disquieting. Leaders coping with problem situations, both foreign and domestic, usually show some kind of alteration in complexity. For example, the complexity levels of Saddam Hussein and George Bush moved up and down as events developed from the invasion of Kuwait to the end of the Gulf War in 1991 (Wallace, Suedfeld, and Thachuk, 1993; Suedfeld, Wallace, and Thachuk, 1993).

In considering the significance of our findings for the future of the administration, what may we infer from President Clinton's overall low level of complexity and from his failure to show an increase in complexity when the situation appears to call for such a change? To sum up the implications briefly, this pattern has been consistently associated in the past with a record of failure. This association has held true across a number of studies with a wide diversity of people facing an even more diverse set of problems.

What about the general (i.e., non-situation-specific) trend toward decreasing complexity that Clinton has exhibited since before the election? In other leaders, such consistent decreases have been found under conditions of increasing fatigue, failure, and frustration. Robert E. Lee, for example, showed such a trend during the last years of the Civil War as the Confederacy's war-waging ability eroded and his army went short of replacements, supplies, and equipment. This trend, interpreted as connoting a progressive loss of energy and initiative, ended in, and with, Lee's surrender at Appomattox (Suedfeld, Corteen, and McCormick, 1986). Increasing difficulty in mustering the cognitive energy and resources to deal optimally with problems may also explain the findings of a terminal drop in complexity: that is, a negative association between complexity and the number of years of life remaining to the individual, independent of age (Suedfeld, 1985; Suedfeld and Piedrahita, 1984).

We hypothesize that steadily declining complexity over time may be the result of severe, prolonged, and/or repeated stress and that the outcome represents the exhaustion phase of Hans Selye's (1978) General Adaptation Syndrome. There is a parallel with the well-replicated finding that when statesmen who have been trying to resolve an international confrontation exhibit a lowering of complexity, they may be near to abandoning negotiations in favor of armed conflict (e.g., Suedfeld and Tetlock, 1977; Suedfeld, Tetlock, and Ramirez, 1977). In Clinton's case, the pattern may show a course of growing fatigue and frustration. If this interpretation is correct, a period of lower stress and perhaps a few important victories may reverse the trend.

Image and Reality

As we mentioned previously, the public and expert image of President Clinton is that of a man who operates at high levels of complexity. We now know that view to be wrong. But why is it so widespread? Although we cannot answer that question definitively, a few hypotheses seem reasonable and could be explored through further research.

One is that throughout the 1992 campaign many commentators in the media and in academe found Clinton's politics and policies much more to their taste than those of his two immediate predecessors, both of whom were frequently portrayed as being insensitive to the complexities of the world and domestic situations. By contrast, Clinton was seen as being much more like the commentators themselves, not only in having a complex cognitive structure, but—because many such analysts are political liberals—also in promoting a particular ideological content (see Suedfeld, 1992). His impressive academic credentials, obviously high intelligence, and verbal skill are likely to have reinforced that view. These observers may have looked at the *content* of the president's speeches and activities, whereas integrative complexity scoring deals with *structure*. This would not be the first time that the two foci led to opposite conclusions (Suedfeld et al., 1977).

However, an interesting quirk appeared as the shortcomings of the president's decisionmaking style became increasingly prominent during a series of salient early failures. Without giving up the view that Clinton is a highly intelligent, knowledgeable, and complex thinker, observers began to focus on drawbacks of his purported intellectual style. Attributes that had formerly been cited as assets now started to attract criticism.

Tetlock (1991) proposed that both high and low levels of complexity have positive as well as negative social perception concomitants. Complex decisionmakers may be seen as flexible, intelligent, thoughtful, calm, and openminded; but they may also appear weak, confused, and indecisive (see Table 11.6). Having to explain the president's setbacks, experts increasingly emphasized the latter set of images while increasingly ignoring the former. It may be expected that if he runs up a series of successes, the original positive interpretation of his supposed intellectual complexity will reappear. Of course, given that Clinton has not actually been a complex decisionmaker, the changes of his image in that role may be unimportant.

Questions for Further Exploration

The images of complexity deserve closer examination. We have found two intriguing paradoxes in the course of our research on Clinton. One is his widely accepted *persona* as a highly complex decisionmaker, which the data indicate that he is not; the other is the fact that in his case, commentators have emphasized the flaws associated with high complexity rather than—as is much more usual—its advantages (see Suedfeld and Tetlock, 1991). The interaction between cognitive style and public image is of interest for complexity theory in general as well as for an understanding of Clinton's treatment by the media and by policy analysts.

Our future research will also consider factors that may affect, and be affected by, Clinton's performance as a cognitive manager. Among these factors is the relation between Clinton's complexity level and that of his closest advisers or surrogates on particular policy domains: for instance, Vice President Al Gore on the environment and Hillary Rodham Clinton on health care. The influence of advisers is among a variety of circumstances that may ameliorate the adverse impact of his simple and rigid cognitive style on the outcome of policy dilemmas. In the future, the president may also face problems more amenable to his approach—that is, those that are best handled in a relatively simple way. It is also possible that he will demonstrate higher and more flexible integrative complexity as he gains more experience or learns to adjust his framing of a situation to allow for better decision strategies (e.g., by not imposing unnecessarily tight deadlines). The relationships between all of these factors and the future accomplishments and shortcomings of the Clinton administration will continue to be of interest and will have implications beyond this particular presidency.

Notes

Some of the data in this chapter were reported at a meeting of the American Political Science Association (Suedfeld, 1993). This research was made possible by grants to both authors from the Humanities and Social Sciences Research Council of Canada. We are grateful to Phyllis J. Johnson for her very helpful comments on previous versions of this chapter and to the following for their assistance in collecting and/or scoring the material: Erin Callaway, David Eichhorn, Karen Guttieri, and Kim Thachuk. Correspondence should be addressed to Peter Suedfeld at the Department of Psychology or to Michael D. Wallace at the Department of Political Science, both at the University of British Columbia, Vancouver, B.C. V6T 1Z4, Canada.

1. We are grateful to Eric Stern for an interesting suggestion concerning President Clinton's failure to show a complexity increase from before to after his election. Stern remarked that this could be explained by the frequently made comment that the president is "constantly running for election," even *since* the election. If the effort to maintain and increase one's popularity leads to simple cognitive strategies, a politician who is centrally concerned with popularity may indeed remain fixated on such strategies. One must wonder whether this will become a more common phenomenon as poll results become increasingly important in guiding policy decisions.

References

Baker-Brown, G., E. J. Ballard, S. Bluck, B. de Vries, P. Suedfeld, and P. E. Tetlock (1992). "The Conceptual/Integrative Complexity Scoring Manual." In *Motiva-*

tion and Personality: Handbook of Thematic Content Analysis, ed. C. P. Smith, 400–418. Cambridge: Cambridge University Press.

Ballard, E. J. (1983). "Canadian Prime Ministers: Complexity and Political Issues." *Canadian Psychology* 24:125–130.

Elkins, D. (1993). *Manipulation and Consent: How Voters and Leaders Manage Complexity.* Vancouver: University of British Columbia Press.

Herek, G., I. L. Janis, and P. Huth (1987). "Decisionmaking During International Crises: Is Quality of Process Related to Outcome?" *Journal of Conflict Resolution* 31:203–226.

Janis, I. L. (1989). *Crucial Decisions: Leadership in Policymaking and Crisis Management.* New York: Free Press.

Schroder, H. M., M. J. Driver, and S. Streufert (1967). *Human Information Processing.* New York: Holt, Rinehart, and Winston.

Selye, H. (1978). *The Stress of Life.* New York: McGraw-Hill.

Simonton, D. K. (1993). "Putting the Best Leaders in the White House: Personality, Policy, and Performance." *Political Psychology* 14:537–548.

Suedfeld, P. (1985). "APA Presidential Addresses: The Relation of Integrative Complexity to Historical, Professional, and Personal Factors." *Journal of Personality and Social Psychology* 49:1643–1651.

———— (1988). "Are Simple Decisions Always Worse?" *Society* 25, no. 5:25–27.

———— (1992). "Cognitive Managers and Their Critics." *Political Psychology* 13:435–453.

———— (1994). "President Clinton's Policy Dilemmas: A Cognitive Analysis." *Political Psychology* 15:337–349.

Suedfeld, P., R. S. Corteen, and C. McCormick (1986). "The Role of Integrative Complexity in Military Leadership: Robert E. Lee and His Opponents." *Journal of Applied Social Psychology* 16:498–507.

Suedfeld, P., and L. E. Piedrahita (1984). "Intimations of Mortality: Integrative Simplification as a Precursor of Death." *Journal of Personality and Social Psychology* 47:848–852.

Suedfeld, P., and A. D. Rank (1976). "Revolutionary Leaders: Long-Term Success as a Function of Changes in Conceptual Complexity." *Journal of Personality and Social Psychology* 34:169–178.

Suedfeld, P., and P. E. Tetlock (1977). "Integrative Complexity of Communications in International Crises." *Journal of Conflict Resolution* 21:169–184.

———— (1991). "Psychological Advice About Foreign Policy Decision Making: Heuristics, Biases, and Cognitive Defects." In *Psychology and Social Policy,* ed. P. Suedfeld and P. E. Tetlock, 1–30. New York: Hemisphere.

Suedfeld, P., P. E. Tetlock, and C. Ramirez (1977). "War, Peace, and Integrative Complexity: UN Speeches on the Middle East Problem, 1947–1976." *Journal of Conflict Resolution* 21:427–442.

Suedfeld, P., P. E. Tetlock, and S. Streufert (1992). "Conceptual/Integrative Complexity." In *Motivation and Personality: Handbook of Thematic Content Analysis,* ed. C. P. Smith, 393–400. Cambridge: Cambridge University Press.

Suedfeld, P., M. D. Wallace, and K. Thachuk (1993). "Changes in Integrative Complexity Among Middle East Leaders During the Persian Gulf Crisis." *Journal of Social Issues* 49:183–199.

Tetlock, P. E. (1981). Pre- to Postelection Shifts in Presidential Rhetoric: Impression Management or Cognitive Adjustment?" *Journal of Personality and Social Psychology* 41:207–212.

_____ (1983). "Accountability and Complexity of Thought." *Journal of Personality and Social Psychology* 45:285–292.

_____ (1985a). "Accountability: A Social Check on the Fundamental Attribution Error." *Social Psychology Quarterly* 48:227–236.

_____ (1985b). "Accountability: The Neglected Social Context of Judgement and Choice." *Research in Organizational Behavior* 7:297–332.

_____ (1991). "An Integratively Complex Look at Integrative Complexity." Paper presented at the Annual Meeting of the American Psychological Association, San Francisco, California, August.

_____ (1992). "Good Judgment in International Politics: Three Perspectives." *Political Psychology* 13:517–539.

Tetlock, P. E., D. Armor, and R. S. Peterson (1994). The Slavery Debate in Antebellum America: Cognitive Style, Value Conflict, and the Limits of Compromise. *Journal of Personality and Social Psychology* 66:115–126.

Wallace, M. D., and P. Suedfeld (1988). "Leadership Performance in Crisis: The Longevity-Complexity Link." *International Studies Quarterly* 32:439–451.

Wallace, M. D., P. Suedfeld, and K. Thachuk (1993). "Information Processing Among Leaders Under Stress: Findings from the Gulf Crisis." *Journal of Conflict Resolution* 37:94–107.

12

Psychological Dimensions of Post–Cold War Foreign Policy

RICHARD NED LEBOW

The Cold War is over and the international system is in a state of flux. The threat of superpower nuclear war has receded and has been replaced by new and more diffuse threats about the stability of the post–Cold War world order. The momentous structural changes of the past few years have reshaped the psychological context in which leaders and peoples make foreign and domestic policy. As in the past, this context can be expected to influence the nature of the problems that engage public attention, the solutions seen as appropriate, and the ways in which leadership is won and held.

Among the many changes in the post–Cold War psychological context, two in particular stand out: the absence—at least for the time being—of an external enemy and the shifting nature of domestic constraints on foreign policy. I examine these changes and their implications for American foreign policy. My treatment is of necessity speculative. The post–Cold War world is still taking shape, and there is only fragmentary evidence on which to base an analysis.

Enemies

The Cold War was fought against powerful and seemingly ruthless communist enemies: the Soviet Union, which ruled an empire stretching from the Elbe to the Pacific, and "Red" China, a totalitarian behemoth almost one billion strong that fought the West to a standstill in Korea by repeated human wave assaults.

Powerful enemies are dangerous, but they also confer advantages. They permit leaders to organize the world into simple "them" and "us" dichotomies, with all the advantages this has for the formulation of foreign policy, coordination of bureaucracies charged with its implementation, and mobilization of public support needed to sustain and pay for an active role in world affairs. It seems unlikely, for example, that the American people would have supported Marshall Plan aid for Europe or the permanent deployment of U.S. forces in Europe and Asia in the absence of a perceived communist threat.[1]

Powerful enemies also allow leaders to mobilize populations in support of domestic goals. The "Red Scare" of the 1920s provided the cover for a war against organized labor. The Cold War spawned McCarthyism and its decade-long suppression of liberal-left nonconformists. The 1950s also saw the rise of "the military-industrial complex," with its cozy relationships between corporations in search of lucrative government contracts and politicians in search of contributions government expenditure in the districts. This vast and often wasteful expenditure was justified in the name of national security.

Powerful enemies are useful in explaining away failures. The "loss of China" and vilification of Americans throughout the Third World were blamed by many on betrayal and subversion by communists at home and abroad. So, too, were rock n' roll, the civil rights movement, marijuana, cohabitation, feminism, and, for the far far Right, fluoridation of the reservoirs. Psychologists have long observed that such explanations are appealing because they exonerate the values and policies of those who resort to them.

Powerful enemies legitimate otherwise repugnant foreign and domestic policies. There is always some discrepancy between a country's declared goals and its policies. In the United States, where foreign policy has always been justified with reference to its moral content, the disparity between theory and practice has at times been acute. The cognitive dissonance this generates can be reduced by assertions to oneself and to others that unsavory means are sometimes necessary to achieve a larger, worthwhile end. During the Cold War, the allegedly life-or-death struggle against the evil of communism was repeatedly invoked to justify American support of corrupt and repressive regimes. In 1961 Vice President Lyndon Johnson brushed off a question about what he really thought about South Vietnamese strongman Ngo Dinh Diem with the reply, "Shit, man, he's the only boy we got out there."[2] In the 1980s Oliver North and other members of the Reagan administration justified their illegal transfer of laundered funds to the Nicaraguan Contras as essential to protect the hemisphere from communist penetration.

From the vantage point of the United States, the most striking feature of the post–Cold War world is the absence of powerful adversaries. To be sure, there are Saddam Hussein, Muhammar Qadaffi, and fundamentalist Iran, but they are small fry in comparison to Joseph Stalin's Soviet Union or even Mao Zedong's China. At best, they provide the Defense Department with some justification for its budget. Six months before Saddam Hussein's invasion of Kuwait, U.S. forces had staged an exercise that entailed the expulsion of Iraqi forces from Kuwait. The exercise was not the result of political foresight—the Iraqi invasion took the State Department and intelligence community by surprise—but a response to the Defense Department's need to find an enemy.

Military planners were instructed to invent a scenario, any scenario, that would justify a large and diverse force structure. Iraq was picked on the basis of its military capabilities.[3]

Attempts are under way to bestow the mantle of enemy on Japan. Japan bashing was on the upswing even before the end of the Cold War, and there has been a noticeable attempt to hold that Asian colossus responsible for some of America's economic problems. A recent bestseller describes a future war with Japan.[4] Elite opinion has begun to contemplate the possibility of a hostile People's Republic of China.[5] A nuclear power, run with an iron hand by the butchers of Tiananmen Square, who swamp American markets with the products of prison camp labor, keep Tibet in thralldom, and seem on the verge of snuffing out the political liberties of the residents of Hong Kong, has lots of adversarial potential.

Enemy images of either Japan or China could also draw on residual racial prejudices and memories of Pearl Harbor or Korea, the latter fought with a communist regime that still hangs on to power. These are still distant forebodings, and in the case of Japan, there is reason to believe that there is enough goodwill and common sense in both countries to weather whatever economic conflicts strain their relationship. Whatever the long-term relationship with either country, for the foreseeable future neither is likely to fill the size fourteen extrawide jackboots vacated by the Soviet Union.

Without powerful enemies leaders confront fewer external constraints. This apparent advantage also has its drawbacks. A comparison of Hungary and Bosnia indicates that in a world without powerful enemies, contradictions between policies and values can become painfully evident.

In the 1952 presidential campaign, the Republicans made political capital over the alleged failure of the Democrats to keep Eastern Europe from falling under Soviet control. In an appeal for the white ethnic vote, Dwight Eisenhower promised to "roll back" Soviet influence in Eastern Europe. However, when workers rioted in East Germany in 1953 and Hungarians overturned their Stalinist regime in 1956, the Eisenhower administration made clear to Moscow that it would not intervene. Eisenhower was very careful to do nothing that could provoke a military confrontation with the Soviet Union. In 1992 candidate Bill Clinton was openly critical of the Bush administration's failure to come to the aid of Bosnia. Once in the White House, President Clinton found it in his interest to remain just as detached from Bosnia.

Hungary and Bosnia confronted presidents with different kinds of political-psychological dilemmas. In 1956 President Eisenhower and Secretary of State John Foster Dulles felt enormous frustration at not being able to come to the aid of Hungary's freedom fighters. They were further embarrassed by their prior public commitment to roll back communism in Eastern Europe. We can surmise that the contradiction between their campaign promises and foreign policy created dissonance for both men. They could reduce this dissonance by convincing themselves that American intervention in either East Germany or Hungary would have provoked a war-threatening confrontation with the Soviet Union and that anything short of intervention would not have been effective. Faced with the reality of Soviet power, Eisenhower and Dulles believed that they had no choice but to exercise restraint, and this must have made it easier for them to live with their failure to honor their pledge. Many conservative Republicans and voters of Eastern European ancestry felt betrayed. Their anguish was deep and not so easily assuaged.

A much smaller constituency demanded intervention in Bosnia, and Clinton had never made the same kind of promises as Eisenhower. The president and some of his advisers nevertheless felt themselves on the horns of a political and moral dilemma. They were troubled by the atrocities committed in Bosnia but were reluctant to intervene because the European allies were unenthusiastic and the American military establishment and secretary of defense were opposed. Any prolonged foreign entanglement would threaten the success of the administration's domestic legislative agenda. In the absence of the Soviet threat, they had to face up to their responsibility for making the choice for nonintervention or conjure up constraints that would justify inaction to the American people and themselves.

The administration chose to conjure. Secretary of State Warren Christopher was sent to Europe to sound out the Europeans on the possibility of intervention and returned to report that they were opposed. Subsequent leaks indicated that the real purpose of his trip had been to elicit an expression of opposition to intervention that the administration could then use to justify its reluctance to proceed. The Pentagon provided another justification. The Joint Chiefs of Staff insisted that intervention would encounter serious resistance and lead to an open-ended and costly commitment. Some experts questioned this self-serving estimate, but Clinton accepted it uncritically and used it to buttress his decision not to intervene.

The debate on Bosnia reflected two different conceptions of American interests. Former Cold Warriors, on the whole hostile to intervention, maintained that nothing that happened in the former Yugoslavia directly threatened American security. Together with other opponents to intervention, they were prone to portray the civil war in Yugoslavia as the latest episode in a historical struggle among hostile ethnic groups that could not be resolved or significantly ameliorated by third parties. Many of the Americans who favored a more interventionist policy by then had been active in or were generally sympathetic to the goals of the peace movement. They believed that it was imperative for the United States and its European allies to prevent "ethnic cleansing" and uphold the most basic principles of international justice. They maintained that Bosnia was the test case of the post–Cold War order, the same claim made by many former Cold Warriors to justify intervention in Kuwait.

The Cold War and its larger-than-life communist enemies helped create a consensus about foreign policy that endured until America's failure in Vietnam. The American response to Bosnia, Somalia, and other major international issues revealed widely varying opinions among elite and public opinion. There is no consensus about America's role in the world, how and where its influence should be expressed or sought, the nature and gravity of the threats the country faces, or the appropriate strategies for dealing with them. In the absence of the Cold War, there is no obvious frame of reference for ordering the world.

Congress mirrors the wider public confusion. It has swung widely between support and opposition to foreign deployments of U.S. forces. Thomas Mann, a noted congressional scholar at the Brookings Institution, observed that "members of Congress are absolutely without anchor here. They find themselves responding on an ad hoc basis, responding to public opinion and pictures on television screens, and also by short-term ideological considerations, and such that responsible members end up embracing extraordinary inconsistent imperatives on foreign policy."[6]

Such uncertainty and vacillation reflect a deeper contradiction. The American people and their leaders cling to a belief that they are the chosen people and have a god-given mission to export their liberties and way of life to the rest of the world. But they are increasingly reluctant to expend the lives and money such responsibility entails. Most Americans seem unprepared to renounce their country's putative mission. They want to believe that they are morally superior to everyone else—and more courageous. No other nations have bumper stickers of their flag with the slogan "These Colors Don't Run." So American leaders vainly search for some way to exercise influence on the cheap. Their frustration will continue until such time as they and the American people are willing to come to terms with themselves and, by extension, the world.

Domestic Constraints

Cold War commitments could sometimes be exploited for domestic ends. On other occasions, perceived strategic imperatives threatened important domestic goals and confronted leaders with difficult choices. Lyndon Johnson agonized over military intervention in Vietnam, fearful that it would consume the funds required by the Great Society. The post–Cold War political environment confronts presidents with choices more reminiscent of Vietnam.

In his first year in office, Bill Clinton repeatedly shied away from international involvements that put American lives and his domestic legislative agenda at risk. The consensus among Washington leaders is that Bosnia was sacrificed for health care. Clinton's reluctance to pursue a more active policy in Bosnia was also a response to public opinion. In the early 1960s, Lyndon

Johnson worried that the loss of Vietnam to the communists could lead to the loss of the presidency to the Republicans. Clinton recognized that his administration could easily survive the loss of Bosnia to the Serbs but not the loss of the American lives that it might take to prevent this outcome. Bosnia is indicative of a broad shift in public attitudes toward foreign commitments. During the Cold War, Congress appropriated billions for military assistance. Today it is reluctant to vote funds to help revitalize the Soviet economy. Congress and the American people have also become increasingly antagonistic to military intervention.

The Gulf War, the country's first post–Cold War military action, was preceded by a massive allied military buildup and diplomatic effort designed to bring about an Iraqi withdrawal from Kuwait. Most Americans supported the president, but a significant minority opposed the use of force; some urged the adoption of economic sanctions instead. When war broke out, public opinion rallied to the troops. Support for the president remained high throughout the conflict because it was short, ended in victory, and entailed remarkably few American casualties. This support waned considerably over the next few months as it became apparent that Saddam Hussein retained his grip on power and that the United States and its allies could do little short of direct involvement to halt his murderous campaigns against the Shiites and the Kurds.

In Somalia, another Bush administration initiative, Americans were initially supportive of intervention because of its humanitarian motive. Subsequent firefights in Mogadishu between American soldiers and the irregular forces of warlord Mohammed Farah Aidid rapidly shifted opinion against the operation. Voicing a widely shared feeling, one concerned citizen interviewed by ABC News explained that he would rather see starving Somalis on television every night than the dead bodies of American soldiers. In October 1993 Congress began debating the wisdom of the intervention, and the president, to head off criticism, committed himself to a date for the withdrawal of all American troops.

In Haiti, President Clinton took the lead in organizing international pressure on the military to allow the return to power of exiled President Jean-Bertrand Aristide. To compel the obviously reluctant Haitian military to step down from power, the administration convinced the United Nations to authorize the dispatch of peacekeeping forces to that country. In October 1993 as blue-helmeted soldiers prepared to disembark at Port-au-Prince, "attachés" in the pay of Haiti's generals conducted a reign of terror in the country's capital and murdered a prominent member of the opposition. The crescendo of violence in Haiti prompted Republican senator Robert Dole to declare that "restoring Jean-Bertrand Aristide to power was not worth a single

American life and that the American people wanted more restraint on the use of troops abroad."[7] Concerned that this policy would alienate public opinion, the Clinton administration ordered American ships and the forces they carried to return to American ports.

The general reluctance of the American people and their elected representatives to support military intervention in Europe, Africa, and the Caribbean is in the first instance attributable to the end of the Cold War and the collapse of the Soviet Union. Without a powerful enemy to deter and prevent from exploiting instability, there was no compelling strategic need to act.

Congress and the public have also come to doubt the efficacy of military intervention in situations of civil war or breakdown. In the Gulf, military intervention succeeded in expelling Iraqi forces from Kuwait but failed to remove Saddam from power, protect the Shiite minorities in Iraq, or encourage greater democracy in liberated Kuwait. Somalia was even more of a watershed. Foreign military forces were welcomed at first by a starving and terrified population as providers and liberators. They gradually became the enemy to at least one clan, whose influence they threatened. Unable to restore civil authority but unable to leave in its absence, and handicapped by squabbles among their governments and between them and the United Nations, these forces seem trapped and vulnerable in a situation not of their own making.

The Somali experience made Americans more cautious about intervention in Bosnia and Haiti. Even for thoughtful people not easily seduced by superficial analogies, the experience in Somalia seemed to highlight the difficulty of using military means to resolve complex and sometimes poorly understood local antagonisms. The failure of compellence in Haiti and the suffering caused to the local population—but not the military junta—by the subsequent economic blockade will most likely reinforce the general conclusion that it is very difficult for outsiders to ameliorate civil conflicts in developing countries.

One important respect in which Haiti was different from Somalia was motive. Intervention in Somalia was prompted by largely humanitarian concerns. This sentiment was not absent in Haiti, but it took a second seat to a more practical consideration: stemming the flow of boat people to the United States. The administration sought to do this by restoring a popularly elected but avowedly left-wing government to Haiti but changed its mind when it concluded that the political costs of intervention were almost certain to exceed those of illegal emigration, detention camps, and deportations.

More practical considerations were also apparent in the public's reaction to Somalia and Haiti. In Congress and the media, many voices urged the administration to focus its attention and resources on domestic problems. They drew attention to "domestic Haitis" where impoverished and underfed inner-city residents were terrorized by criminal elements armed with automatic weapons.

Greater public interest in domestic versus foreign problems is nothing new. But it has become more pronounced in recent years in response to the recession and its aggravation of many preexisting social ills. The political agenda has been dominated by unemployment, drugs, crime, corruption, and how to respond to them. There are interesting parallels between the domestic and international debates, just as there were during the heyday of the Cold War.

The 1960s witnessed activist policies at home and abroad. The Johnson administration conducted a war on poverty in the United States while it waged war on communism in Vietnam. Both struggles were rooted in the premise that enlightened, committed, and well-funded government could reshape unpleasant and threatening social realities and had a responsibility to do so. The 1990s is characterized by widespread pessimism about social engineering at home or abroad and lack of faith in government at all levels. Almost everybody recognizes the need to do something about the national debt, unemployment, crime, drugs, and international instability, but few people believe that government can do much about them. The combination of grave social problems and seemingly helpless government constitutes the political crisis of the late twentieth century.

How do leaders respond to this dilemma? One approach, adopted by Ronald Reagan and George Bush, is to do nothing and to claim that nothing is something. Both presidents promised that deep cuts in expensive social programs and lower taxes for upper-income brackets would create trickle-down prosperity. Another approach, characteristic of Bill Clinton and his administration, might be called half-hearted activism. Clinton announced a series of reforms (e.g., homosexual rights, the environment, taxation, health care) but accepted major compromises when his proposals encountered opposition.

The Reagan and Clinton strategies reflect at least in part the different class bases of their parties. Many more Republicans are well-to-do and untouched by the recession. They live and often work in the suburbs, send their children to private schools, and may never set foot in dangerous neighborhoods. They confront social problems in their tax bills, and many deeply resent the sacrifice this entails. By denying the efficacy and value of government programs and proclaiming that individual greed had beneficial social consequences, Reagan and Bush rewarded their supporters financially while at the same time legitimizing their avarice.

Democrats have a more diverse constituency, at least some of which demands government intervention on behalf of minorities, the underprivileged, and the average citizen who is the victim of well-organized special interests. Many of these constituents have contradictory desires. Compelling the military to accept homosexuals antagonizes many officers and enlisted personnel, banning logging in certain tracts in the Cascades threatens the livelihood of entire communities, and higher taxes on gasoline adversely affect the poor. Reluctant to choose between competing constituencies, the president has sought to placate all of them by introducing reforms and then backing away from them to varying degrees.

There is little indication that the Clinton strategy has worked; public opinion polls indicate that the president's support declined precipitously during his first year in office. A longer-term failure of the administration would only deepen the country's political crisis.

The City on the Hill

The French, the Germans, and the Japanese know who they are because of their language, culture, and ancestry. For the United States, where immigration has been the national rite of passage, it has been necessary to forge an identity from an idea. Being American means being committed to "the American way of life" and its belief in the perfectibility of the individual through democratic institutions, economic progress, and tolerance.

The American ideology has always had universalist pretensions. The American dream was for export, and Americans saw themselves as a modern-day chosen people with a divine mission to carry their ideas, products, and way of life to the far corners of the globe. American power and influence were a means to this end and a validation of the nation's mission.

For two centuries American foreign policy struggled under the burden of two masters. It had to be pragmatic and safeguard the security and economic interests, first, of a fledgling power and, ultimately, of a world power, with all its attendant interests and responsibilities. Foreign policy also had to advance the American ideology and its political, economic, and social values. From the time of the French Revolution on, Americans have been divided over the respective primacy of these missions.

In our time this struggle has been acute and complex. Cold Warriors described their policies as pragmatic. They defended American support of authoritarian regimes and intervention in Third World struggles as unpleasant necessities vital to the struggle against communism. Their critics, often referred to as peaceniks, accused the national security establishment of conducting a crusade that sacrificed the real interests of the nation to ill-conceived ideological goals. Cold Warriors in turn bitterly derided the efforts of the Carter administration to make a country's respect for human rights a litmus paper test for American support. Such ideological objectives, they insisted, could be pursued only at the expense of America's real interests.

Cold Warriors and peaceniks represented different blends of ideology and pragmatism. Their competing conceptions of foreign policy reflected different understandings of the national interest. For Cold Warriors, all other considerations were secondary to the containment of the Soviet Union and its allies. For peaceniks, the preservation of American liberties required a foreign policy that did not trample on those liberties and nourished their development in other parts of the world. Both groups claimed to be pragmatic in their approach to foreign policy but justified that approach with reference to their broader moral purpose.

Throughout the twentieth century, American military commitments—and opposition to them—have always been justified in terms of moral and even altruistic goals. World War I was sold to the American people as the war to end all wars, World War II was fought to make the world safe for democracy, and the Vietnam War was a struggle to keep Southeast Asia from communist enslavement. Opposition to Vietnam was a crusade to maintain constitutional liberties within the United States.

Since the end of the Cold War, there has been a noticeable change in the rhetoric of the foreign policy debate. One increasingly hears arguments devoid of ideological packaging. Opponents of intervention in Somalia and Haiti suggested that the absolute benchmark for assessing foreign policy should be the possible loss of American life. Opponents and proponents of NAFTA made direct, unvarnished appeals to the pocketbook. In the past, appeals to naked, individual self-interest would have been regarded as embarrassing and unpersuasive. Presumably, those making such arguments today do so in the expectation that it will enhance the effectiveness of their appeals.

This rhetorical evolution suggests that self-interest is coming out of the closet in American public life. This is most apparent in domestic politics, where private greed was more or less portrayed as a public virtue by Ronald Reagan. Throughout the 1980s, economic self-interest was legitimized as the standard for assessing the merits of any policy proposal. It has even affected the world of scholarship, where rational choice, which identifies the individual as the unit of analysis and self-interest as the motive for behavior, has increasingly come to dominate the social sciences.

This emphasis on self-interest may reflect the triumph of materialist values and another assault on what remains of our civic culture. It may also be a sign that Americans feel more comfortable with their national identity. American foreign policy has always been harnessed to build, shape, and strengthen that identity. The demystification of that policy and its partial retreat from the pretension of divine mission have been paralleled on the domestic front by the demise of that other great myth: the melting pot. It is gradually giving way to a conception of the United States as a salad bowl composed of different ethnic and religious groups that retain their distinctive cultures. For better or worse, America may be on its way to becoming a normal nation.

Notes

1. See Melvyn Leffler, *A Preponderance of Power: National Security, the Truman Administration, and the Cold War* (Stanford: Stanford University Press, 1992).

2. Quoted in David Halberstam, *The Best and the Brightest* (New York: Random House, 1969), 135.

3. Interviews with U.S. Army planners, Washington, D.C., 1992–1993.

4. George Freedman and Meredith LeBard, *The Coming War with Japan* (New York: St. Martin's Press, 1991).

5. On November 10, 1993, Richard L. Solomon, president of the United States Institute of Peace, gave a lecture at the Council on Foreign Relations entitled "China and the United States: The Next Cold War?"

6. Quoted in Adam Clymer, "Foreign Policy Tug-of-War: Latest in a Long String of Battles," *New York Times,* October 19, 1993, A4.

7. Thomas L. Friedman, "Dole Plans Bill to Bar the Use of G.I.'s in Haiti," *New York Times,* October 18, 1993, A41.

About the Book

The Clinton presidency faced a basic set of public questions at the outset regarding its real intentions, strategies, and competence. Would the administration be able to develop and implement policies that were constructive in intent, fair in formulation, and successful in result? Would President Clinton be able to govern as successfully as he campaigned? Would there be a productive fit between Clinton's leadership style and the needs of the public?

Additional questions arise about Clinton personally. Many admire him; others distrust him. What realistic basis is there for either view?

This book explores these questions and develops an initial appraisal of the Clinton presidency. The chapters herein are framed by theories of political leadership and psychology. They draw on a diverse body of theories, including psychological theories of character and personality, cognitive psychology and communication theory, theories of presidential leadership and performance, and theories of public psychology. The goal is to examine the many facets of leadership and governing that constitute the modern presidency and to locate Bill Clinton's emerging presidency within that framework.

Bill Clinton is and likely will remain a controversial president. One objective of this analysis is to provide a clearer, more objective framework in which to evaluate both the man and his approach to political leadership and executive power and the consequences of his approach for public psychology and policy.

About the Editor and Contributors

W. Lance Bennett is a professor of political science at the University of Washington. His most recent books include: *News: The Politics of Illusion* and *The Governing Crisis: Media Money and Marketing in American Elections*.

Betty Glad is Carolina Research Professor of Political Science at the University of South Carolina. Her most recent books include *The Psychological Dimensions of War* (editor and contributor), *Key Pittman: the Tragedy of a Senate Insider*, and *Jimmy Carter: In Search of the Big White House*.

Fred I. Greenstein is a professor of politics at Princeton University and the director of its Program in Leadership Studies. He has recently coauthored, with John B. Burke, *How Presidents Test Reality: Decision in Vietnam, 1954 and 1965*.

Margaret G. Hermann is a professor of political science at Ohio State University and an associate of the Mershon Center. Among other works, she is the author of *A Psychological Examination of Political Leaders* and *Political Psychology*.

Lawrence R. Jacobs is a professor of political science at the University of Minnesota. He has written articles on American and British health care policy and is the author of *Health of Nations*.

Martha Joynt Kumar is a professor of political science at Towson State University. She is the author of *Wired for Sound and Pictures: The President and White House Communication Policies* and a coauthor of *Portraying the President: The White House and the News Media*.

Richard Ned Lebow is director of the Program in International Relations and a professor at the University of Pittsburgh's Graduate School of Public and International Affairs. His most recent book, coauthored with Janice Gross Stein, is *We All Lost the Cold War*.

Jerrold M. Post is a professor of international relations and political psychology at George Washington University. He is the author of *The Captive King*.

Stanley A. Renshon is a professor of political science at the City University of New York and a psychoanalyst and clinical faculty member at the Training and Research Institute for Self Psychology. He is the editor of the journal *Political Psychology*. His most recent book is *The Political Psychology of the Gulf* War: Leaders, Publics and the Process of Conflict.

Robert Y. Shapiro is a professor of political science at Columbia University. He is a co-author of *The Rational Public: Fifty Years of Trends in Americans' Policy Preferences* and a coeditor of *Research in Micropolitics: New Directions in Political Psychology.*

Peter Suedfeld is a professor of psychology at the University of British Columbia and a fellow of the Royal Society of Canada. He has conducted experimental studies on decisionmaking and information processing and originated the structural analysis of integrative complexity in archival materials. His most recent book is *Psychology and Social Policy.*

Michael D. Wallace is a professor of political science at the University of British Columbia. He has recently published two papers on the Gulf War and a monograph on small navies in the post–Cold War world. He is working on a major study of Russian leadership before, during, and after the collapse of the Soviet Union.

David G. Winter is a professor of psychology at the University of Michigan. He has published several articles on measuring personality at a distance and the motives of political leaders. Among his published books are *The Power Motive* and *A New Case for the Liberal Arts.*

Index